The Autumn House Anthology of Contemporary American Poetry

The Autumn House Anthology of Contemporary American Poetry

second edition

edited by
Michael Simms

Autumn House Press

PITTSBURGH

iv

"Autumn House" and "Autumn House Press" are registered trademarks owned by Autumn House Press, a nonprofit corporation whose mission is the publication and promotion of poetry and other fine literature.

Autumn House Press Staff
Editor-in-Chief and Founder: Michael Simms
Executive Director: Richard St. John
Community Outreach Director: Michael Wurster
Co-Founder: Eva-Maria Simms
Fiction Editor: Sharon Dilworth
Associate Editor: Ziggy Edwards
Assistant Editors: Evan Oare, Kriscinda Meadows, Adrienne Block
Media Consultant: Jan Beatty
Publishing Consultant: Peter Oresick
Tech Crew Chief: Michael Milberger
Interns: Athena Pappas, D. Gilson

Autumn House Press receives state arts funding support through a grant from the Pennsylvania Council on the Arts, a state agency funded by the Commonwealth of Pennsylvania and the National Endowment for the Arts, a federal agency.

ISBN: 978-1-932870-48-0
Library of Congress: 2010919239

Landscape with Onlooker

One night shy of full, the moon
looks not lonesome shining through the trees, but replete

with the thoughtless sensuality of well-being.
A chill in the air? No, under the air, like water

under a swimmer. The unsteadfast leaves grow crisp
and brittle, the better to fall away. Some nights

fear, like rising water in a well, fills these hours—
the dead of night, as the phrase goes, when you quicken

and the dank metallic sweat beads like a vile dew.
But tonight you stand at your window, framed and calm,

and the air's as sweet as a freshly peeled orange.
There's a moon on the lake, and another in the sky.

William Matthews

Contents

About This Book

When my son Nicholas was twelve years old, we received a DVD from our friend Jo McDougall. On the disc was a recording of *Emerson County Shaping Dream*, a dramatic performance of a dozen of Jo's poems. After watching the video, Nicholas turned to me and said, "Dad, that wasn't really poetry, was it?" And I answered, "Well, yes, it was. In fact it was very fine poetry." Puzzled, he exclaimed, "But it sounded just like people talking!" Nicholas was right—poetry is just like people talking. He was confused by the fact that the poetry he'd been studying in school was like nineteenth-century people talking, not at all like the speech he was accustomed to hearing among his family and friends. And yet, as Nicholas intuitively knew (and Jo, I'm sure, would agree), poetry is also more than everyday speech. It is everyday speech that has something special or amazing about it, something that makes us think, wonder, or marvel. It makes us angry, or it makes us serene. It helps us to remember and to forgive. Poetry captures the essence of what it is to be alive at a particular time and place.

For instance, try reading aloud this short poem by Jo McDougall:

Telling Time

My son and I walk away
from his sister's day-old grave.
Our backs to the sun,
the forward pitch of our shadows
tells us the time.
By sweetest accident
he inclines
his shadow, touching mine.

What makes this poem so quietly powerful? Immediately, we notice the poem's brevity, just thirty-five words in eight lines plus a two-word title. Strange, we may think, how so few words can recreate such a significant moment, a woman and her son walking away from the fresh grave of his sister. Next, we may notice the musicality of the language: the alliteration of the title echoed in the fifth line, the long open vowels of *away, grave, shadows, time*, and the rhyming couplet that concludes the poem. We may be struck by the images of the grave, the sun, and the shadows, and the originality and beauty of the phrase *by sweetest accident*. And finally we may notice how these different elements work together to represent the experience: the rhyming pair of lines at the end corresponding to the mother and son sharing their grief—their shadows rhyming, so to speak. One quality I especially admire is that the poet never tells us how to feel—words like "sadness" and "grief" never appear—but rather she lets the music, the phrasing, the imagery, and the dramatic moment carry the weight of the experience. A marvelous, authentic poem like this embodies some of the guiding principles that inform this selection of poetry.

What did I hope to achieve with this particular anthology? When I look over the landscape of contemporary American poetry, I see an impressive range of subjects and styles. This anthology attempts to capture that diversity. In these pages the reader will find elegies and epigrams, pantoums and prose poems, humor and horror, soulful prayers and revolutionary manifestos, screams of madness and statements of commonsense. You'll also find a family recipe for bread pudding with whiskey sauce, as well as a number of recipes for family disaster with and without whiskey.

The selection of poems in an anthology necessarily reflects the personal tastes of the editor, but ideally it should also represent a larger aesthetic shared by the culture. Currently this ideal presents a challenge to the anthologist because the American poetry scene is so varied in its range of aesthetics—from personal narratives rendered in free verse, to poems in fixed forms, to experimental "language poetry." I've included representative poems from each of these "schools"—although personal narratives tend to predominate here just as they do in the field as a whole—while trying to remain true to certain principles—some of the same principles that animate Jo McDougall's poem.

First, a poem needs to feel *authentic*, which is not the same as *autobiographical*. The former refers to truth, the latter to fact. In other words, poetry does not necessarily report verifiable information about a person's life; instead it creates an experience on its own terms. Instead of autobiographical fact, the measure of a poem's truth depends on a pair of mutually dependent qualities: whether the utterance sounds like a real person is saying the words; and whether the experience of listening to the poem moves the reader toward a profound insight. Related to authenticity, there also needs to be an urgency about the poem, a sense that the words need to be said.

Second, although a poem can employ many strategies—such as describing a scene, defining a term, experimenting with language, or arguing a point—to my mind, the most important is the creation of *song* and *story*. We want to hear the music of our language. Rhythm, rhyme, repetition of words and sounds, pattern and syntax, the clash and meld of different kinds of language—abstract and concrete, formal and colloquial, short words and long words, basic Anglo-Saxon and fancy French. Besides these technical considerations, there's the simple pleasure of hearing certain phrases. Edgar Allan Poe thought that "cellar door" is the most beautiful phrase in the English language; I would nominate the phrase "all summer long" for that honor although Jo McDougall's "by sweetest accident" would be in the running as well.

In addition to enjoying the sound of language, we also want to connect with something deeply human: character, plot, setting, voice, morality, theme—to paraphrase Faulkner, the struggle of the human heart in conflict with itself. And I would stretch the usual meaning of *song and story* to include poems by poets such as Lynn Emanuel, Leonard Gontarek, Matthea Harvey, and Thom Ward that push the boundaries of language far beyond simple lyric and linear narrative to create realities that need to be accepted on their own unique terms; these authors impinge on the listener's consciousness in unusual ways. Also, it should be said that although lyric and narrative both give pleasure to the reader, they don't necessarily appear in equal measure. Some poems, such as Sarah Gridley's, lean more toward music, while others—Ed Ochester's come to mind—resemble anecdotes. What the work of Gridley and Ochester share is an extreme efficiency of language. Poetry, you might say, provides the fastest route to the center of our lives.*

Though song and story are touchstones throughout, the poems in this anthology vary widely in subject matter. Love in its many forms is a traditional focus of literature and no less so in contemporary poetry: Chana Bloch's "Sometimes I Want to Sink into Your Body" describes the erotic love between a man and a woman while "Some Days" by Matthew Dickman is a rich evocation of the tension and tenderness between siblings. Dysfunctional families, a favorite topic for contemporary poets, are depicted in "Scary Parents" by Michael Dickman, who, one might guess from their photographs, is Matthew's twin brother.

Poetry itself is another recurring subject, for example, "Ars Poetica" by Linda Pastan, "Snow for Wallace Stevens" by Terrance Hayes, "Selecting a Reader" by Ted Kooser, and "The Wandering Poets" by Philip Levine. Grief has always been an important engine of inspiration for poets—besides Jo McDougall's "Telling Time" quoted above, one of my favorites is the beautiful elegy "What the Living Do" by Marie Howe. Landscape description is another traditional subject made new by contemporary poets, whether quietly meditative, for example "Landscape with Onlooker" by William Matthews, or energetically urban, such as "Tire Shop" by Jimmy Santiago Baca.

Contemporary social issues, such as the stain of racism in "Confederate Pride Day at Bama" by Honorée Fanonne Jeffers, are also well represented here. The horror of war is vividly portrayed in John Samuel Tieman's "Ed-

---

*I'm tempted to say that poetry captures the *ineffable*, but then I remember my teacher William Matthews saying in class one day, "The ineffable is that which cannot be effed." Ever since then, I haven't been able to say the word *ineffable* with a straight face.

iting" and its lingering effects on veterans in "At a Barbecue for R. C. One Week after He Is Out of Iraq" by James Tyner. Gender differences are portrayed in a number of poems, perhaps most surprisingly in Charles Harper Webb's "Tenderness in Men." Popular culture is invoked in "The Burning Bush of Basketball" by Gary Margolis and "Ode to My 1977 Toyota" by Barbara Hamby. Ed Ochester and Liam Rector describe Fred Astaire in contrasting ways: Ochester portrays the great Hollywood star as a proletarian hero while Rector compares him to a tragic dandy. Among my other favorites are Anne Marie Macari's elegant meditations on animals, Laure-Anne Bosselaar's ironic reversal of received wisdom in "The Pleasures of Hating," and the strange and wonderful spirituality of Jane Mead.

The poems gathered here vary in style, as well as in subject matter. Although most are composed in free verse, many use fixed forms, for example, "Sestina for the Beloved" by Sheryl St. Germain; "Ballad of the Returnee" by Samuel Hazo; and "Pantoum for Attachment" by Mary Crocket Hill. Readers interested in the use of allegory and extended metaphor might look at "Famous" by Naomi Shihab Nye and "The Blessing of the Old Woman, the Tulip, and the Dog" by Alicia Suskin Ostriker. Many poets make use of personal narrative to give their work verisimilitude and emotional energy: Jan Beatty's poems about her father and Elizabeth Kirschner's sequence about her mental breakdown affect me profoundly every time I read them. Readers who prefer a lighter touch will enjoy the poems of Billy Collins and George Bilgere, as well as Ada Limón's "Selecting Things for Vagueness" with its surprise ending.

Although translations of poetry from other languages are an important part of contemporary American poetry, influencing many poets with the possibility of new voices and images, I decided early on that translation is outside the scope of this anthology. However, I've made one exception—"Little Soul" by W.S. Merwin. This poem is so perfectly rendered in English that it can stand on its own, quite apart from Hadrian's Latin original.

As a reader, I value clarity, originality, passion, and craftsmanship. My models for the best in American poetry are found in the work of five twentieth-century masters: Theodore Roethke, Elizabeth Bishop, Sylvia Plath, Frank O'Hara, and James Wright. Their mastery of craft and form, their evocative music, their focused passion, their authenticity of voice are the criteria for the selection of poems in this twenty-first-century anthology.

Finally, let me point out that this is an anthology of poetry, not of poets. I've selected poems based on their importance to me, not on the fame of their authors, so some readers may be surprised at the absence of a few well-known poets who have won major prizes. I make no apology for these omissions; however, I do apologize to the many practicing poets who are doing fine work, but for reasons of economy I was not able to include here. Ultimately, it is the reader who will decide whether the poems in this collection move, inspire, and provoke with the power, in James Wright's phrase, "of the pure clear word."

Much has been written about the craft of poetry—rhythm, imagery, meta-phor—and about the spiritual essence of poetry—its relationship to myth, ritual, and revelation. For the serious student of poetry, both of these ap-proaches are invaluable. For discussions of craft I recommend Ted Kooser's commonsense guide *The Poetry Home Repair Manual: Practical Advice for Beginning Poets* and, for more advanced students, *The Poet's Companion: A Guide to the Pleasures of Writing Poetry* by Kim Addonizio and Dorianne Laux. For a discussion of the spiritual aspects of poetry, I refer the reader to Robert McDowell's inspired *Poetry as Spiritual Practice: Reading, Writing, and Using Poetry in Your Daily Rituals, Aspirations, and Intentions*. As a sup-plement to McDowell's insights, I recommend *Joyful Noise: An Anthology of American Spiritual Poetry* edited by Robert Strong, which doubles as an effective survey of American poetry over the last four hundred years.

The anthology you are holding in your hand, however, tries to do some-thing more basic and perhaps more enjoyable than these explorations of technique and mysticism. It brings together a substantial collection of po-ems that represent the wide diversity of poetry in America today while attempting to stay true to certain principles of quality. My hope is that the reader will find poems that give voice, through song and story, to what Samuel Hazo calls in a different context "the holy surprise of right now."

Many people have helped make this book possible. Limitations of space permit me to name only a few. My wife Eva-Maria Simms, co-founder of Autumn House Press, has stood beside me at every turn in the road: I am more grateful to her than I can say. Rick St. John, Executive Director of Au-tumn House since 2007, has brilliantly managed the press, freeing me of much of the administrative work—fund-raising, accounting, community-building—inherent in running a thriving independent publisher. Our assistant editors, Evan Oare, Adrienne Block, and Kriscinda Meadows, and our intern Athena Pappas, have put in many hours typing and proofread-ing our books, including this one. Kathy Boykowycz has brought skill and creativity to the tasks of layout and design. Frederick T. Courtright of The Permissions Company arranged for the inclusion of many of these poems. Sue Ellen Thompson, the editor of the first edition of this title, and Andrea Hollander Budy, the editor of *When She Named Fire: An Anthology of Con-temporary Poetry by American Women*, provided a template for this volume. And most of all, I want to thank the poets for dedicating their craft and vision to an art that I love.

Michael Simms

Kim Addonizio

Kim Addonizio has authored five poetry collections, most recently *What Is This Thing Called Love* and *Lucifer at the Starlite* (W.W. Norton), along with *Ordinary Genius: A Guide for the Poet Within*. Addonizio also has two novels, *Little Beauties* and *My Dreams Out in the Street*, from Simon & Schuster. Her awards include two fellowships from the National Endowment for the Arts and one from the Guggenheim Foundation. She teaches privately in Oakland, California, and on-line, and also plays blues harmonica. Her website is <u>www.kimaddonizio.com</u>.

Collapsing Poem

The woman stands on the front steps, sobbing.
The man stays just inside the house,
leaning against the doorjamb. It's late, a wet
fog has left a sheer film over the windows
of cars along the street. The woman is drunk.
She begs the man, but he won't let her in.
Say it matters what happened between them;
say you can't judge whose fault this all is,
given the lack of context, given your own failures
with those you meant most to love.
Or maybe you don't care about them yet.
Maybe you need some way
to put yourself in this scene, some minor detail
that will make them seem so real you try to enter
this page to keep them from doing
to each other what you've done to someone,
somewhere; think about that for a minute,
while she keeps crying, and he speaks
in a voice so measured and calm he might be
talking to a child frightened by something
perfectly usual: darkness, thunder,
the coldness of the human heart.
But she's not listening, because now
she's hitting him, beating her fists against the chest
she laid her head on so many nights.
And by now, if you've been moved, it's because
you're thinking with regret of the person
this poem set out to remind you of,
and what you want more than anything is what
the man in the poem wants: for her to shut up.
And if you could only drive down that street
and emerge from the fog, maybe you

could get her to stop, but I can't do it.
All I can do is stand at that open door
making things worse. That's my talent,
that's why this poem won't get finished unless
you drag me from it, away from that man;
for Christ's sake, hurry, just pull up and keep
the motor running and take me wherever you're going.

The Moment

The way my mother bent to her car door, fumbling the keys, taking
    forever it seemed
to find the right one, line it up with the lock and feebly push it in and
    turn,
the way she opened the door so slowly, bending a bit more, easing herself
finally into the leather seat—She'd hurt her ribs, she explained, but it
    wasn't injury
that I saw, not the temporary setback that's followed by healing, the
    body's tenacious renewal;
I saw for the first time old age, decline, the inevitable easing towards
    death. Once in the car, though,
settled behind the wheel, backing out and heading for the steady traffic
    on the highway,
she was herself again, my mother as I'd always known her: getting older,
    to be sure,
in her seventies now, but still vital, still the athlete she'd been all her life;
    jogging, golf,
tennis especially—the sport she'd excelled at, racking up champion-
    ships—they were as natural
to her as breath. All my life she'd been the definition of grace, of a
    serenely unshakeable confidence
in the body; impossible ever to imagine her helpless, frail, confined to
    walker or wheelchair.
She was humming now as she drove, that momentary fumbling erased,
    no trace of it.
No acknowledgment of pain, of the ache she must still be feeling in her
    side. My mother
refused all that, she would go on refusing it. She peered ahead at the busy
    road, the past all but forgotten—
somewhere behind us griefs, losses, terrible knowledge, but ahead of us a
    day we'd spend together,
we were going there now, while there was still time, none of it was going
    to be wasted.

Onset

Watching that frenzy of insects above the bush of white flowers,
bush I see everywhere on hill after hill, all I can think of
is how terrifying spring is, in its tireless, mindless replications.
Everywhere emergence: seed case, chrysalis, uterus, endless manu-
    facturing.
And the wrapped stacks of styrofoam cups in the grocery, lately
I can't stand them, the shelves of canned beans and soups, freezers
of identical dinners; then the snowflake-diamond-snowflake of the rug
beneath my chair, rows of books turning their backs,
even my two feet, how they mirror each other oppresses me,
the way they fit so perfectly together, how I can nestle one big toe into
    the other
like little continents that have drifted; my God the unity of everything,
my hands and eyes, yours, doesn't that frighten you sometimes,
    remembering
the pleasure of nakedness in fresh sheets, all the lovers there before you,
beside you, crowding you out? And the scouring griefs,
don't look at them all or they'll kill you, you can barely encompass your
    own;
I'm saying I know all about you, whoever you are, it's spring
and it's starting again, the longing that begins, and begins, and begins.

Maggie Anderson

Maggie Anderson was born in New York to parents who were both teachers. Her books of poetry include *Cold Comfort*, *A Space Filled with Moving*, and *Windfall: New and Selected Poems*. Anderson is also the editor of the new and selected poems of Louise McNeill and co-editor of *Learning by Heart: Contemporary American Poetry about School* and *A Gathering of Poets*, an anthology of poems read to commemorate the 20th anniversary of the shootings of students in an anti-war protest at Kent State University in 1970.

And then I arrive at the powerful green hill

Up, up, I follow
        the creek bed through downed branches
                on spongy leaves, rimed and slippery.
The way is clear because
it is late winter,
        wet snow patches
          the runoff cold, cold to the touch
          a tang of ice still in it.

And then I arrive at the powerful green hill,
my place, my exact location,
        where I most began and started from
          where I will end beneath this ground.
I have brought everything I've left undone—
letters and resolutions, almost loves,
        hard grudges—to give to the wind that takes them up,
        tosses them down, down until
my hands are empty and I am as thin and light as a girl.

How the Brain Works

Like a peony. Full white blossoms,
so heavy. Heavy and damp with the scurrying
of a hundred ants over each petal.
From this comes language:
Morning sun. Afternoon shower. This, that.
I think can do to say.
Gathers to fit in open palms, heart shape
that wants to carry one flower as far
as it has to, as fast as it's able, to the dark
oak table, the red cut glass bowl.
Blank ants will drop and crawl to the windowsill.

Soft petals will brown and slime,
fall down to re-enter the earth.
And the brain says *Over to do*.
The brain says *Happy, happy*.

Try

To move the language toward happiness,
or failing that, toward love. Like this:
the trees have undone their sandals and silk saris,
thrown light scarves down onto the brickwork.
One red thread is caught mid-air on an updraft,
held by a spider web. Remember the way
he described the green soup he moved through
coming out of surgery? *A swift current
of warm water, swirling and turning among
floating cylinders, friends inside them talking.*
Next door the little boy swings higher and higher.
His half-scream is also half-laugh—*more, more*.
Follow the vowels; laudanum, potpourri, chrysanthemum.
Trust the verbs: to meander, to sashay, to bear up.

Beautiful War

   March-September 2003

Photographs   painted, cropped, rearranged
            into smoke   soldier   tank   desert sky
                        red on red
horizon line of dreamed landscape

so that it does not look like war—
wounded Marines, no blood—
                        no detonations, conflagrations
only the white onion tops of minarets, billowing black clothes
on the screen   digitalized   e-mailed   unsigned.

How photogenic the desert is!
The black and whites, uncaptioned, could be
Ansel Adams   moon over desert
quiet   clean   lucky
I collect the pictures from *The New York Times*.
This is the least I can do;
            to remember what happens.

March 2003   in Paris   I saw the blue peace sign
hanging from the fourth floor apartment window
            in the Ninth Arrondissement,

hurried back to my small hotel   between *Pigalle* and *St. Georges*
        watched the news in French   on the tiny black and white TV
        bolted to the ceiling above the bed.
The first clippings I saved were from *Le Figaro* and *Paris Match*.

In West Virginia in April I cut and pasted, full-page,
full-color   Jessica Lynch,
        girl from my own country of mud road and canebrake,
filth by the highway   loud and steamy in summer,
low white high school building at the edge of the forest
        her silent friends stand in a straight row—
She was my best good friend—
        they answer the reporters' questions,
country polite   they say   *yes ma'am   no, sir*

I have filled five books so far   stacked them
under the window that faces the maple turning
        red in late September.
Still clipping and pasting   my hands
smudged black with newsprint   gummy with rubber cement,
my painless war wounds.
Little enough to do   to remember what happens,
to remember the war in my books.

Jimmy Santiago Baca

Born in New Mexico of Chicano and Apache descent, Jimmy Santiago Baca was raised first by his grandmother and later sent to an orphanage. A runaway at age thirteen, it was after Baca was sentenced to five years in a maximum security prison at the age of twenty-one that he began to turn his life around: there he learned to read and write and found his passion for literature. His poetry, fiction, and memoirs have won many prizes, including the Pushcart Prize, the American Book Award, the National Poetry Award, and the International Hispanic Heritage Award.

Tire Shop

I went down yesterday
to fix a leak in my tire. Off Bridge street
there's a place 95 cents
flats fixed,
smeary black paint on warped wood plank
between two bald tires.
I go in, an old Black man
with a Jackie Gleason hat greasy soft
    with a mashed cigar stub in mouth
and another old Chicano man
working the other
pneumatic hissing tire changer. The walls are black with rubber
soot blown black dust everywhere
and rows of worn tires on gnawed board racks for sale,
air hoses snaking and looped over the floor.
I greet the two old men
    "Yeah, how's it going!"
No response.
They look up at me as if I just gave them a week to live.
    "I got a tire needs a tube."
Rudy, a young Chicano emerges from the black part of the room
pony tailed and plump
walks me out to my truck and looks at the tire.
"It'll cost you five bucks to take off and change."
    I nod.
He tells the old Chicano, who pulls the roller jack
    with a long steel handle outside,
and I wait in the middle of the grunting oval tire
changing machines,
while the old guy goes out and returns with my tire.
    He looks at me like a disgruntled Carny
    handling the ferriswheel

for the millionth time
and I'm just another ache in the arm,
        a spoiled kid.
I watch the two old men work the tire machines
        step on the foot levers that send the bars around
flipping the tire from the rim
and I wonder what brought these two old men to work here
        on this gray evening in February—
        are they ex-cons?
Drunks or addicts?
He whips the tube out, "Rudy" he yells
        and I see a gaping hole in the tube,
"Can't patch that," Rudy says
        Then in Spanish Slang says, "*no podemos pachiarlo*,"
"we got a pile of old tubes over there, we'll do it for ten
dollars."
At first I think he might be taking me
        but I hedge away from that thought
        and I watch the machines work
the spleesh of air
the final begrudging phoof! of rubber popped loose
        then the holy clank of steel bar
against steel
and very gently the old Chicano man, instead of throwing the bar
on the floor,
takes the iron bar and wipes it clean of rubber bits
        and oil
and slides it gently into his waist belt,
        in such a way
I've only seen a mother wipe her infant's mouth.
And I wonder where they live these two old guys
I turn and watch MASH on a tv suspended from the ceiling
        six o'clock news comes on
Hunnington beach blackened with oil.
Rudy comes behind me and says,
"Fucking shame they do that to our shores."
I suddenly realize how I love these working men
working in half dark with bald tires
like medieval hunchbacks in a dungeon.
They eat soup and scrape along in their lives—
how can they live I wonder on 95 cents a tire change
in today's world?
I am pleased to be with them
and feel how barrio Chicanos love this too—
how some give up nice jobs
in foreign places
to live by friends working in these places
and out of these men revolutions have started.
        The old Chicano is mumbling at me
        how cheap I am

when he learns my four tires are bald
    and spare flat,
    shaking his head as he works the tube into the tirewell.
I notice his heels are chewed to the nails
his fingernails black
his face a weary room and board stairwell
    of a downtown motel
given over to drunks and derelicts, his face hand worn
    by drunks leaning their full weight on it
wooden steps grooved by hard soled men just out
    of prison, a face condemned by life to live out more days
    in futility.
I bid goodbye to the Black man chomping his ancient cigar
the Chicano man with his head down
and I feel ashamed, somehow, that I cannot live
    their lives a while for them.
Grateful they are here, I respect such men, who have stories
that will never be told, who bring back to me
    my simple boyish days, when men
in oily pants and grubby hands talked in rough tones
    and worked at simply work, getting three meals a day
    on the table the hard way.
They live in an imperfect world,
unlike men with money who have places
to put their shame
these men have none,
others put their shame on planes or Las Vegas
these have no place
but to put their shame on their endurance
    their mothers
their kids
    themselves
unlike men who put their shame
on new cars
condos
bank accounts
so they never have to face their shame
    these men in the tire shop
    have become more human with shame.
And I thought of the time my brother betrayed
    me leaving me at 14
when we vowed we'd always be together
    he left to live with some rich folks
and I was taken to the Detention Center for kids
with no place to live—
    I became a juvenile
    filled with anger at my brother who left me alone.
These tire shop men made choices
never to leave their brothers,

in them I saw shame with no place to go
　　　but in a man's face, hands, work and silence.
　　　And as I drove away, nearing my farm
I saw a water sprinkler shooting an arc of water
　　　far over the fence and grass
it was intended to water—
　　　the fountain of water hitting a weedy stickered spot
that grew the only single flower anywhere around
　　　in the midst of rubble brush and stones
　　　the water hit
and touched a dormant seed that blossomed all itself
　　　into what it was
despite the surroundings.
Something made sense to me then
and I'm not quite sure what—
　　　an unconditional love of being and living,
　　　and taking what came one's way
　　　with dignity.
That night in my dream
I cried for my brother as he was leaving,
　　　all the words I used against myself
　　　rotten, no good, shitty, failure,
　　　dissolved in my tears,
my tears poured out of me in my dream and I wept
for my brother and wept when I turned after he left
　　　and I reached for my sister and she was having coffee
with a friend—
　　　I wept in my dream because she was not available for me
when I needed her,
and all my tears flowed, and how I wept, my feeling my pain
　　　of abandonment,
　　　all my tears became that arc of water
　　　and I became the flower, by sheer accident in the middle
　　　of nowhere, blossoming....

Jan Beatty

Jan Beatty's most recent collection of poems is *Red Sugar* (University of Pittsburgh Press, 2008). Her previous books include *Boneshaker* and *Mad River*, winner of the Agnes Lynch Starrett Prize. She is director of creative writing at Carlow University, where she teaches the Madwomen in the Attic workshops and in the MFA program. Beatty also co-hosts and produces "Prosody," a public radio show on which she interviews prominent writers. She is a Pittsburgh Steelers fan and likes muscle cars.

My Father Teaches Me Light

7 AM I get the call you have died.
To get to the hospital before my mother &
sister & their arsenal of sorrows:
I rush to your bedside, nothing
has ever been this important.
I'm standing in the shaft of morning,
the light through the window splitting
the room in half: the dead body of you/
the living me. I talk to the air, tell you
it will be alright, look to the ceiling
for floating bodies: there is no you there.
The part of me in your heart, where is it?
And what is the body now, old empty house?
You said you'd come to haunt me,
pound your cane on the floorboards,
I'd hear you say, *Pay your bills!*
I hang your cane on my bedroom door,
I wear your VFW jacket & sometimes
old men stop me to make sure I'm not
mocking the War. I want to tell them: You
were the one who spun me into the fire
of myself; I am the one you left behind,
the one you saved while you were here.

My Father Teaches Me Desire

Once it starts you can't stop it:
My father leans into it like a hunchback
at the particle-board table in the light

of our kitchen, arranging his little world:
Vidalia with paring knife; Iron City next
to French's; open sardine tin/no plate.

His left hand grabs the onion/the right
slashes a fat slice/the right dips into
the briny swamp of sardine/lifts one
by the tail/down to the French's/then
plunges it headfirst into his cavernous mouth.

Crunch of Vidalia, then pump an Iron, and
we are livin now, baby, we are home—
me watching my Dad from the dining room,
the grunt and slosh of it all, thinking,
My god, he's eating the head—where
are its eyes?

What world is this? He's god and brute,
half quake/half precision, what kind of man
can stare down the milky eye of the sardine
sans flinch, then sever its head with
those same incisors he grew in his mother's belly?

Now he's starting again, reaching
for the onion, two-fisted and ravenous,
king of kings in this 6X6 tabernacle,
he's the holy spirit of torque and focus,
and this is more action than
I've ever seen in church.

I'm standing here at age 12, learning
that sweet seduction of revulsion/desire,
I'm learning real good that the guy I want
to marry is the one who can do the worst
thing without blinking, a man who eats life
raw, the heads of things—and what else
won't scare him?

Oh Father, oh terrible primate, I am one of you.
Together we can skin the rabbit, stuff
the apple in the pig's mouth, in this kitchen
there is so much I don't know yet:
That I can write this poem.
That I will want to die many times in this life.
That in ten years I will drive back to this house,
to this kitchen, looking for your glasses.
I'll drive back to you at the funeral home
and gently place them on your face

in the casket, with no flash
or fanfare, just the music
of my heart playing:
too soon,
too soon.

My Father Teaches Me Longing

Empty eye of your onyx ring where
the diamond used to be; iron tack-hammer,
wooden cane, hat, hat—things I
dream on to conjure you back: thick
knuckles of your freckled hands, quick
laugh, Old Spice & Beeman's gum, your
life of work, work—everywhere, *love*—
over me, through, a wash of bloom, I'm
crossing Morewood, I'm the flood
of students, rolling buses, I pass
a tulip path and there you are:
Yellow tulip, singular, brutal fire,
is it here I find my foothold?
Pin of light that curses & saves.

Modern Love

Early evening, five minutes before
you're due home, I slam the dishes
in the dishwasher, squeeze rivers
of 409 onto the kitchen floor and
counters, smear it white with too many
paper towels, check the clock, listen
for the doorbell of your arriving—
Love, this is not my dreamscape,
my answer to romance's longing—but Love,
still I grab old food from the refrigerator
and sail it into the trash, call for
take-out with the breathy voice of
a woman in want—burritos again,
with enough jalapeño to make our eyes
water; Strange new world this shape
of our love: the details of our lives
stacked in piles of tabloids, month-
old pretzels in their lonely bag, and yes,
the paint peeling off the porch since spring,
no time now to wash the clothes. I do
the only thing a woman in love can:
clear papers off the bed with a wide sweep,
slide in the video, pour the soft drinks,

so we can eat in our element, our little city;
so we can tear open time to find the heart,
heart enough for us to fill our bellies and
fill our bodies with each other until
we surface to ourselves again, until we're
the only ones here tonight, and the look
in your eyes looking at me is the beautiful
sight, and my only complaints are two:
that I didn't make myself ready
for you sooner in life, that
I can't give better,
love you more.

Jacqueline Berger

Jacqueline Berger is the author of three books of poetry: *Things That Burn*, winner of the Agha Shahid Ali Prize, University of Utah Press, *The Mythologies of Danger*, winner of the Bluestem Award and the Bay Area Book Reviewers Award, and *The Gift That Arrives Broken*, winner of the 2009 Autumn House Poetry Prize. Her poetry has also appeared in numerous journals. She teaches creative writing and directs the graduate program in English at Notre Dame de Namur University in Belmont, California. Born and raised in Los Angeles, she now lives in San Francisco with her husband.

At the Holiday Crafts Fair

My friend and I sell compasses
next to a girl selling goddess magnets.
She's so female the air around her
is perfumed—crushed lavender,
curry soup. She's in her twenties
and has a baby who all day travels
from hip to lap. Both of them
blond and every part of their bodies
pumped full, the abundance
of nature bursting into life.
I remember learning to shade in art class,
circles darkened from below
until they were globes.
A useful skill considering the lips
and cheeks, the belly and ass.
Watching the girl as she walks across the room—
her hips in a stretch skirt,
her milk-rich breasts straining the cotton tee—
almost makes me a believer.
And when she pops a breast
out of her shirt to nurse, I can feel
it in my mouth, both the nipple
and the firm swell of flesh around it.
Midday, her friend comes to join her.
They talk of remedies, essential essences,
they praise the Goddess,
passing the child between them.
Then the dad arrives.
He's Venezuelan, tall and so thin his hips
jut out where his stomach dips in.
He's loose as a hinged board, slow as oil.
Now I want to marry both of them,

let the swollen river of their nights
gush over me.
Okay, the woman's views are daft
and the man's English needs work,
and they just moved out of their one-bedroom
to a converted garage. But youth,
that country I never felt at home in,
is bright as sun on water
and shines on them.
Their skin is a place to settle,
a philosophy, a way of life.
He comes back from the food booth carrying pie
with whipped cream. They eat it
together, the spoon dipping
into one mouth then the other.
The baby is happy, gurgling
at the nipple. The woman
is blessed, she tells us during a lull
between customers, and I believe it,
blessed in a way I've never been,
cradled in her body, using it
for every purpose it was intended for.
Thanksgiving's just around the corner,
the feast day's table around which
my own family will gather.
My father being helped to his place
by the caregiver, who settles him in,
ties a napkin around his neck.
He's messy as a toddler now,
suddenly left-handed, his whole
right side refusing to work.
Next to him, my mom, hunched
but tough, my brother who is loud,
the husband I married in my forties.
We will drink wine left over from the wedding,
lift our glasses to each other, here at the table
at the start of one more winter, then
lower our heads to the meal.

The Magic Show

Six of us go on a Saturday night
to a magic show.
The magician stuffs a red silk scarf
into the top of his fisted hand,
pulls out a green one from the other end,
then opens his hand to show
it's empty.

He swallows a deck of cards,
then pulls a black heart
from under his tongue,
circles his neck with diamonds.
A twenty dollar bill that's burned
is later peeled from an orange.
This guy is good,
the sleight of hand, faster
than the eye that tries to follow,
but it's nothing compared
to what I saw the day you died.
I lay on the floor beside you
when the vet gave the shot
and I watched life
vanish into thin air.
No cloth draped then removed
with a flourish, no crate
with a hidden, inner panel.
Death replaced life,
and I have no idea how it's done.

My friends and I sit in the dark
with our drinks, happily baffled.
After the show, we walk out into the night.
The new moon is drawn with invisible ink.
Summer is disappearing into autumn
and we pull our jackets closer.
By morning the mind will want answers.
For a little while amazement is enough.
Good thing the floor is there
the magician said when an ace
flipped loose from the deck,
otherwise this card would fall forever.

Celebrity Cooking

I've set the timer, am doing sit ups
on the exercise ball
and watching the food channel
where the actress is making a salad.
There's green dressing in the blender.
She doesn't eat carbs, no bread or fruit,
they cause cravings, she tells the host,
an ample woman who nods in agreement.
Just vegetables and meat.
The camera is indifferent,
capturing the actress and the host

but also the actress's sullen and beautiful
teenage daughter. Ignored by the adults,
she's a prop, the helper, and at the moment
is digging a spoon into the blender,
again and again, and shoveling the dressing
into her mouth. She must have gotten some
on her hand because now she's sucking
her knuckles, such vigor, her whole fist
seems to be making its way in.
Whether she's oblivious to the camera
or knows exactly what she's doing
is hard to say. If she crammed her hand
down her pants, it wouldn't surprise me.
I call my husband into the room to watch.
Mother and daughter are playing chicken.
The girl, bleak and hard, steps off the curb,
crossing against the light.
The actress, sun-bleached,
doesn't slow, but swerves
at the last minute to miss her.
My husband and I are rapt.
We know something about swallowing rage,
surviving the family.
It's like looking down the wrong end of a telescope,
small and far away, the girl
I'd like to take in my arms but who never
in a million years would let me.

George Bilgere

George Bilgere's most recent books are *The White Museum* (Autumn House), *The Good Kiss* (winner of the University of Akron Poetry Prize) and *Haywire*, which won the 2006 May Swenson poetry Award. He has received grants and fellowships from the National Endowment for the Arts, the Ohio Arts Council, the Society of Midland Authors, the Fulbright Foundation, and the Witter Bynner Foundation. In 2009 he won a Pushcart Prize. Bilgere teaches at John Carroll University in Cleveland, Ohio.

Greatness

Monet came in from the cold,
stomping his boots and shaking off the snow.
He was in his haystack period
and he was working on the haystack of winter,
which was proving to be much harder than the haystack of fall.

That one had been easy. The mellow afternoons
turning cool with a hint of wood smoke at twilight.
The ducks coming low over the wheat stubble.
But now his hands and feet, even his paints, were frozen.
However, he was great—a great painter,
the inventor of Impressionism—
which was a consolation.

Alice took his coat, unlaced his boots,
and sat him down at the dinner table.
She knew what was coming: a long talk about the haystack
over wine and her *coq au vin*. She thought,
I eat my suppers with a man who spends his days
staring at a haystack. Week after week. Month after month.
She loved him for his passion,
his steady, bulldog fidelity, but sometimes
she felt a twinge of jealousy toward the haystack.

Soon it would be spring, and Monet
would be painting the haystack of spring. She sighed,
a mixture of contentment and restlessness.
The funny thing was, her *coq au vin*,
on the scale of greatness, was actually superior
to his haystack paintings. Alice was a genius
of the *coq au vin*, and also of the *crêpe*.
Her *crêpes* were miracles, levitating above the plate.

Finally, she had a way of tossing her hair
away from her high, pale forehead
while at the same time
scrunching her lips into a little *moue*,
and she could do this better than any woman in Giverny—
indeed, better than any woman in all of France.

But Greatness, historically speaking, does not concern itself
with *coq au vin* or hair-tossing,
or even that irresistible little *moue*. Greatness, in this case,
is the steady haystack of a man's love,
burning, freezing, coalescing,
but enduring
in the changing light.

Trash

> *Each morning I place on my writing table*
> *a carnation and a hammer.*
>   Neruda

In fifth grade, I think it was, or even sixth,
the teacher got so fed up
with the trash stuffed into my desk,
she made me dump it out on the floor
in front of the whole classroom.
And there, amidst the detritus
I'd spent the spring collecting
on my one-mile morning walk
to Lowell Elementary—the lost keys
and toy soldiers, the scraps of smut,
the pencil stubs and broken protractors,
my half-eaten peanut butter sandwiches—
was a dead bird and a pink garter belt.
This from a time when folk still walked,
when the sidewalks were peopled
with travelers, when Fuller Brush men
and encyclopedia salesmen, and blind
sellers of brooms still walked the earth.
When every morning I left the house
in my blue Dodgers jacket, my eyes
peeled for odd stuff along the way,
like the sparrow, mummified
in the dry California air, flightless
and silent on the mica-glitter
of the sidewalk. And the garter belt,
balled up in some ivy. I didn't know
what to make of it, only that the silver
hooks meant to catch the invisible
waist of girl—a girl not my mother—

frightened me, like the empty
little talons of the sparrow, curled
around death. Mrs. Eicker turned red
and made me throw all of it—sparrow,
garter belt, rotting sandwiches,
the wads and clumps—in the trash,
although nothing is ever really lost.

The Fall

Although there were no witnesses
in the hallway outside the woman's room
of the Hotel Coronado,
when my aunt stumbled
and fell to her knees on the ancient marble,

it must have been like the swordsman
falling in *The Seven Samurai*,
a whole dynasty collapsing,
falling out of its bones
into the mud. I was reading
the sports section in the lobby
when a boy, probably sixteen or so,
ran in and called my name.
An old woman has fallen,
he said, frightened that something
so enormous could happen, that fate
should cast him as an emissary
announcing dynastic collapse
instead of just a high school kid,

and I stood up and ran to her
although I'm fifty-six now, and breaking
into a spontaneous run feels like
trying out a first language you'd lost
as a kid who swapped countries.

And there she sat, lean and elegant,
like an athlete who'd collapsed
from sheer exhaustion, her legs
drawn up to her chin as she fought
to lift the whole city again,

the crumbling Coronado,
where Miles Davis used to play,
and the Continental, where the Gershwins
hung out at the Tack Room,
and the abandoned Fox Theater
where she saw Olivier's *Hamlet*,

and even the boarded up
Forest Park Boat House, where her father
used to take her for ice cream
in the sweltering summers.

An old woman has fallen.

Laundry Chute

In go the dirty socks and underwear,
last week's stale shirts. The slacks
with their drizzle of bisque.

It's so easy
that while I'm at it
I throw in the car's old brakes
and the weird new sound
the fridge has started to make,

along with that nasty crack of my father's
from last night's nightmare. And the fact
that I can't quite manage to unremember
what I didn't manage to say to my mother
the last time we ever saw each other.

Into the black hole
go the lies I've told, the big ones
that certain people I love
still carry around like wounds.
And something I'd rather not mention
involving a couple of women
and a lot of gin.

Meanwhile, far beneath me,
the steady, reassuring hum
of subterranean machinery.

I've got a few days
before everything finds its way back up,
cleaned, pressed, and folded.

Peter Blair

Peter Blair's first full-length book, *Last Heat*, won the 1999 Washington Prize and was published by Word Works Press. *The Divine Salt* (2003) and *Farang* (2009) were published by Autumn House Press. Born in Pittsburgh, he has worked in a psychiatric ward, a steel mill, and in Thailand as a Peace Corps member. Currently, he teaches at the University of North Carolina at Charlotte.

Discussing the Dream of Culture with Professor Kwaam

At the corner of Somprasong and Petchaburi
we sit at a rickety metal table. Our soup steams
in sidewalk sunlight. Cars crawl on the street
like the streams of ants up and down the shop wall.
His shiny head fuzzed with new hair,
eyebrows shaved clean, Kwaam smiles, ethereal,
kind: *Thai and American cultures, two dreams*
of one world, the Dharma. A few months ago
he taught me Thai and how to read palms:
A good way to hold hands with a girl. He winked.
Now, he's one day out of a monastery and saffron
robes. Noodles slip off my novice chopsticks.
My soup darkened by soy sauce, peanuts,
sugar, the strands disappear in my bowl.
Kwaam's noodles twine in clear broth.

At the plywood counter, I buy another soup.
The cook dunks a strainer of beef chunks
in boiling water. The red meat turns gray
and rubbery in bubbling froth. He dumps them
into a bowl with cilantro, sprouts, broth
and a fleshy lump of noodles. *So, what is Dharma?*
I set the dish on the table. *Dharma is the empty*
bowl. Joking, again. The sky's blue, like a bowl
overturned on market stalls and bleached
white buildings. *The abbot took us to an autopsy.*
They cut open a woman, removed the heart,
liver, intestines. He tells me about shriveled skin,
hollow rib cages arching over tables,
pails of limp, gray organs. *Dharma*.

My soup steams. My abdomen's distended.
The market gurgles ageless sounds around us.
I can't look at Kwaam's sad, triumphant smile,
or the emptiness deepening in his sunlit bowl.

November Full Moon

It's *Loy Krathong*, the night lovers float lit candle-boats
on waves, wish for luck from water spirits.
We two couples walk to the river. Yingna curses Harry
in bar-girl Thai I can't follow. Siripan drops my hand,
runs ahead of us into the shadows between streetlights.
Your girlfriend doesn't want to hear that shit, Harry says.
I chase Siripan down the narrow street under high walls
topped with jagged glass, glinting green in the moonlight.
When I touch her shoulder, Siripan's crying:
She said she'll sleep with every man on Patpong.
Sweat seeps into my shirt like ignorance.
I'm always insulting her with the best intentions.
I sit on the curb. She hails a cab, then waves it off.
Yingna followed Harry home one night and stayed.
She's pregnant. He won't marry her. Siripan gazes
down the road where a blue neon light flickers.

We find them again by the Chao Phraya River.
The rainy season over, China winds blow into Bangkok.
At the water's edge, Siripan calms Yingna.
Their silhouettes sway against the dark waves:
Siripan's Western pants and Yingna's peasant sarong
together in this city of walls. My palms cradle
a bamboo boat strung with jasmine,
sheltering a small yellow candle. We drift apart
into the privacy the night provides every few paces.
Her arm around Harry, Yingna shouts, *Ours is still lit!*
Some boats crowd together. Some spin
and float back to shore. Most flames die at ten yards.
Siripan and I squat on the muddy bank. My hissing match
whispers to the night air, and kisses the candle-wick
with fire. We push our boat into the current,
give the flame to the wind and waves.

The Day after the Coup

A green wall of jungle blazes outside
the window of the English Department room.
The professors wear their uniforms today,
creased and rumpled from being folded in trunks.

In stifling heat, we're made to stand at attention
like laurel leaves shrunk stiff in a cold snap.
Stocky soldiers in camouflage fatigues
weave between us. The sergeant grunts sharp
questions. Like a schoolmaster, he jabs at papers
with the grooved steel tip of his bayonet.

Later, we take chicken and *som tam* salad,
to three teachers in jail. Kwaam sits
cross-legged on cement in striped
prison shorts, his shirt draped over his neck
like a towel. Purple bruises shine
through the sweat on his chest.
We pass packets of yellow papaya
between the bars. His house burned down
last night. *Professor*, he whispers to me,
how do you like our Thai prisons?

Professor Som's still missing. *I hope he stays
in the mountains*, Sutape says. It's night.
We talk on his porch as frogs whistle
love calls in the canals. He's my boss, the newly
appointed dean. Moths fly into the candlelight
and fall, splashing, in a wide water pan
he set on the table to catch them. Turned low,
his police radio murmurs about students barricaded
in a Bangkok university, fighting tanks.

Communist dogs, he growls. *They have guns
in their rooms, make trouble for everyone.*
I ask what will happen. He shrugs.
The soldiers will kill them. I take the pan
and pour the moths onto the ground,
set it back on the table again. One flops over,
legs grasping at air. Others lie drowned
on the grass. Sutape says good night,
pinches out the flame with his thumb.

Planting Rice with Nipun, Ubol Province

My bare feet wading ankle-deep water,
I face a buffalo's tapered back flanks,
and the leathery black zero
of its anus. We work a glassy rice paddy
among hundreds of gleaming squares
checkering the flat valley. In the distance, the blue
mounded Petchabun mountains rise into Laos.

Don't push the plow down.

I guide the curved wood-tip through soft mud.
He clicks his tongue, tugs a rope
strung through the buffalo's spongy nose.
It turns at the dike and we slosh along,
shattering the sky below us.
Soon Nipun drapes my neck with a cloth,
gives me a green bundle of rice shoots.

Do three rows, like this.

He plants a shoot off his left foot,
one below his crotch, and one off his right.
I bend, thumb-jam the seedlings' roots
into cool viscous muck. The mud
holds them, tight as my ankles.

Don't raise your back. Sing with me.

Forced to grip new soil,
the green spears totter and wave.
We step, reach, stretch, swinging
our arms and singing
the planting song's tonal Thai words:

During the twelfth full moon,
canals overflow their banks.
All the rice farmers dance
under the village locust tree.

That night, we sip rice wine
around an open fire. Heat-lightning flashes
off the capes of horizon clouds.
Overhead, Orion, old silver warrior,
wields his starry shield and sword, forever locked
in battle with the bull. Nipun smiles.

For Thai farmers, it's a turtle
with a plow on its back. See?
The belt and the sword make a plow.

I nod and stretch my muddy feet to the fire,
my body stiff and sore from plunging
hundreds of roots into earth.

Chana Bloch

Chana Bloch's four books of poetry are *The Secrets of the Tribe, The Past Keeps Changing, Mrs. Dumpty*, winner of the Felix Pollak Prize in Poetry, and *Blood Honey* (Autumn House, 2008), winner of the Poetry Society of America's Di Castagnola Award. She is co-translator of *Hovering at a Low Altitude: The Collected Poetry of Dahlia Ravikovitch, The Song of Songs, The Selected Poetry of Yehuda Amichai* and his *Open Closed Open*, winner of the PEN Award for Poetry in Translation. She has received fellowships from the NEA, the NEH, and the Rockefeller Foundation. Bloch taught English Literature for many years at Mills College, where she directed the Creative Writing Program.

The New World

My uncle killed a man and was proud of it.
Some punk with a knife came at him in Flatbush
and he knocked the sucker to the ground.
The sidewalk finished the job.

By then he'd survived two wives
and a triple bypass. He carried
a bit of the plastic tubing in his pocket
and would show it to anyone.
He'd unbutton his shirt right there on the street
and show off the scar.

As a boy, he watched a drunken Cossack
go after his father with an ax.
His sister tried to staunch the bleeding
with a hunk of dry bread.

That's the old country for you:
they ate with their hands, went hungry to bed,
slept in their stink. When pain knocked,
they opened the door.

The bitter drive to Brooklyn every Sunday
when I was a child—
Uncle George in the doorway snorting and laughing,
I'm gonna take a bite of your little behind.

He was a good-looker in a pin-striped suit
and shoeshine shoes.
*This is America, we don't live
in the Dark Ages anymore, sweetie.
This is a free country.*

Brothers

When I was the Baba Yaga of the house
on my terrible chicken legs,
the children sat close on the sofa as I read,
both of them together
determined to be scared.

Careful! I cackled, stalking them
among the pillows:
*You bad Russian boy,
I eat you up!*
They shivered and squirmed, my delicious sons,

waiting for a mighty arm
to seize them.
I chased them screeching down the hall,
I catch you, I eat you!
my witch-blade hungry for the spurt
of laughter—

                What stopped me
even as I lifted my hand?
The stricken voice that cried: *Eat him!
Eat my brother.*

The Messiah of Harvard Square

Every year some student would claim to be the Messiah.
It was the rabbi who had to deal with them.
He had jumped, years ago, from a moving boxcar
on the way to a death camp. That leap
left him ready for anything.

This year at Pesach, a Jewish student proclaimed
Armageddon. "Burn the books! Burn the textbooks!"
he shouted to a cheerful crowd,
sang Hebrew songs to confuse the Gentiles,
dressed for the end like Belshazzar.
People stopped to whisper and laugh.

"I have a noble task," the boy explained.
"I must prepare myself to endure
the laughter of fools."

The rabbi was a skeptic.
Years ago he'd been taught, If you're planting a tree
and someone cries out, *The Messiah has come!*
finish planting the tree. Then
go see if it's true.

Still, he took the boy into his study
and questioned him slowly, meticulously,
as if the poor soul before him might be,
God help us, the Messiah.

Reprieve

We were drinking coffee in her pre-war flat,
four walls, Pompeiian gray
to match her complexion.
An old Jewish woman in Prague.
Her dead husband laughing in a dapper suit,
fedora, cigarette, one arm around a life
flash-frozen and set at the table
beside the Czech pastries.

She held me with her skinny hand.
"I could have left after the war with my baby
and started over." And then,
half to herself: "Did I make a mistake?"
Her baby was translating
into a broken German I could manage.

What a question to ask a green girl like me,
still too married to regret a marriage
I thought I chose.
Still three or four wars away from knowing
when a question
isn't a question, just a gasp of loss—
but mine to translate.

She poured coffee, passed the kolacky, awaited
my verdict. Yes, you should have left.
No, you did the right thing.

As if one could reprieve a life even now
by pointing a finger
left or right.

Sometimes I Want to Sink into Your Body

Sometimes I want to sink into your body
with the fever that spikes inside me
to be a woman
who can open a man.

Why must I be only softness and haunches,
a satin cul-de-sac?

You ought to know what sharpens me
like a barbed arrow.
Do you think we're so different?

How you tease me, twiddle me,
hustle me along,
just when I'd like to splay you
tooth and nail.

Laure-Anne Bosselaar

Laure-Anne Bosselaar grew up in Belgium and moved to the United States in 1987. Her books are *The Hour Between Dog and Wolf* (BOA Editions, 1997), *Small Gods of Grief* (BOA Editions, 2001), winner of the Isabella Gardner Prize for Poetry, and *A New Hunger* (Ausable, 2007). She is also editor of four anthologies and translator, with her husband, poet Kurt Brown, of a book by Flemish poet Herman de Coninck. Recipient of a 2007 Pushcart Prize, Bosselaar taught at Sarah Lawrence College and currently teaches at the low-residency MFA Program of Pine Manor College. She and her husband live in California.

The Pleasures of Hating

I hate Mozart. Hate him with that healthy
pleasure one feels when exasperation has

crescendoed, when lungs, heart, throat,
and voice explode at once: *I hate that!* —

there's bliss in this, rapture. My shrink
tried to disabuse me, convinced I use Amadeus

as a prop: *Think further, your father perhaps?*
I won't go back, think of the shrink

with a powdered wig, pinched lips, mole:
a transference, he'd say, *a relapse*: so be it.

I hate broccoli, chain saws, patchouli, bra-
clasps that draw dents in your back, roadblocks,

men in black kneesocks, sandals and shorts—
I *love* hating that. Loathe stickers on tomatoes,

jerky, deconstruction, nazis, doilies. I delight
in detesting. And love loving so much after that.

After a Noisy Night

The man I love enters the kitchen
with a groan, he just
woke up, his hair a Rorschach test.
A minty kiss, a hand
on my neck, coffee, two percent milk,
microwave. He collapses
on a chair, stunned with sleep,
yawns, groans again, complains
about his dry sinuses and crusted nose.
            I want to tell him how
much he slept, how well,
the cacophony of his snoring
pumping in long wheezes
and throttles—the debacle
of rhythm—hours erratic
with staccato of pants and puffs,
crescendi of gulps, chokes,
pectoral sputters and spits.
            But the microwave goes *ding*!
A short little *ding*!—sharp
as a guillotine—loud enough to stop
my words from killing the moment.
            And during the few seconds
it takes the man I love
to open the microwave, stir,
sip and sit there staring
at his mug, I remember the vows
I made to my pillows, to fate
and God: I'll stop eating licorice,
become a blonde, a lumberjack,
a Catholic, *anything*,
but bring a man to me:
            so I go to him: *Sorry, honey,
sorry you had such a rough night*,
hold his gray head against my heart
and kiss him, kiss him.

Plastic Beatitude

Our neighbors, the Pazzotis, live in a long
narrow canary-yellow house with Mrs. Pazzotti's old
father, their 2 daughters, *their* husbands, 4 kids,
a tortoise shell cat and a white poodle.
            Their yard is my childhood dream: toys,
bicycles, tubs, bird cages, barbeques, planters, pails, tools
and garden sculptures: an orange squirrel eating a nut,

Mickey Mouse pushing a wheelbarrow, St. Joseph
carrying a lantern, his other blessing hand
broken at the wrist, and two tea-sipping toads
in an S-shaped love seat, smiling at each other
under a polka-dotted parasol.
          On the yellow railing around the deck,
a procession of nine pinwheels. This May morning,
they thrash the air with each breeze like clumsy
angels nailed to their posts. On the garage wall
at the end of the yard an electric cord
shoots up to the roof. One half connects to a blue
neon insect electrocuter, the other half snakes to, then
disappears into a pedestal cemented on the cornice.
          And there she stands, in plastic
beatitude—and six feet of it—the Madonna,
in her white robe and blue cape, arms
outstretched, blessing the Pazottis, their yard
and neighbors, lit from within day and night,
calling God's little insects to her shining light,
before sending them straight
          to the zapper—tiny buzzing heretics
fried by the same power that lured them
to their last temptation.

Andrea Hollander Budy

Andrea Hollander Budy is the author of three full-length poetry collections, *House Without a Dreamer*, *The Other Life*, and *Woman in the Painting*, and the editor of *When She Named Fire: An Anthology of Contemporary Poetry by American Women* (Autumn House Press, 2009). Recipient of two poetry fellowships from the National Endowment for the Arts, she is also winner of such national honors as the Nicholas Roerich Poetry Prize, the D.H. Lawrence Fellowship, and a Pushcart Prize for prose memoir. The Writer-in-Residence at Lyon College, she lives in Mountain View, Arkansas.

In the Garden

Mill Cottages, Donnington, England

A squirrel fidgets at the tip of a swaying branch
and I wonder if he clings without knowing he clings.

Sometimes I remember my first time
and wonder if that girl I was held any regrets.

I think about the boy I believed I would cling to forever,
whatever I understood *forever* to mean,

no more reliable than the wind that is blind to us
and invisible.

Of course we were both young and knew
only how much we didn't know,

both of us giddy with wanting.
The squirrel leaps. The branch holds.

That's where he is now, worrying another pine cone.
I've seen this before. And him. Or one just like him.

Later there were other men
and the hopes of a young woman,

a little older now, a little more equipped,
steadying herself and more sure of her place

in her own life, not counting on
even the sturdiest looking

branch to hold her.

Ex

Long after I married you, I found myself
in his city and heard him call my name.
Each of us amazed, we headed to the café
we used to haunt in our days together.
We sat by a window across the paneled room
from the table that had witnessed hours
of our clipped voices and sharp silences.
Instead of coffee, my old habit in those days,
I ordered hot chocolate, your drink,
dark and dense the way you take it,
without the swirl of frothy cream I like.
He told me of his troubled marriage, his two
difficult daughters, their spiteful mother, how
she'd tricked him and turned into someone
he didn't really know. I listened and listened,
glad all over again to be rid of him, and sipped
the thick, brown sweetness slowly as I could,
licking my lips, making it last.

Nineteen-Thirty-Eight

I remember the way my mother
answered when people asked
where she'd gone to school:

South Side High, 1938,
adding the year in the same breath
though I knew

she never graduated,
yanked out
when her father lost his job.

Now it was her turn
to make herself
useful, he told her.

Hadn't he put
food on the table
all her life and all her little sister's?

How necessary
to tell a lie like hers, to answer
South Side High, 1938, and smile

without betraying
the blaze in her chest, her envy
for the questioner who likely met

her own husband at some university.
But wasn't my mother *the lucky one*,
my grandfather was fond of telling her

even into my childhood, sometimes
in front of my friends, lucky
to have got my father, a college man

who sat beside her at a ballgame
in 1939? *Just look at her*
who didn't finish high school!

Didn't I tell her then it wouldn't matter?

Graveyard Shift

While the family slept, he scraped out innards.
Fox, badger, rabbit, mink—the rich
would have their jackets and stoles,
their long coats. The uniform he wore
belonged to the factory, but the boots
were his own. Blood on their soles, the perpetual
stench of blood in his nostrils. He did it
for his mother, good woman his father
had left, and his four siblings. During his break
in the factory courtyard, he'd nibble yesterday's
dark bread, gulp watered-down milk
from the thermos he'd used at school,
the air ruined by cigarettes and the blood
they'd all dragged with them. Light blared
from the building's windows.
If there were stars, he couldn't find them.
He'd shuffle back through the steel doors
and hold his breath like the brown boy
who would amaze him decades later
holding his breath for tourists who threw
coins into deep water for him to retrieve.
They'd shine from his palms
or his teeth when he surfaced, rising
from his poverty.

Rick Campbell

Rick Campbell is the author of *The Traveler's Companion, Setting the World in Order*, which won the Walt McDonald Prize, and *Dixmont* (Autumn House, 2008). His poems and essays have been widely published, and he has won an NEA Fellowship, a Pushcart Prize, and two fellowships from the Florida Arts Council. The director of Anhinga Press and the Anhinga Prize for Poetry, Campbell teaches English at Florida A&M University in Tallahassee. He lives with his family in Gadsden County, Florida.

Fair Warning

These stones are from my daughter's collection,
pebbles washed in the river of days. She
asks which is my favorite and I

work against my will to say all of them are nice—
the line that means Daddy's not really paying
attention now; his mind is in another part of the house

somewhere in Clifton's poems,
or counting dollars
for the Bank of America bill.

Below my heart, where things are tight,
where I keep my father, I remember my promise
not to be him, and say this one, the one

that looks like a blue dinosaur's tooth,
and this one too, the way the dark
swirls so deep into the brown like love,

like how I look at you and know there is no excuse
for not giving the world, all your blood,
every inch of skin and bone, for your child.

Then we slide the box under her bed
and wash our hands for dinner.

Road House

After the kids had gone back to town,
to rock and roll bars and bodies
like their own, the owner
would unplug the jukebox

and start his reel of favorite songs.
Popcorn was free and sometimes beer too.
And we'd listen, And we'd dance.
And he'd sit and tell us some story

we were privileged to know by heart
because all good stories are already ours.
After midnight, I'd look up at the bar,
the neon beer signs, a dead elk on the wall.

The fat man I imagined sad, long eyes
of a Basque sheepherder, would look at his wife
sleeping on the bar, head in her arms,
and then whisper to his dog—who waited for this moment—

wanna dance. Between bar and empty tables
he'd wrap his big arms around the mutt and sway
in the yellow light. They danced a slow circle,
no matter what the music said.

Poetry Makes Nothing Happen

I want to claim that I don't understand genocide,
That I have not read history; that I don't
Understand the circulation of the blood
And how we can die from its
Spilling on the ground
From hacked off limbs.

I am against genocide
But who is for it? Do
Those who murder in genocide's
Name, favor it? Do they say
I am a genocidist? I fly
The flag of genocide. I sever
Your wife's head in the name
Of genocide.

Do they even say *I hate you?*
I killed you because you're not like me.
You are too much like me.

And how, if we go back
Can I not understand Wounded Knee,
The Trail of Tears, Manifest Destiny,
Major Mason's massacre of the Pequot?

How can I forget lynching,
Carpet bombing, Napalm, My Lai?
How can we go back?

Poetry makes nothing happen,
Auden so famously said. Yet
We are here, often. Ready to stop
The war, to end Apartheid, to bring
About justice.

We will rail and weep in verse
Against other atrocities, against air-
Tight containers of Chinese immigrants,
Trailers of dead Mexicans in the big armed
Cactus of the Sonora.

We will gather again.

Heart of Dependent Arising

My wife is rolled into surgery
and as the drugs wash over her
she tries to remember her
Medicine Buddha meditation.

Her heart is still at the center
of her chest, the lotus flower
still eight-petalled and white.

The Healing Buddha, though
his light's still blue, has begun
to float off his moon disc. The
icons that surround him: *Actualized
Wisdom, Simultaneous Wealth*
are only colors now. But *Peacock's
Throat*, she remembers. Remembers
too blissful, radiant light.

I figure this is enough
to let her go with the nurses
to the hands and scalpel
of her Georgia gynecologist
who yesterday told us
that the ovary is the size of a pecan.
I am left to sit in the cafeteria
with pager 209—that will flash
and beep when her doctor wants me.

We go for refuge to the Buddha.
We go for refuge to the empty clarity
of our minds. She prays too
to the Virgin, but skips
in the hour of our death.

I have echoed our doctor's mantra
that this surgery is routine, a quick
in and out. But nothing
to the terminally nervous
is routine, anesthesia's 2% death rate
looms in her thoughts.

She dislikes hospital staff's blanket
reassurances and rolls
to surgery with yak bone *mala*
twisted in her right hand,

her Immaculate Heart of Mary scapula
wrapped around her wrist.
My pager blinks every three seconds
like a slowed heart beat,

and I wait in the secular world
I've made for myself through subtraction,
through sloughing off catechism, prayer,
Jesus, God, the saints and archangels.

I've nothing left but sin and hope.
A resolute faith in whom and what I love.
Many paths in a wood.
Many shafts of light.

Lucille Clifton

Lucille Clifton (1936-2010) was the 2007 recipient of the Ruth Lilly Poetry Prize, as well as the 2010 Frost Medal from the Poetry Society of America. She wrote dozens of books of poetry, fiction, and books for children, including *Blessing the Boats: New and Selected Poems 1988-2000*, which won the National Book Award. Appointed a Chancellor of The Academy of American Poets and elected a Fellow in Literature of The American Academy of Arts and Sciences, Clifton lived for many years in Columbia, Maryland, where she was a Distinguished Professor of Humanities at St. Mary's College.

the times

it is hard to remain human on a day
when birds perch weeping
in the trees and the squirrel eyes
do not look away but the dog ones do
in pity.
another child has killed a child
and i catch myself relieved that they are
white and i might understand except
that i am tired of understanding.
if this
alphabet could speak its own tongue
it would be all symbol surely;
the cat would hunch across the long table
and that would mean time is catching up,
and the spindle fish would run to ground
and that would mean the end is coming
and the grains of dust would gather themselves
along the streets and spell out:

these too are your children   this too is your child

moonchild

whatever slid into my mother's room that
late june night, tapping her great belly,
summoned me out roundheaded and unsmiling.
is this the moon, my father used to grin,
cradling me?   it was the moon
but nobody knew it then.

the moon understands dark places.
the moon has secrets of her own.
she holds what light she can.

we girls were ten years old and giggling
in our hand-me-downs. we wanted breasts,
pretended we had them, tissued
our undershirts. jay johnson is teaching
me to french kiss, ella bragged, who
is teaching you? how do you say; my father?

the moon is queen of everything.
she rules the oceans, rivers, rain.
when I am asked whose tears these are
I always blame the moon.

what i think when i ride the train

maybe my father
made these couplers.
his hands were hard
and black and swollen,
the knuckles like lugs
or bolts in a rich man's box.
he broke a bone each year
as if on schedule.
when i read about a wreck,
how the cars buckle
together or hang from the track
in a chain, but never separate,
i think; see,
there's my father,
he was a chipper,
he made the best damn couplers
in the whole white world.

august

for laine

what would we give,
my sister,
to roll our weak
and foolish brother

back onto his bed,
to face him with his sins
and blame him
for them?

what would we give
to fuss with him again,
he who clasped his hands
as if in prayer and melted

to our mother?   what
would we give
to smile and staple him
back into our arms,

our honey boy, our sam,
not clean, not sober, not
better than he was, but
oh, at least, alive?

study the masters

like my aunt timmie.
it was her iron,
or one like hers,
that smoothed the sheets
the master poet slept on.
home or hotel, what matters is
he lay himself down on her handiwork
and dreamed.   She dreamed too, words:
some cherokee, some masai and some
huge and particular as hope.
if you had heard her
chanting as she ironed
you would understand form and line
and discipline and order and
america.

to my last period

well girl, goodbye,
after thirty-eight years.
thirty-eight years and you
never arrived
splendid in your red dress
without trouble for me
somewhere, somehow.

now it is done,
and i feel just like
the grandmothers who,

after the hussy has gone,
sit holding her photograph
and sighing, *wasn't she*
beautiful? wasn't she beautiful?

my dream about being white

hey music and
me
only white,
hair a flutter of
fall leaves
circling my perfect
line of a nose,
no lips,
no behind, hey
white me
and i'm wearing
white history
but there's no future
in those clothes
so I take them off and
wake up
dancing.

Billy Collins

Billy Collins' latest collection is *Ballistics*. He served as U.S. Poet Laureate 2001–03.

Consolation

How agreeable it is not to be touring Italy this summer,
wandering her cities and ascending her torrid hill towns.
How much better to cruise these local, familiar streets,
fully grasping the meaning of every road sign and billboard
and all the sudden hand gestures of my compatriots.

There are no abbeys here, no crumbling frescoes or famous
domes and there is no need to memorize a succession
of kings or tour the dripping corners of a dungeon.
No need to stand around a sarcophagus, see Napoleon's
little bed on Elba, or view the bones of a saint under glass.

How much better to command the simple precinct of home
than be dwarfed by pillar, arch, and basilica.
Why hide my head in phrase books and wrinkled maps?
Why feed scenery into a hungry, one-eyed camera
eager to eat the world one monument at a time?

Instead of slouching in a café ignorant of the word for ice,
I will head down to the coffee shop and the waitress
known as Dot. I will slide into the flow of the morning
paper, all language barriers down,
rivers of idiom running freely, eggs over easy on the way.

And after breakfast, I will not have to find someone
willing to photograph me with my arm around the owner.
I will not puzzle over the bill or record in a journal
what I had to eat and how the sun came in the window.
It is enough to climb back into the car

as if it were the great car of English itself
and sounding my loud vernacular horn, speed off
down a road that will never lead to Rome, not even Bologna.

Taking Off Emily Dickinson's Clothes

First, her tippet made of tulle,
easily lifted off her shoulders and laid
on the back of a wooden chair.

And her bonnet,
the bow undone with a light forward pull.

Then the long white dress, a more
complicated matter with mother-of-pearl
buttons down the back,
so tiny and numerous that it takes forever
before my hands can part the fabric,
like a swimmer's dividing water,
and slip inside.

You will want to know
that she was standing
by an open window in an upstairs bedroom,
motionless, a little wide-eyed,
looking out at the orchard below,
the white dress puddled at her feet
on the wide-board, hardwood floor.

The complexity of women's undergarments
in nineteenth-century America
is not to be waved off,
and I proceeded like a polar explorer
through clips, clasps, and moorings,
catches, straps, and whalebone stays,
sailing toward the iceberg of her nakedness.

Later, I wrote in a notebook
it was like riding a swan into the night,
but, of course, I cannot tell you everything—
the way she closed her eyes to the orchard,
how her hair tumbled free of its pins,
how there were sudden dashes
whenever we spoke.

What I can tell you is
it was terribly quiet in Amherst
that Sabbath afternoon,
nothing but a carriage passing the house,
a fly buzzing in a windowpane.

So I could plainly hear her inhale
when I undid the very top
hook-and-eye fastener of her corset

and I could hear her sigh when finally it was unloosed,
the way some readers sigh when they realize
that Hope has feathers,
that Reason is a plank,
that Life is a loaded gun
that looks right at you with a yellow eye.

Workshop

I might as well begin by saying how much I like the title.
It gets me right away because I'm in a workshop now
so immediately the poem has my attention,
like the Ancient Mariner grabbing me by the sleeve.

And I like the first couple of stanzas,
the way they establish this mode of self-pointing
that runs through the whole poem
and tells us that words are food thrown down
on the ground for other words to eat.
I can almost taste the tail of the snake
in its own mouth,
if you know what I mean.

But what I'm not sure about is the voice,
which sounds in places very casual, very blue jeans,
but other times seems standoffish,
professorial in the worst sense of the word
like the poem is blowing pipe smoke in my face.
But maybe that's just what it wants to do.

What I did find engaging were the middle stanzas,
especially the fourth one.
I like the image of clouds flying like lozenges
which gives me a very clear picture.
And I really like how this drawbridge operator
just appears out of the blue
with his feet up on the iron railing

and his fishing pole jigging—I like jigging—
a hook in the slow industrial canal below.
I love slow industrial canal below. All those *l*'s.

Maybe it's just me,
but the next stanza is where I start to have a problem.
I mean how can the evening bump into the stars?
And what's an obbligato of snow?
Also, I roam the decaffeinated streets.
At that point I'm lost. I need help.

The other thing that throws me off,
and maybe this is just me,
is the way the scene keeps shifting around.
First, we're in this big aerodrome
and the speaker is inspecting a row of dirigibles,
which makes me think this could be a dream.
Then he takes us into his garden,
the part with the dahlias and the coiling hose
though that's nice, the coiling hose,
but then I'm not sure where we're supposed to be.
The rain and the mint green light,
that makes it feel outdoors, but what about this wallpaper?
Or is it a kind of indoor cemetery?
There's something about death going on here.

In fact, I start to wonder if what we have here
is really two poems, or three, or four,
or possibly none.

But then there's that last stanza, my favorite.
This is where the poem wins me back,
especially the lines spoken in the voice of the mouse.
I mean we've all seen these images in cartoons before,
but I still love the details he uses
when he's describing where he lives.
The perfect little arch of an entrance in the baseboard,
the bed made out of a curled-back sardine can,
the spool of thread for a table.
I start thinking about how hard the mouse had to work
night after night collecting all these things
while the people in the house were fast asleep,
and that gives me a very strong feeling,
a very powerful sense of something.
But I don't know if anyone else was feeling that.
Maybe that was just me.
Maybe that's just the way I read it.

Steven Cramer

Steven Cramer is the author of five poetry collections: *The Eye That Desires to Look Upward* (1987), *The World Book* (1992), *Dialogue for the Left and Right Hand* (1997), *Goodbye to the Orchard* (2004), and *Clangings* (2012). Recipient of fellowships from the Massachusetts Artists Foundation and the National Endowment for the Arts, he directs the low-residency MFA program in creative writing at Lesley University in Cambridge, MA.

The Benevolence of the Butcher

He's not history yet. He's as proud
of his work as a blood-spatter expert

breaking the code of sprayed gore.
Next door left, in the gourmet shop,

brie and baguettes; *Love-Lies-Bleeding*
in the garden center next door right.

Two witches, catty-corner, run
a crystal shop. Self is the artful

lies it tells itself, Mind is no more
than neural chuck. We know

it's only human to wait in line
for the choicest cuts, to forecast

when our number's up, to tense
what feels a lifetime for the shutter—

all that forbearance just to end up
a rat-eyed stiff. Blood-gouted

apron in a hamper, the butcher
drives home by instinct. At red

stoplights he clicks the seconds past
with his tongue, our strongest muscle.

On Hold

Press #1 to languish in English,
wait time estimated anywhere
between death and rebirth. Askew
skull pinioning the handset to

your collarbone's hollow, listen:
your dead kin traffics in and out
of memory's rest stop, the rents
of past loves disjointed Legos now.

Whatever you do, don't touch
zero. It defaults to queue's end
or worse, the ohms of nothingness.
You skeptic of intervention you,

thumb and index compassing
your temples, what *was* at heart
in your appeal? Oh, just hit star,
or pound, or mute. Then rage, rage.

Sketches at the Hayden Rec Center

A solitary clock behind bars, floors
forbidden to street shoes, exit signs—

one, two, three, four: fine—and waxy cries
of boys, one mine, practicing their dribbling

and bank shots. My eyes closed, the volley
of Spauldings pounds like opening night

of *Operation Desert Storm*, or *Shield*, or
whatever war our Sonys dust up next . . .

Opening my eyes, I glimpse, time-lapse,
the pierced, lovely lips and eyebrows

of the future for these boys. Give them,
please, their share of nitrogen, oxygen,

and the less-than-one-percent of "other"
my son & I idled in, *en route* to Hayden,

in line at Walgreen's new drive-through,
watching a man cradle tulips to his van.

To study electricity, you need lights,
a Baghdad schoolteacher said on NPR—

after which we learned the hawk sees
eight times better than us. What gives

deadly eyesight to that beauty of a bird,
what gave those tulips an edgy splash

of apricot against the parking lot's
fresh tarmac and knolls of sod—is that

what can't simmer down in these boys?
Oh, they're trying, as the coach requires,

to stretch their fingers, rotate their necks.
When his whistle fires them down-court,

into the 30-second zone, they're home—
targeting each other, being themselves

targeted. At my son's age, I drilled
my blue and gray sharpshooters, and had

by heart the total killed and wounded
at Bull Run . . . A few more chest-shots

and time's up. I peel my son off the pine
handholds bolted to cinder-block walls;

navigate him toward the snack machine
for cheddar fries and Sprite; then to the car

where, sliding him into the back, I get
this burst of scent: part cheese-product,

part lemon-lime and sweat-tang in his hair;
and from the drugstore lot across the street

where a man hugged color like a pass
completed, the mix of damp earth and tar.

Jim Daniels

Jim Daniels, the Thomas Stockman Baker Profes-
sor of English at Carnegie Mellon University, has
published 13 books of poetry and three collections
of short stories, including *From Milltown to Mall-
town* with Charlee Bodsky and Jane McCafferty,
and *Having a Little Talk with Capital P Poetry*. He
has also written and produced three films based
on his short stories and edited or co-edited four
anthologies. His poems have been featured on
Garrison Keillor's "Writer's Almanac," in Billy Col-
lins' *Poetry 180* anthologies, and in Ted Kooser's
"American Life in Poetry" syndicated column. His
poem "Factory Love" is displayed on the roof of a
race car. Daniels was born in Detroit, and currently
lives in Pittsburgh with his wife, the writer Kristin
Kovacic, and their two children, near the boyhood
homes of Andy Warhol and Dan Marino.

Short-order Cook

An average joe comes in
and orders thirty cheeseburgers and thirty fries.

I wait for him to pay before I start cooking.
He pays.
He ain't no average joe.

The grill is just big enough for ten rows of three.
I slap the burgers down
throw two buckets of fries in the deep frier
and they pop pop spit spit . . .
pss . . .

The counter girls laugh.
I concentrate.
It is the crucial point—
they are ready for the cheese:
my fingers shake as I tear off slices
toss them on the burgers/fries done/dump/
refill buckets/burgers ready/flip into buns/
beat that melting cheese/wrap burgers in plastic/
into paper bags/fries done/dump/fill thirty bags/
bring them to the counter/wipe sweat on sleeve
and smile at the counter girls.
I puff my chest out and bellow:
"Thirty cheeseburgers, thirty fries!"
They look at me funny.
I grab a handful of ice, toss it in my mouth

do a little dance and walk back to the grill.
Pressure, responsibility, success,
thirty cheeseburgers, thirty fries.

Where Else Can You Go

to get those wonderful T-shirts
with the pocket for your smokes
  the pocket for your smokes?

In all colors all sizes
blue and dark blue and light blue
and black   and brown   green and red
light brown   dark red   all colors.

Where else can you go
for the blue light   the blue light
    the blue light specials?

You know what I'm talking about
that place   that savings place
you've been there
wandering the aisles dazed.
You have to be in the right mood
to go in. You have to be slow
and happy   and sad.

I am buying T-shirts and basketball shoes
I am buying a Hula Hoop and a can of oil
I am buying a travel alarm and an eraser
in the shape of Mr. T's head—
oh, Mr. T where are you now?

Good cheap stuff, don't you love it
cheeseballs and vitamins
a bag of cement   a light-up fish

a lightbulb with three speeds
a lightbulb that lasts forever.
It's cotton candy on my tongue—
it disappears   yet is so sweet
yet is so sickening.

Why did I come here, what did I really need?
I am lonely and it is raining.
I am tired of flossing.
I want to wander these cluttered aisles
till what brought me here

slides off into shoe boxes and dish drainers
into stale bags of caramel corn

and circus peanuts, into disposable lighters
and sugar-free gum. I want to be emptied
emptied of it all, I want to pass through
the checkout counter past the security guard
having mumbled all my sins to the plastic dolls.
I want to be purified by the smells of ammonia
and Colorforms, the taste of junk America
the sweet sweet blues—I hope I can afford it.

Todd Davis

Todd Davis, winner of the Gwendolyn Brooks Poetry Prize, teaches creative writing, environmental studies, and American literature at Penn State University's Altoona College. He is the author of three books of poetry—*The Least of These, Some Heaven*, and *Ripe*—and co-editor of *Making Poems: 40 Poems with Commentary by the Poets*. In addition to his creative work, Davis is the author or editor of six scholarly books. When he's not working at poems, he's in Gamelands 158 above Tipton, PA, hiking or hunting with his wife and two sons.

Craving

In the dust of a February snow the coyote's track
follows the deer's track. He sees in the hoof-dragged

line of her stride a weariness that lengthens with winter's
spiteful width, a labor he longs to release with the clean

tear of canine, easy flow of artery. Along the banks
the river runs faster, snow-melt and the quickening of time

as sun throws down more light each day. A mink scores
its trail, countering the river's course, and every twenty yards

a pool of piss sugared with blood, with estrus' craving.
We're always giving ourselves away, smallest parts

of our bodies flying through space, neutrinos hauling
the blood and dust and piss of our existence.

How surprised the buck was when he approached
my wife, her menses thick in his nostrils, and even

when he realized her bottom was clothed, no doe's
red vulva beckoning, he could not turn away.

The coyote must be fed; the mink joined to her mate.
My wife ran the dirt trail back to our house, collapsed,

and later laughed at her own allure. Alone, wind
coming up from the river, the buck must have raised

his head, barely aware of the heart's insistent thump,
as he tried once again to catch the stinging scent

that spurs us on.

Accident

They tell the son, who tells his friends
at school, that the father's death was
an accident, that the rifle went off
while he was cleaning it. I'm not sure
why he couldn't wait. We understand
the ones who decide to leave us in February,
even as late as March. Snows swell.
Sun disappears. Hunting season ends.
With two deer in the freezer any family
can survive. I know sometimes
it feels like you've come to the end
of something. Sometimes you just want
to sit down beneath a hemlock and never go
back. But this late in the year, when plum
trees have opened their blossoms?
Yesterday it was so warm we slept
with the windows open. Smell of forsythia
right there in the room. I swear
you could hear the last few open,
silk petals come undone, a soft sound
like a pad sliding through a gun's barrel,
white cloth soaked in bore cleaner,
removing the lead, the copper, the carbon
that fouls everything. My son knows
you don't die cleaning your rifle:
the chamber's always open.
I told him to nod his head anyway
when his friend tells the story,
to say *yes* as many times as it takes,
to never forget the smell of smoke
and concrete, the little bit of light
one bulb gives off in a basement
with no windows.

Puberty

Among the last of the raspberries
we find scat seeded about, canes
pushed over without care, tufts of hair
sticking to the black juice of berries.
Arms carry the proof of hours

reaching between thorns, lower leaves
pushed aside to find the darkest,
ripest part of our delight. My son,
who has begun to change, stands
thirty yards away, picks disinterestedly,
asking how soon before we can leave.
Hair sprouts everywhere on his body:
forearms, legs, balls. When you're older
there's more in the nose and ears, eyebrows
gone mad. I'd like to say this siren song
that calls him away will disappear in time,
music fading into the hollow bend of a tree,
but no one knows where the notes will lead him.
Instead I bow my head, a penitent working
through prayers to the sweet forgiveness
of this precious wood that feeds us, to these
brief moments we have before this boy refuses
to spend even a few hours in our company.
It's his shout that interrupts my failed attempt
at something holy, that brings me around
to his jabbing finger, harried eyes pointing
to a young bear scrambling across the path
and into the brush. In the silence that follows
the crash, I'm afraid I've lost something
I won't be able to retrieve, though I know
my son still stands among these brambles.

Theodicy

If the air is suffused with light, if the very air
brushes against your skin, illuminating the mole
on your right cheek or the softest, smallest hairs
along your left arm, will you then believe?
Wind has come up in the night and rushes
over the tops of ridges. Shutters shake
and we take care to close the door firmly.
What does it mean to say God is with us,
to say one should not put the Lord to the test?
To the north, along the interstate, five bear,
restless as wind, cross in front of a line
of cars. One of them is struck and dies.
The others bound to the edge of the trees
where they watch as cars come over the hill
only to crash into each other, again and again.

Toi Derricotte

Toi Derricotte's recent poetry books include *Tender*, winner of the Paterson Poetry Prize, and *Captivity*. Her memoir, *The Black Notebooks*, published by W.W. Norton, won the 1998 Annisfield-Wolf Book Award for Nonfiction. An essay is included in *The Best American Essays 2006*. Her honors include the Lucille Medwick Memorial Award from the Poetry Society of America, two Pushcart Prizes, the Distinguished Pioneering of the Arts Award from the United Black Artists, and fellowships from the National Endowment for the Arts, the Rockefeller Foundation, and the Guggenheim Foundation. She is a Professor of English at the University of Pittsburgh.

Boy at the Paterson Falls

I am thinking of that boy who bragged about the day he threw
    a dog over and watched it struggle to stay upright all
    the way down.
I am thinking of that rotting carcass on the rocks,
and the child with such power he could call to a helpless
    thing as if he were its friend, capture it, and think of
    the cruelest punishment.
It must have answered some need, some silent screaming in a
    closet, a motherless call when night came crashing;
it must have satisfied, for he seemed joyful, proud, as if he
    had once made a great creation out of murder.
That body on the rocks, its sharp angles, slowly took the shape of
    what was underneath, bones pounded, until it lay on the bottom
    like a scraggly rug.
Nothing remains but memory—and the suffering of those who
    would walk into the soft hands of a killer for a crumb of bread.

Shoe Repair Business

"This shoe is shiny
as a nigger's heel,"
his customer bursts out
approvingly. Then, remembering
the shop owner is black, he
tactfully amends, "I mean
shiny as a *Negro's* heel."

After Reading at a Black College

Maybe one day we will have
written about this color thing
until we've solved it. Tonight
when I read my poems about
looking white, the audience strains
forward with their whole colored
bodies—a part of each person praying
that my poems will make sense.
Poems do that sometimes—take
the craziness and salvage some
small clear part of the soul,
and that is why, though frightened,
I don't stop the spirit. After,
though some people come
to speak to me, some
seem to step away,
as if I've hurt them once
too often and they have
no forgiveness left. I feel myself
hurry from person to person, begging.
Hold steady, Harriet Tubman whispers,
Don't flop around.
Oh my people,
sometimes you look at me
with such unwillingness—
as I look at *you*!
I keep trying to prove
I am not what I think you think.

Bird

The secret is
not to be afraid, to
pour the salt, letting your wrist
be free—there is almost
never too much; it sits on top of the skin like a
little crystal casket. Under it the bird might
imagine another life, one in which it is grateful
for pleasing, can smell
itself cooking—the taste
of carrots, onions, potatoes stewed
in its own juice—and forget
the dreams of blood
coursing out of its throat like a river.

Not Forgotten

I love the way black ants use their dead.
They carry them off like warriors on their steel
backs. They spend hours struggling, lifting,
dragging (it is not grisly as it would be for us,
to carry them back to be eaten),
so that every part will be of service. I think of
my husband at his father's grave—
the grass had closed
over the headstone, and the name had disappeared. He took out
his pocket knife and cut the grass away, he swept it
with his handkerchief to make it clear. "Is this the way
we'll be forgotten?" And he bent down over the grave and wept.

Matthew Dickman

Matthew Dickman was born in Portland, Oregon. He is the author of two chapbooks, *Amigos* and *Something about a Black Scarf*. His full-length collection *All-American Poem* won the APR/Honickman First Book Prize and was published by Copper Canyon Press.

Some Days

It's winter in Oregon
and I'm thinking about the snow in Ann Arbor
where my brother lives in his happiness,
the masculine huskiness
of corned beef stewing inside its own juices,
filling the heavy-bottomed pot,
big enough to hide a small teenager,
the grease of a thousand mornings
darkening the iron and copper,
the two brown eggs lying on the cutting table, femininity
doubled up, a stereotype in stereo,
the sun breaking over the ladles and knives like water.
Any cook would want to hold them,
their perfectly formed shells,
the yolk inside its yellow limbo, both
in one hand, my brother cracks them over the steel bowl
while the snow falls
like really expensive French sea salt,
the kind that comes in little blue bowls
with cork tops and the words
Sel de Mer written in French loops and flourishes,
like someone's number on a pack of matches
after you've closed a bar or maybe
not even that, not even closed it
but drank real fast so everything
was French and flourishy.
In the morning you can take your hangover to work,
when everything feels more German than French, and work
will straighten you out. Work will make you
see clearly even if, like my friend Mike,
you wake up early so you can deliver candy bars
and soda-pop to the machines
scattered across the University campus

where you used to go to school before taking this job,
putting on the gray jumpsuit, starting up
the truck, the robins staring at you from the barbed wire
fence. He is working
so students can drop their parents' coins
into little slots so that THUNK!
a piece of chocolate or can of cold
Coca-Cola will fall into a larger slot.
Slot to slot Mike worked all day and drank
on the Sabbath with a book or two in his head
and some car in his heart.
When I worked the job opening a café
at five in the morning, I knew beautiful women
were getting out of the shower, drying off, not even thinking
of coffee yet, or the croissants I was making,
folding and re-folding the dough
over the cold marble slab, some hopefulness
pouring out of me, waiting
for them to arrive, the bell
around the doorknob jingling
a little behind them, the bell
somehow like a dimple
above the ass
of a person you love, I can't explain it,
it's somehow silver
and supernatural. It didn't matter.
I never saw them. I worked
in the back, behind the closet
filled with detergents and toilet paper,
until the soups were done and the chicken cleaned,
the guts tossed, the boning knife
washed and sheaved, my apron
covered in blood
darker than the darkest cigar.
Some days a kitchen can
save your life. Carl would
come in and have one piece of brown
pumpkin bread, reading the *Times* or the *Oregonian*
or that late, great magazine, *The Sciences*,
where even a guy from Harvard, Illinois could understand
biophysics. Every time he opened
The New Yorker, each time he picked up
the warm bread
and placed it to his red mouth, he was not
thinking of how much he'd lost
or who he would love desperately
with nothing but wind
moving through his hands like a rope.

When I was broke and hungry and worried about the dogwood trees
I thought of my brother
making croutons and blintzes in Michigan,
the corned beef steaming,
the sun with its yolk running over everything.
I thought of him, and almost,
as if he had pulled it from his own wallet,
a ten dollar bill lay folded
on the sidewalk where I picked it up
and went directly out to lunch, a bowl of onion soup, a pint of dark
beer, the bread was free, and all because
of my brother, that old apron,
that great and mythic friend of mine,
that lucky charm.

Michael Dickman

Michael Dickman was born in 1975 and raised in Portland, Oregon. His poems have appeared in *American Poetry Review, Field, New Yorker,* and *Tin House.* His first collection, *The End of the West,* was a Lannan Literary Selection published by Copper Canyon.

Scary Parents

I didn't shoot heroin in the eighth grade because I was afraid of
           needles and still am

My friends couldn't
not do it—

Black tar
a leather belt
and sunlight

Scary parents

They filled holes
all afternoon
then we went to the movies

*

The shit-faced gods swam upstream inside them and threw wild parties

and stayed up
all night

Under their tongues
between their toes
their stomachs

All over their arms
wings

did not descend to wrap them up like babies

As promised

Still
there is a lot to pray to
on earth

*

Everyone is still alive
if not here then
someplace else

Climbing out of their arms

Resting their heads

On what?
No one is singing us
to sleep

Ian broke his mother's nose because she burned the pancakes

She left hypodermics
between the couch cushions
for us to sit on

Pat Dobler

Pat Dobler is the author of *UXB* and *Talking to Strangers*, which won the Brittingham Prize in Poetry. She also completed a third collection, *Now*. Dobler taught at Carlow College in Pittsburgh and directed the Women's Creative Writing Center. She died in 2004. Her *Collected Poems* was published by Autumn House Press in 2005.

An Afterlife

I climbed to the third floor,
I climbed and could still breathe
the thin bright air.
Last year I thought I never would again
climb and breathe.

The attic door opened a crack
to a table set for one,
a silver spoon and fork,
a vase with white roses, bowls filled with food,
all of it smelling delicious: borscht
sprinkled with dill, salmon in a kind of sauce,
a bright red vegetable

I couldn't name, for I was on a porch
somewhere in Russia somewhere in the country,
long shadows fell on the white table,
I thought it must be a white night,
the vines were heavy, the porch's lattice-work
was carved with rooster, horse, man.

The one chair, pulled away
from the table, was ready to hold me.

Field Trip to the Mill

Sister Monica has her hands full
timing the climb to the catwalk
so the fourth-graders are lined up
before the next heat is tapped, "and no
giggling no jostling, you monkeys!

So close to the edge!" She passes out
sourballs for bribes, not liking
the smile on the foreman's face,
the way he pulls at his cap,
he's not Catholic. Protestant madness,
these field trips, this hanging from catwalks
suspended over an open hearth.

Sister Monica understands Hell
to be like this. If overhead cranes clawing
their way through layers of dark air
grew leathery wings and flew screeching
at them, it wouldn't surprise her.
And the three warning whistle blasts,
the blazing orange heat pouring out
liquid fire like Devil's soup
doesn't surprise her. She understands
Industry and Capital and Labor,
the Protestant trinity. That is why
she trembles here, the children clinging
to her as she watches them learn their future.

Your Language Is Lost at Sea

for Grandma

Since you didn't speak their language
and besides were scared of the big Russian girls
with their oiled black hair and coarse gestures,
silence became your sister, she kept everything
in her heart, in the chill dark, in the hold
of your ship bound for the new country.
Silence was the chosen one in whose deep lap
you buried the Hunkie gutturals and sibilants,
keeping back only the few consonants and vowels
you thought your children would need in Ohio.
So your story trickles down the years: "Say nothing
if you are hungry, tired, poor. And wish to be
nothing as your syllables fall, break the ocean's skin.
With empty hands touch your body,
its boundaries and frontiers. Whoever invades,
hold tight, hold your tongue. Silence will bless
like a sister the tears you keep to yourself."

Uncle Rudy Explains the Events of 1955

We laid the last course of firebrick
in the big 3-story kiln when something broke upstairs.
Us brickies on the kiln bottom held our breath
at the first whiff of lime, we knew that stuff
could blind you, burn your lungs.
Each man found another man's hand
before shutting his eyes, so we inched out
that way—like kids, eyes shut tight
and holding hands. Climbed the ladder, finally up
to sweet air, the lime falling like snow
and burning our skin all the way.
That was the winter I found a rabbit
in one of my traps still alive.
The noise he made. "Quit it quit it quit it."
Lord, just like a person. So I quit.

On Murray Avenue

I don't know the boy who runs
toward me, holding out his arms.
You look so pretty, he shouts,
and grabs me round the shoulders.
I see that only his mind
is young—some mother's hand
still combs his hair, though it's graying,
but maybe he chose the red tee-shirt,
it looks brand-new, and if
my heart were less a closed fist
I would not shudder
out of this sidewalk two-step,
I'd hug him back, tell him
he looks pretty too.

Stephen Dobyns

Stephen Dobyns' most recent book of poems, *Winter's Journey*, was published in 2010 by Copper Canyon. His most recent work of fiction is a book of short stories, *Eating Naked* (Holt, 2000). His other work includes *Next Word, Better Word* (Palgrave, 2011), which is a book of essays on poetry, and *Velocities* (Penguin, 1994), a volume of new and selected poems. He has published eleven other books of poetry and twenty novels. Two of his novels and two of his short stories have been made into films. He has received a Guggenheim fellowship, three fellowships from the National Endowment of the Arts and numerous prizes for his poetry and fiction. His novel *The Church of Dead Girls* (Holt, 1997) was translated into twenty languages. Born in New Jersey in 1941, he now lives with his wife in Westerly, Rhode Island.

Stars

The man took the wrong fork in the road.
It was out in the country. They saw
no signs. It was getting dark. They began
to blame each other. Should they keep

going straight or should they turn around?
They drove past farms without lights.
The man said, If we reach a crossroad,
we can just turn right. His wife said,

I think you should turn around. The man
was driving. They kept going straight.
There's got to be a road up here someplace,
he said. His wife didn't answer. By now

it was pitch black. In their lights, the trees,
pressing close to the road, looked like people
wanting to speak, but deciding against it.
The farther they drove, the farther they got

from one another until it seemed they sat
in two separate cars. Who's this person
next to me? This thought came to them both.
They weren't newlyweds. They had children.

He's trying to upset me, thought the woman.
She thinks she always knows best, thought
the man. They were on their way to dinner
at a friend's farmhouse in the country. Now

they'd be late. It would take longer to go back,
than to go straight, said the man. The woman
knew he hated it when she remained silent,
so she said nothing. The woods were so thick

one could walk for miles and never get out.
The stars looked huge, as if they had come down
closer in the dark. The woman wanted to say
she could see no familiar constellations,

but she said nothing. The man wanted to say,
Get out of the car! Just to make her speak!
Where had they come to? They had driven
out of one world into another. They began

to recall remarks each had made in the past.
Only now did they realize their meanings,
hear their half-hidden barbs. They recalled
missing objects: a favorite vase, a picture

of his mother. How foolish to think they had
only been misplaced. They recalled remarks
made by friends before the wedding, remarks
that now appeared to be warnings. Ice crystals

grew between them, a cold so deep that only
an ice axe could shatter it. Who is this monster
I married? They both thought this. Soon they'd
think of lawyers and who would get the kids.

Then, in the trees, they saw a brightly lit house.
They had come the long way around. The man
parked behind the other cars and opened the door
for his wife. She took his arm as they walked

to the steps. They heard laughter. Their friends
were just sitting down at the table. On the porch
the man told his wife how good she looked,
while she fixed his tie. Both had a memory

of ugliness, like a story told them by somebody
they had never liked. As he opened the door,
she glanced upward and held him for a second.
How beautiful the stars look tonight, she said.

Wisdom

With the door shut the child sat in the closet
with his fingers pressed in his ears. Tell me
the truth, wasn't it wisdom? Hadn't he had

a sudden insight into the nature of the world?
One time my stepson in third grade stopped
taking tests. His reason? If you take one test,

they only give you another. Better call a halt
right now. He had caught on to the grown-ups'
stratagem to drag him into adulthood. What

was in it for him? he asked. Nothing nice.
Likewise the boy in the closet had become
temporarily resistant to the blandishments

of the world. Two hours later, his own body
turned against him and he crept downstairs
to dinner. But when his parents pointed out

the joys of growing up, he remained in doubt.
Who knew how the thought had come to him?
TV, a friend's chatter? Perhaps he had seen

a picture of a conveyor belt. Click, click—
so he'd go through life until he was dumped
on a trash heap. Or perhaps he had deduced

what he was leaving behind, the shift from
innocence to consequence, from protection
to fragility. Fortunately, stories like the boy

shutting himself up in the closet are scarce,
and his parents joked about it to their friends.
By now, I don't know, he's on his second or

third marriage, has a job that's made him rich,
but that time in the closet, five years old and
calculating what life was destined to deal out,

how different it must have seemed from what
he had ever imagined, so he made his decision
and crept into the closet, wasn't it wisdom?

Leaf Blowers

That autumn morning he awoke to the crying
of lost souls that quickly changed to the roar
of leaf blowers up and down the street. Still,
the lost souls hung on, although only as idea,
as if the day's cloudy translucence had become
the gathered dead circling the earth. Nothing
he believed, of course, but the thought gave flesh
to the skeletal lack, who assumed their places
on fictitious chairs and couches, acquaintances,
old friends, relatives, as impatient as patients
in a doctor's waiting room, an internist late
from a martini lunch. Yet it was him, his attention
they seemed to crave. Did it matter they were false?
They were real as long as he remembered them.
And their seeming need for him, surely the opposite
was true, as if they formed the ropes and stakes
tying down the immense circus tent of his past,
till, as he aged, the world existed more as pretext
to bring to mind the ones who had disappeared.
This morning it was leaf blowers, this afternoon
it might be something else, so as time went by
the palpability of what was not, came to outstrip
the formerly glittering quotidian, till all was seem,
seem, ensuring that his final departure would be
as slight as a skip or jump across a sidewalk's crack,
perhaps on a fall morning with sunlight streaking
the maples' fading abundance. Afternoon, evening,
even in the dead of night, waking to clutch his pillow
as he slipped across from one darkness to the next.

Rita Dove

Rita Dove's ninth book of poetry, *Sonata Mulattica*, was published by W.W. Norton in 2009. She served as Poet Laureate of the United States from 1993–95; her many honors include the 1987 Pulitzer Prize, the National Humanities Medal, and a Fulbright Lifetime Achievement Award. She is Commonwealth Professor of English at the University of Virginia.

Hattie McDaniel Arrives at the Coconut Grove

late, in aqua and ermine, gardenias
scaling her left sleeve in a spasm of scent,
her gloves white, her smile chastened, purse giddy
with stars and rhinestones clipped to her brilliantined hair,
on her free arm that fine Negro,
Mr. Wonderful Smith.

It's the day that isn't, February 29th,
at the end of the shortest month of the year—
and the shittiest, too, everywhere
except Hollywood, California,
where the maid can wear mink and still be a maid,
bobbing her bandaged head and cursing
the white folks under her breath as she smiles
and shoos their silly daughters
in from the night dew… what can she be
thinking of, striding into the ballroom
where no black face has ever showed itself
except above a serving tray?

Hi-Hat Hattie, Mama Mac, Her Haughtiness,
the "little lady" from *Showboat* whose name
Bing forgot, Beulah & Bertha & Malena
& Carrie & Violet & Cynthia & Fidelia,
one half of the Dark Barrymores—
dear Mammy we can't help but hug you crawl into
your generous lap tease you
with arch innuendo so we can feel that
much more wicked and youthful
and sleek but oh what

we forgot: the four husbands, the phantom
pregnancy, your famous parties, your celebrated
ice box cake. Your giggle above the red petticoat's rustle,
black girl and white girl walking hand in hand
down the railroad tracks
in Kansas City, six years old.
The man who advised you, now
that you were famous, to "begin eliminating"
your more "common" acquaintances
and your reply (catching him square
in the eye): "That's a good idea.
I'll start right now by eliminating you."

Is she or isn't she? Three million dishes,
a truckload of aprons and headrags later, and here
you are: poised, between husbands
and factions, no corset wide enough
to hold you in, your huge face a dark moon split
by that spontaneous smile—your trademark,
your curse. No matter, Hattie: it's a long, beautiful walk
into that flower-smothered standing ovation,
so go on
and make them wait.

Daystar

She wanted a little room for thinking:
but she saw diapers steaming on the line,
a doll slumped behind the door.

So she lugged a chair behind the garage
to sit out the children's naps.

Sometimes there were things to watch—
the pinched armor of a vanished cricket,
a floating maple leaf. Other days
she stared until she was assured
when she closed her eyes
she'd see only her own vivid blood.

She had an hour, at best, before Liza appeared
pouting from the top of the stairs.
And just what was mother doing
out back with the field mice? Why,

building a palace. Later
that night when Thomas rolled over and
lurched into her, she would open her eyes

and think of the place that was hers
for an hour—where
she was nothing,
pure nothing, in the middle of the day.

Aircraft

Too frail for combat, he stands
before an interrupted wing,
playing with an idea, nothing serious.
Afternoons, the hall gaped with aluminum
glaring, flying toward the sun; now
though, first thing in the morning, there is only
gray sheen and chatter
from the robust women around him
and the bolt waiting for his riveter's
five second blast.

The night before in the dark
of the peanut gallery, he listened to blouses shifting
and sniffed magnolias, white
tongues of remorse
sinking into the earth. Then
the newsreel leapt forward
into war.

Why *frail*? Why not simply
family man? Why wings, when
women with fingers no smaller than his
dabble in the gnarled intelligence of an engine?

And if he gave just a four second blast,
or three? Reflection is such

a bloodless light.
After lunch, they would bathe in fire.

Straw Hat

In the city, under the saw-toothed leaves of an oak
overlooking the tracks, he sits out
the last minutes before dawn, lucky
to sleep third shift. Years before
he was anything, he lay on
so many kinds of grass, under stars,
the moon's bald eye opposing.

He used to sleep like a glass of water
held up in the hand of a very young girl.
Then he learned he wasn't perfect, that
no one was perfect. So he made his way
North under the bland roof of a tent
too small for even his lean body.

The mattress ticking he shares in the work barracks
is brown and smells
from the sweat of two other men.
One of them chews snuff:
he's never met either.
To him, work is a narrow grief
and the music afterwards
is like a woman
reaching into his chest
to spread it around. When he sings

he closes his eyes.
He never knows when she'll be coming
but when she leaves, he always
tips his hat.

Roast Possum

The possum's a greasy critter
that lives on persimmons and what
the Bible calls carrion.
So much from the 1909 Werner
Encyclopedia, three rows of deep green
along the wall. A granddaughter
propped on each knee,
Thomas went on with his tale—

but it was for Malcolm, little
Red Delicious, that he invented
embellishments: *We shined that possum*
with a torch and I shinnied up,
being the smallest,
to shake him down. He glared at me,
teeth bared like a shark's
in that torpedo snout.
Man he was tough but no match
for old-time know-how.

Malcolm hung back, studying them
with his gold hawk eyes. When the girls
got restless, Thomas talked horses:

Strolling Jim, who could balance
a glass of water on his back
and trot the village square
without spilling a drop. Who put
Wartrace on the map and was buried
under a stone, like a man.

They liked that part.
He could have gone on to tell them
that the Werner admitted Negro children
to be intelligent, though briskness
clouded over at puberty, bringing
indirection and laziness. Instead,
he added: *You got to be careful*
with a possum when he's on the ground;
he'll turn on his back and play dead
till you give up looking. That's
what you'd call sullin'.

Malcolm interrupted to ask
who owned Strolling Jim,
and who paid for the tombstone.
They stared each other down
man to man, before Thomas,
as a grandfather, replied:
                        Yessir,
we enjoyed that possum. We ate him
real slow, with sweet potatoes.

Denise Duhamel

Denise Duhamel's most recent books are *Ka-Ching!*, *Two and Two*, and *Queen for a Day: Selected and New Poems*, all from University of Pittsburgh Press. *Mille et un sentiments* was published in a limited edition by Firewheel in 2004. She teaches creative writing at Florida International University in Miami.

How It Will End

We're walking on the boardwalk
but stop when we see a lifeguard and his girlfriend
fighting. We can't hear what they're saying,
but it is as good as a movie. We sit on a bench to find out
how it will end. I can tell by her body language
he's done something really bad. She stands at the bottom
of the ramp that leads to his hut. He tries to walk halfway down
to meet her, but she keeps signaling Don't come closer.
My husband says, "Boy, he's sure in for it,"
and I say, "He deserves whatever's coming to him."
My husband thinks the lifeguard's cheated, but I think
she's sick of him only working part-time
or maybe he forgot to put the rent in the mail.
The lifeguard tries to reach out
and she holds her hand like Diana Ross
when she performed "Stop in the Name of Love."
The red flag that slaps against his station means strong currents.
"She has to just get it out of her system,"
my husband laughs, but I'm not laughing.
I start to coach the girl to leave the no-good lifeguard,
but my husband predicts she'll never leave.
I'm angry at him for seeing glee in their situation
and say, "That's your problem—you think every fight
is funny. You never take her seriously," and he says,
"You never even give the guy a chance and you're always nagging,
so how can he tell the real issues from the nitpicking?"
and I say, "She doesn't nitpick!" and he says, "Oh really?
Maybe he should start recording her tirades," and I say
"Maybe he should help out more," and he says
"Maybe she should be more supportive," and I say
"Do you mean supportive or do you mean support him?"

and my husband says that he's doing the best he can,
that he's a lifeguard for Christ's sake, and I say
that her job is much harder, that she's a waitress
who works nights carrying heavy trays and is hit on all the time
by creepy tourists and he just sits there most days napping
and listening to "Power 96" and then ooh
he gets to be the big hero blowing his whistle
and running into the water to save beach bunnies who flatter him
and my husband says it's not as though she's Miss Innocence
and what about the way she flirts, giving free refills
when her boss isn't looking or cutting extra large pieces of pie
to get bigger tips, oh no she wouldn't do that because she's a saint
and he's the devil, and I say, "I don't know why you can't admit
he's a jerk," and my husband says, "I don't know why you can't admit
she's a killjoy," and then out of the blue the couple is making up.
The red flag flutters, then hangs limp.
She has her arms around his neck and is crying into his shoulder.
He whisks her up into his hut. We look around, but no one is watching us.

Blue Beard's One-Hundredth Wife

This was before battered women's shelters,
before serial killers were called serial killers,
before divorce, even before handguns.
Blue Beard's one-hundredth wife found his dead ninety-nine others
stored in a forbidden room. Some said he tired of a woman
once her mystery faded. Others thought
he was too quick to temper. He went on
long business trips before there were business trips,
trying perhaps to curb his domestic violence.
His beard was blue before punk rock was fashionable
which manipulated some women into feeling bad for him.
They stroked his speckled mustache—his navy bristles
and his soft gray hairs which grew in aqua.
He curled into their breasts, playing sensitive,
his big rough hands stroking the backs of their necks.
In a week or two a wedding, in another month
she'd drop a dish or smell up the outhouse
and it was all over. No one ever found his weapon.
Certain forensics guess he used his bare hands,
pulling his wives apart as though they were roasted chickens.
Luckily for them, this was before magic was obsolete
and Blue Beard's one-hundredth wife knew how to sew.
When she found that pile of dead wife parts
she pieced them together like Butterick patterns
and took to arms and heads with a needle and thread.
After two afternoons of non-stop work,

the women breathed again, all perfectly proportioned.
Some said, "Thank you, I've always wanted red hair."
Or, "Wow! I wondered what it was like to have big breasts!"
Blue Beard's one-hundredth wife sewed the light eyes
to the light skin, the small ankles on the small legs.
This was before plastic surgery, this was before women's magazines,
before body doubles were used in movies. Yet here were ninety-nine
untouchable pin-ups, their creator a Plain Jane
with a good eye for detail. When Blue Beard came home
his grief shook the stained glass windows of his castle.
He tried to kill his one-hundredth wife,
using the excuse of her entrance into the forbidden room,
but his ninety-nine exes pushed him out his heavy oak front door.
This was before lawyers, but the one hundred wives still got the house.

Oriental Barbie

She could be from Japan, Hong Kong, China,
the Philippines, Vietnam, Thailand, or Korea.
The little girl who plays with her can decide.
The south, the north, a nebulous
province. It's all the same, according to Mattel, who says
this Barbie still has "round eyes,"
but "a smaller mouth and a smaller bust"
than her U.S. sister. Girls, like some grown men,
like variety, as long as it's pretty, as long
as there's long hair to play with.
On a late-night Manhattan Cable commercial,
one escort service sells *Geishas to Go*,
girls from "the Orient, where men are kings..."
White Ken lies on his stomach
while an Oriental Barbie walks on his back.
Or is it a real woman stepping on Ken?
Or Oriental Barbie stepping on a real man?
You have to travel to Japan
to buy this particular Barbie doll. A geisha girl
can be at the door of your New York apartment
in less than an hour. Of course,
there is no Oriental Ken.
Those who study the delicate balance
of American commerce and trade understand.

Stephen Dunn

Stephen Dunn is the author of 14 collections of poetry, including *What Goes On: Selected and New Poems 1995–2009*. His *Different Hours* was awarded the 2001 Pulitzer Prize for poetry.

Empathy

Once in a small rented room, awaiting
a night call from a distant time zone,
I understood one could feel so futureless
he'd want to get a mermaid

tattooed on his biceps. Company
forever. Flex and she'd dance.
The phone never rang, except for those
phantom rings, which I almost answered.

I was in D.C., on leave from the army.
It was a woman, of course, who didn't call.
Or, as we said back then, a girl.
It's anybody's story.

But I think for me it was the beginning
of empathy, not a large empathy
like the deeply selfless might have,
more like a leaning, like being able

to imagine a life for a spider, a maker's
life, or just some aliveness
in its wide abdomen and delicate spinnerets
so you take it outside in two paper cups

instead of stepping on it.
The next day she called, and it was final.
I remember going to the zoo
and staring a long time

at the hippopotamus, its enormous weight
and mass, its strange appearance
of tranquility.
And then the sleek, indignant cats.

Then I went back to Fort Jackson.
I had a calendar taped inside my locker,
and I'd circle days for which I
had no plans, not even hopes—

big circles, so someone might ask.
It was between wars. Only the sergeants
and a few rawboned farm boys
took learning how to kill seriously.

We had to traverse the horizontal ladder,
rung after rung, to pass
into mess hall. Always the weak-handed,
the weak-armed, couldn't make it.

I looked for those who didn't laugh
at those of us who fell.
In the barracks, after drills,
the quiet fellowship of the fallen.

Don't Do That

It was bring-your-own if you wanted anything
hard, so I brought Johnnie Walker Red
along with some resentment I'd held in
for a few weeks, which was not helped
by the sight of little nameless things
pierced with toothpicks on the tables,
or by talk that promised to be nothing
if not small. But I'd consented to come,
and I knew what part of the house
their animals would be sequestered,
whose company I loved. What else can I say,

except that old retainer of slights and wrongs,
that bad boy I hadn't quite outgrown—
I'd brought him along too. I was out
to cultivate a mood. My hosts greeted me,
but did not ask about my soul, which was when
I was invited by Johnnie Walker Red
to find the right kind of glass, and pour.
I toasted the air. I said hello to the wall,

then walked past a group of women
dressed to be seen, undressing them
one by one, and went up the stairs to where

the Rottweilers were, Rosie and Tom,
and got down with them on all fours.
They licked the face I offered them,
and I proceeded to slick back my hair
with their saliva, and before long
I felt like a wild thing, ready to mess up
the party, scarf the hors d'oeuvres.
But the dogs said, No, don't do that,
calm down, after a while they open the door
and let you out, they pet your head, and everything
you might have held against them is gone,
and you're good friends again. Stay, they said

The Sacred

After the teacher asked if anyone had
    a sacred place
and the students fidgeted and shrank

in their chairs, the most serious of them all
    said it was his car,
being in it alone, his tape deck playing

things he'd chosen, and others knew the truth
    had been spoken
and began speaking about their rooms,

their hiding places, but the car kept coming up,
    the car in motion,
music filling it, and sometimes one other person

who understood the bright altar of the dashboard
    and how far away
a car could take him from the need

to speak, or to answer, the key
    in having a key
and putting it in, and going.

Cornelius Eady

Cornelius Eady's books include *Brutal Imagination, Autobiography of a Jukebox, You Don't Miss Your Water, The Gathering of My Name*, and *Victims of the Latest Dance Craze*. He is Associate Professor of English at the University of Notre Dame and co-founder of Cave Canem, a center for African-American poets.

Dance at the Amherst County Public Library

Fellow poets,
My Brothers and Sisters,
Comrades,
Distinguished guests and visitors,
Yes,
Even the tourists
In their T-shirts and mirrored sunglasses.

Before our attention begins to wander
Let me ask this:
In one hundred years,
No,
Say fifty years,
If, through grand design or fluke
The world still stands
And leads our descendants to this branch library in Amherst, Va.,

Which poets would they find on the shelves?

The answer probably is
They will only find
What I found this afternoon:
Shakespeare
And Paul Laurence Dunbar.

In view of
And in spite of this awful truth
I would still like to leave one or two thoughts behind:

If you are an archaeologist and find these items slipped into
    Mr. Dunbar's Collected Works:
        This poem,
        A pair of red laces

Please understand that this was how I defined myself,
A dancing fool who couldn't stay away from words
Even though they brought me nothing but difficulties.
I was better when I danced,
The language of the body so much cleaner.

I was always in jealous awe of the dancers,
Who seemed, to me at least, to be honest animals.
When I danced

I imagined myself a woman,
Because there is no sight more lovely
Than a woman kicking her heels up in a dive.

This is how I wasted my time,
Trying to become the Henry Ford of poetry,
And mass produce a group of words
Into a thing that could shake
And be owned by the entire world.

Naturally, I failed.

Of course, even the failure was a sort of dance.

My friend,
I bequeath to you what I know:
Not the image of a high, glistening city
But the potential in tall grass, flattened
    by a summer's storm.
Not the dance
But the good intentions of a dance.

This was the world I belonged to,
With its symphony of near-misses,
And in its name
And in the names of all those omitted
I dance my small graffiti dance.

Almost Grown

My father loves my sister so much he has to strike her. He cares for her so
deeply that he has crossed, for the first and only time, into my mother's
domain.

    He has caught his daughter red-handed at the front door, trying to
sneak home late from her boyfriend's house.

    And my father, poor ghost, knows too much. Without ever leaving the
house, he has overheard every sweet thing this man, an old buddy of his,
has whispered to her in bed.

Tonight, my sister discovers her only power. As she tussles with him on the front porch, she is all heat and righteous passion.

He will never try this hard again to tell anyone how much he loves them. With his belt, my father tries to tell my sister what he knows a man is capable of, but all he does is tell her fortune.

Lynn Emanuel

Lynn Emanuel's third book of poetry, *Then, Suddenly*, won the Eric Matthieu King Award from The Academy of American Poets. Her work has often appeared in the Pushcart Prize and Best American Poetry anthologies. She has been a member of the Literature Panel for the National Endowment for the Arts, and a judge for the National Book Awards and for the James Laughlin Award from the Academy of American Poets. She has taught at the Bread Loaf Writers' Conference, the Bennington Writers' Conference, the Warren Wilson Program in Creative Writing, and the Vermont College Creative Writing Program. Currently she is a Professor of English at the University of Pittsburgh.

Dear Final Journey

Dear Final Journey,
Dear Noose, Dear Necktie, Dear Cravat,
Salutations, big ship, toiling the dark waters
Of death. Dear Freighter, in whose hold the oily links
Of the anchor's chain, like snakes, are coiled. Dear Oily
Waters, salve and balm, black disk of ocean across which,
Dark Craft, you creak, loom, until your black gobbles
The horizon up. Dear black firmament and earth,
Ditch of the kicked in. World shut and over,
Mingy and dim. Dear Line, Dear Sinker,
Noose and Hook,

Hello.

The Murder Writer

The living teetered at the edge of a cliff.
Below the living lay the lake, that slick, black
plate of water, and just behind them purred

a car as dark and hollow as a hearse.
I dipped my pen into that inky place.
I sat behind the windshield of my face.

The cloudy brow of night
was furrowed in concern,
because the living did not seem to know
that they were being stalked by me.

Night after night I tried to nudge them
into the water, the path of a train,
or my oncoming speed.

But they were always busy:
The woman in red waxed
and waned, smoldered like a mine fire

just beneath the surface of the page.
And the woman in white was always
asleep inside the simple moonbeam of herself.

The car was ready, and the cliff;
the moon was a drop of mercury
that rolled back and forth across

the night and beside the black
vat of reservoir I had planted witnesses
like flowers in the rubber pots of their galoshes.

I sat and smoked and lingered.
Inside me a murder sulked and ached
like a lake behind a dam.
I was waiting until the world was on my side
and would turn itself murderous for my sake.

The Revolution

Remember it was early—we were still in the dark
slots of the narrow beds, the room twitching and burning
from all night TV—then voices—almost *lively*

for this place, I think, unsheathing myself from the damp
bedding to the cool and cluttered eight-story commotion—a burn
of sound, those voices, a Braille of noise.

I can't remember what broke the wash of listening,
what turned it (like a boat steered hard into its own wake) into sight:
one or two floors below us, an answer to your question—

(you are up and beside me now)—*what is that?* was dragged by—
window, wall, window, wall—locked in the arms of two men
and trying to bite her way out of their official embrace.

Did I mention—leaning out to put ourselves into the courtyard
where a spill of images lengthened the view—we stared
at a woman in her nightgown

screaming like something metal opening against its will.
We saw her, then she was disappeared by wall, we saw her
naked feet on the stone. Wind blew this way and that

in the immense eight-storied square. And these two facts:
Her gown was torn from her. And we stood staring. What could be done?
There had been trouble, we knew. Betrayals.

Who was to say she was innocent?

Ellipses

Into the clearing of...
she climbed and stood

up from the black boots of her blackouts
into her body.

The coat wept upon her shoulder,
it hung upon her, a carcass heavy on a hook,

and in the sockets of the button holes
the buttons lolled and looked.

As she climbed into that clearing
it shook as it took her.

A fever wrote the sentence
and screwed it tight with ache

and the long hair of the grass grew silvery and weak,
lay greasily against the skull of dirt.
My mother was a figure armed with...
and came toward me

flew to me as though I were a sentence
that must be mended, that must be broken,

then ended, ended, ended.

The Occupation

Personal experiences are chains and balls
fatally drawn to the magnetic personality.
And I have always been a poet
who poured herself into the shrouds
of experience's tight dresses so that a reader could try to get a feel
for the real me, metaphorically speaking, of course,

using only the mind, of course, and a dictionary
that the mind wears like a surgical glove.

I bore experience's leashes and tourniquets.
I stuffed myself deep into the nooses of its collars.
I was equipped. I was like a ship plated with the armor of experience,
nosing the seas which are its seas.

But now I have other things to do. I will not write about dyeing
my hair blonde-on-black for my post post-feminist project. The wicked
    must be punished.
The innocent exalted, butchers called forth for the slaughter of the
    lambs, and doctors
called from their face lifts to perform amputations.

I hear the call to rise out of the trance of myself
into the surcease of the dying world,
Then it went dark. Real dark. Like snow. (9/11 witness.)

I will never again write from personal experience.
Since the war began I have discovered
(1) My Life Is Unimportant and (2) My Life Is Boring.
But now, as Gertrude Stein wrote from Culoz in 1943,
Now, we have an occupation.

Claudia Emerson

Claudia Emerson's poems appear in *Poetry, Smartish Pace, The Southern Review, Shenandoah, TriQuarterly, Crazyhorse* and elsewhere. Louisiana State University Press published *Pharaoh, Pharaoh* (1997), *Pinion, An Elegy* (2002), *Late Wife* (2005), which won the 2006 Pulitzer Prize, *Figure Studies* (2009), and *Secure the Shadow* (2012). Emerson has been awarded fellowships from the National Endowment for the Arts, Virginia Commission for the Arts, and Witter Bynner Foundation. She is Professor of English and Arrington Distinguished Chair in Poetry at Mary Washington College. Emerson is married to musician Kent Ippolito.

Animal Funerals, 1964

That summer, we did not simply walk through
　　the valley of the shadow of death;

we set up camp there, orchestrating funerals
　　for the anonymous, found dead: a drowned mole—

its small, naked palms still pink—a crushed
　　box turtle, black snake, even a lowly toad.

The last and most elaborate of the burials
　　was for a common jay, identifiable

but light, dry, its eyes vacant orbits.
　　We built a delicate lichgate of willow fronds,

supple and green, laced through with chains of clover.
　　Roles were cast: preacher, undertaker—

the rest of us a straggling congregation
　　reciting what we could of the psalm

about green pastures as we lowered the shoebox
　　and its wilted pall of dandelions

into the shallow grave one of us had dug
　　with a serving spoon. That afternoon,

just before September and school, when we would
　　again become children, and blind to all

but the blackboard's chalky lessons, the back
     of someone's head, and what was, for a while

longer, the rarer, human death—there, in the heat-shimmered
     trees, in the matted grasses where we stood,

even in the slant of humid shade—we heard wingbeat,
     slither, buzz, and birdsong—a green racket rising

to fall as though in a joyous dirge that was real,
     and not part of our many, necessary rehearsals.

Cold Room

Her refrigerator full, my mother has stored
     some things in the cold of my brother's

closed-off room, Christmas oranges and pears
     on the floor—the salt-cured ham that hung

for a full year from the cellar rafters
     cooked now and kept on the chest of drawers.

He is far away and ill; she knows
     he will not come home anymore, suspects

she will not see or hold him again in the flesh,
     allowed him now only in smiling photographs

undone by a voice thin on the phone.
     Late afternoons she climbs the slow, complaining

stairs with a platter and carving knife;
     she wears her winter coat, opens the door

to his bed still made, stale light, the scent
     of ripe fruit and cold smoke. Here, in the room

let go for this, she concentrates on carving
     the meat so even and thin she can see through it

to the blade, its clean, practiced passage—*just so*,
     she says as though to no one, *just so.*

Secure the Shadow

"Secure the shadow 'ere the substance fade" was a popular daguerreotypists' advertising slogan for the making of post-mortem images of loved ones.

That it appeared on being
    at first glance an infant asleep

was enough to make me lift it
    from the antique shop box crowded

with albumen prints, daguerreotypes,
    and early photographs of family

gatherings and weddings, most
    of them somber portraits

of the elderly—all in formal
    poses. And then the fact of death

was clear: a boy who still looks
    like a girl—the mother loath

to cut his light fine hair—laid out
    on a couch, its back of ornate,

dark-carved wood all there is
    of the room, which very well

could have been the photographer's
    studio she had traveled to—

how far?—with the body. The photograph
    contains the whole of it: he wears

a white gown that might have been
    for the christening, no shoes,

his plump hands posed with care, folded,
    dimpled, the hands of a healthy child,

the face still round with baby-fat.
    Whatever took him, then,

took him quickly—whooping cough
    or pneumonia, a fever,

something common that left no mark,
    and while the posture is

of sleep, the heavy-lidded inward
　　　gaze of the eyes, not quite

closed, makes no pretense of it.
　　　And I imagined her desperate

for evidence, not of death,
　　　but of what had lived, her anguish

in its grievous failure, then her
　　　resigned survival, becoming at last

one of the women expressionless
　　　in those other photographs.

She might have borne other children
　　　who lived and in surviving her

let go this image they must have feared.
　　　And so I did, with some reluctance,

purchase its further removal from them,
　　　from her—making mine this orphaned

but still secure correspondence
　　　with all that is about to disappear.

B. H. Fairchild

B. H. Fairchild is the recipient of
Guggenheim, Rockefeller, and NEA
fellowships. *Early Occult Memory
Systems of the Lower Midwest*, from
which these poems were taken,
received the National Book Critics
Circle Award and the Gold Medal of
the California Book Awards.

Rave On

> *...wild to be wreckage forever.*
> —James Dickey, "Cherrylog Road"

Rumbling over caliche with a busted muffler,
radio blasting Buddy Holly over Baptist wheat fields,
Travis screaming out *Prepare ye the way of the Lord*
at jackrabbits skittering beneath our headlights,
the Messiah coming to Kansas in a flat-head Ford
with bad plates, the whole high plains holding its breath,
night is fast upon us, lo, in these days of our youth,
and we were hell to pay, or thought we were. Boredom
grows thick as maize in Kansas, heavy as drill pipe
littering the racks of oil rigs where in summer boys
roustabout or work on combine crews north as far
as Canada. The ones left back in town begin
to die, dragging main street shit-faced on 3.2 beer
and banging on the whorehouse door in Garden City
where the ancient madam laughed and turned us down
since we were only boys and she knew our fathers.
We sat out front spitting Red Man and scanned a landscape
flat as Dresden: me, Mike Luckinbill, Billy Heinz,
and Travis Doyle, who sang, *I'm gonna live fast,
love hard, and die young.* We had eaten all the life
there was in Seward County but hungry still, hauled ass
to old Arkalon, the ghost town on the Cimarron
that lay in half-shadow and a scattering of starlight,
and its stillness was a kind of death, the last breath
of whatever in our lives was ending. We had drunk there
and tossed our bottles at the walls and pissed great arcs
into the Kansas earth where the dust groweth hard

and the clods cleave fast together, yea, where night yawns
above the river in its long, dark dream, above
haggard branches of mesquite, chicken hawks scudding
into the tree line, and moon-glitter on caliche
like the silver plates of Coronado's treasure
buried all these years, but the absence of treasure,
absence of whatever would return the world
to the strangeness that as children we embraced
and recognized as life. *Rave on.*
                              Cars are cheap
at Roman's Salvage strewn along the fence out back
where cattle graze and chew rotting fabric from the seats.
Twenty bucks for spare parts and a night in the garage
could make them run as far as death and stupidity
required—on Johnson Road where two miles of low shoulders
and no fence line would take you up to sixty, say,
and when you flipped the wheel clockwise, you were there
rolling in the belly of the whale, belly of hell,
and your soul fainteth within you for we had seen it done
by big Ed Ravenscroft who said you would go in a boy
and come out a man, and so we headed back through town
where the marquee of the Plaza flashed CREATURE FROM
THE BLACK LAGOON in storefront windows and the Snack Shack
where we had spent our lives was shutting down and we
sang *rave on, it's a crazy feeling* out into the night
that loomed now like a darkened church, and sang loud
and louder still for we were sore afraid.
                              Coming up
out of the long tunnel of cottonwoods that opens onto
Johnson Road, Travis with his foot stuck deep into the *soul*
of that old Ford *come on, Bubba, come on* beating
the dash with his fist, hair flaming back in the wind
and eyes lit up by some fire in his head that I
had never seen, and Mike, iron Mike, sitting tall
in back with Billy, who would pick a fight with anything
that moved but now hunched over mumbling something
like a prayer, as the Ford lurched on spitting
and coughing but then smoothing out suddenly fast
and the fence line quitting so it was open field, then,
then, I think, we were butt-deep in regret and a rush
of remembering whatever we would leave behind—
Samantha Dobbins smelling like fresh laundry,
light from the movie spilling down her long blonde hair,
trout leaping all silver and pink from Black Bear Creek,
the hand of my mother, I confess, passing gentle
across my face at night when I was a child—oh yes,
it was all good now and too late, too late, trees blurring
past and Travis wild, popping the wheel, oh too late
too late

and the waters pass over us the air thick
as mud slams against our chests though turning now
the car in its slow turning seems almost graceful
the frame in agony like some huge animal groaning
and when the wheels leave the ground the engine cuts loose
with a wail thin and ragged as a bandsaw cutting tin
and we are drowning breathless heads jammed against
our knees and it's a thick swirling purple nightmare
we cannot wake up from for the world is turning too
and I hear Billy screaming and then the whomp
sick crunch of glass and metal whomp again back window
popping loose and glass exploding someone crying out
tink tink of iron on iron overhead and then at last
it's over and the quiet comes

Oh so quiet. Somewhere
the creak and grind of a pumping unit. Crickets.
The tall grass sifting the wind in a mass of whispers
that I know I'll be hearing when I die. And so
we crawled trembling from doors and windows borne out
of rage and boredom into weed-choked fields barren
as Golgotha. Blood raked the side of Travis's face
grinning rapt, ecstatic, Mike's arm was hanging down
like a broken curtain rod, Billy kneeled, stunned,
listening as we all did to the rustling silence
and the spinning wheels in their sad, manic song
as the Ford's high beams hurled their crossed poles of light
forever out into the deep and future darkness. *Rave on.*

I survived. We all did. And then came the long surrender,
the long, slow drifting down like young hawks riding on
the purest, thinnest air, the very palm of God
holding them aloft so close to something hidden there,
and then the letting go, the fluttering descent, claws
spread wide against the world, and we become, at last,
our fathers. And do not know ourselves and therefore
no longer know each other. Mike Luckinbill ran a Texaco
in town for years. Billy Heinz survived a cruel divorce,
remarried, then took to drink. But finally last week
I found this house in Arizona where the brothers
take new names and keep a vow of silence and make
a quiet place for any weary, or lost, passenger
of earth whose unquiet life has brought him there,
and so, after vespers, I sat across the table
from men who had not surrendered to the world,
and one of them looked at me and looked into me,
and I am telling you there was *a fire in his head*
and his eyes were coming fast down a caliche road,
and I knew this man, and his name was Travis Doyle.

A Photograph of the Titanic

When Travis came home from the monastery,
the ground had vanished beneath him,
and he went everywhere in bare feet

as if he were walking on a plane of light
and he spoke of his sleepless nights
and of a picture in *National Geographic:*

a pair of shoes from the *Titanic* resting
on the ocean floor. They were blue
against a blue ground and a black garden

of iron and brass. The toes pointed outward,
toward two continents, and what had been
inside them had vanished so completely

that he imagined it still there, with the sea's
undersway bellying down each night
as each day after compline he fell into

his bed, the dark invisible bulk of tons
pushing down on the shoes, nudging them
across the blue floor, tossing them aside

like a child's hands in feverish sleep
until the shoestrings scattered and dissolved.
Sometimes he would dream of the shoes

coming to rest where it is darkest,
after the long fall before we are born,
when we gather our bodies around us,

when we curl into ourselves and drift
toward the little sleep we have rehearsed
again and again as if falling we might drown.

Frank X. Gaspar

Frank X. Gaspar is the author of four collections of poetry, most recently *A Field Guide to the Heavens* (Brittingham Prize, 1999) and *One Thousand Blossoms* (Alice James Books, 2004). His novel, *Leaving Pico*, was a Barnes and Noble Discovery Award winner and won the California Book Award for First Fiction.

One Thousand Blossoms

Well, is it really wise to search for guidance in a small room
cluttered with books and papers, with a glass of whiskey
and a box of wheat crackers, with my eyes ticking like
the brass tide-clock on the plaster wall? When the house sleeps
huddled in the city's jasmine night? Night of a thousand blossoms
I can't name? Night of a soft marine layer, Pacific fog
hanging about a hundred yards up, a gauze, a parchment?
I am hidden thus from my duties, I can escape the moral law.
Isn't it written, didn't Lord Krishna himself say that we mustn't
relinquish the action we are born to, even if it is flawed?
Didn't he say a fire is obscured by smoke? You can't see far
into the city on a night like this, the blanket, the cool smell
of the sea, the dampness that sits like velvet on the rose bushes
and the African lilies and the fenders of the neighbor's truck.
You don't want less love—this ground has been covered before—
you want more love, even when you can't say what it means,
even though it binds you to the world, which you can only lose.
Then it is jasmine in the night, night of a thousand blossoms,
and my wife in one room breathing and my son in one room
breathing, and me in one room breathing. It's how loving this
place comes, slowly, then suddenly with great surprise, and then
vanishing again into mystery. Am I dreaming all of this? Is that
a train's long whistle riding the heavenly fog? Am I drunk again
on holy books and the late hours? Now a car rolls down the street,
filling it with light then emptying it again. It's like that. Just like that.

Hurricane Douglas, Hurricane Elida

Here they come again, those Pacific hurricanes,
and here I go in the old white Jeep, sandy and musty
with boards and wetsuits and damp towels, down
the boulevard, down the bougainvillea and the jacaranda,
the red lights and green lights, the Shell station and
the Union 66 station, the 7-11, Anna's Escrows,
Pacific Coast Medical Group, Tiny Naylor's Restaurant,
the Los Altos YMCA, houses and houses behind their
honeysuckled walls, and rows of palm trees curving up
to the muggy sky. A left turn on the highway and watch
the rivers in their concrete bunkers, glassy now because the
wind has not shifted onshore yet. Good. And then turn down
toward the pier and wedge into a parking space and then
down the sand, and there they are again, rolling in like
boxcars, swell after swell, angling off the bar under the
pier, half-again over my head, and then for the first time
ever the thought that I am too old, too weak, too short of
breath. This is fear. How comely, how appealing it is! How
it slows me pulling on the wetsuit and fins, waxing the board,
how it makes my pragmatic heart so ready, knocking against my
ribs in a way that I can hear it all the way up in my head. But
Bang Bang go the breakers, and in I go and dig in with my arms,
and get stuck inside a big set, pulling and pulling and getting
nowhere, duck-diving under the whitewater, heaving a breath
into myself when I come up, digging again to take back the distance
I've already lost, digging and breathing like there's no turning
back because, after all, there isn't now, and this is where I prefer
to leave it, this plain, small poem, digging and breathing like
it wants to avoid some classic fate or some failure of will or some
defect of character, bragging into all the noise and commotion, all
the rips and undertows, that there will be a last time, but this is not it.

Bodhidharma Preaches the Wake-up Sermon

There's no language that isn't the Dharma. Language is essentially free.
It has nothing to do with attachment.
And attachment has nothing to do with language.
        —Bodhidharma

Somehow or another, something is missing in me. I should
be satisfied with the household gods. I should learn my place
and understand that they are enough for any one man or woman.
Of course we are at their mercy. They suffer us every small thing.
And we thank you, god of the kitchen drainboard and goddess of
the gas-log hearth. We thank you for your benevolence and kindness,
and god of the grocery sacks for your capacious heart, and goddess
of linoleum and green lawns, and winged goddess of the laughter

of neighborhood children, but always we are wandering from
your groves and bowers, your gardens, your abundant pantries.
For instance, what does anyone's life mean, now, in this third
millennium, so-called? I am talking about what you can and can't
live without, which is a way of talking about attachment. Is there
a language that isn't the Dharma? *To seek nothing is bliss,*
said the saint Bodhidharma, but isn't he the one who cut off his eyelids
in the search for a more perfect meditation? No, no, this is not
the way, in the heat of night, in the heat of fevers, the blue gas jets
wavering in the hot breeze on the kitchen range (the goddess of
the four burners, the goddess of the coffee pot, our acknowledgment,
our gratitude), not the way when we open the door to the small
empty street and look down its length, first one way and then the other.
It's what you can or can't live without. It's all streetlight and crickets
on this particular night. It's all language and breath in this particular
trial. It's all delicacy and power lines. It's all asphalt and glass. That's
why I am up night after night. That's why I walk so softly on the floors
and rugs. I am bowing and kneeling in every little corner, at every little
helpful shrine, but I couldn't say if I am praying or if I am simply
looking for some small button or short piece of string that I've lost.
Most nights I really couldn't tell you what on earth I'm doing.

Ross Gay

Ross Gay's first book, *Against Which*, was published by CavanKerry Press in 2006, and his second book, *Bringing the Shovel Down*, was published by University of Pittsburgh Press in 2011. His poems have appeared in *American Poetry Review, Margie, Gulf Coast*, and *Sou'wester*. He teaches in the M.F.A. program at Indiana University in Bloomington, and he is on the faculty of Drew University's low-residency M.F.A. program.

Summer

And the sun readies himself for sleep, drowses
backward toward the horizon, and the woods
whisper while the wind massages
the sprawling arms of leaf-thick maples,
heavy shadows cast like dark angels
breast-stroking through the courtyard's grass,
and a man yells to an 8th grade black
kid not to walk around with
white girls, and a sleeveless light blue
shirt flails around his pink chest and pot gut,
and behind him, on the apartment's wall, three
shotguns, and three buildings away the boy's white
mother stirs tomato soup into ground beef
for sloppy joes, and the white girl with the black boy
kicks at the furry clumps of new-mown grass,
stares at her feet, and neighbors whisk the boy
back to his building while the man screams
at the boy, calling him what he does, and kids
play stickball in the tennis courts, and the boy makes
fists in his pockets, and the ice cream truck
slows, passes, and without a word the boy
sits to dinner and lifts the sandwich
to his mouth.

Alzheimer's

She stood in her doorway, asked my name
again—something she would never
remember. A breeze

loosed some cherry blossoms, petals
flipping through her open arms
as she whispered, *Look what God has done,*
look what God
has done.

The Truth

Because he was 38, because this
was his second job, because
he had two daughters, because his hands
looked like my father's, because at 7
he would walk to the furniture warehouse,
unload trucks 'til 3 AM, because I
was fourteen and training him, because he made
$3.75 an hour, because he had a wife
to look in the face, because
he acted like he respected me,
because he was sick and would not call out
I didn't blink when the water
dropped from his nose
into the onion's perfectly circular
mouth on the Whopper Jr.
I coached him through preparing.
I did not blink.
Tell me this didn't happen.
I dare you.

Pulled Over in Short Hills, NJ, 8:00 AM

It's the shivering. When rage grows
hot as an army of red ants and forces
the mind to quiet the body, the quakes
emerge, sometimes just the knees,
but, at worst, through the hips, chest, neck,
until, like a virus, slipping inside the lungs
and pulse, every ounce of strength tapped
to squeeze words from my taut lips,
his eyes scanning my car's insides, my eyes
my license, and as I answer the questions
3, 4, 5 times, my jaw tight as a vise,
his hand massaging the gun butt, I
imagine things I don't want to
and inside beg this to end
before the shiver catches my
hands, and he sees,
and something happens.

Robert Gibb

Robert Gibb was born in Homestead, Pennsylvania. He is the author of eight books of poetry, including *What the Heart Can Bear*, published in 2009 by Autumn House Press. Among his awards are two Poetry Fellowships from the National Endowment for the Arts and seven Pennsylvania Council on the Arts grants.

The Writing Class

Because it's now late November
And because the lights glowing above them
Remind me of something I felt once
As a girl, my voice will not sustain me—
So I've set them writing, face down above
Their desks like the youngest of mothers
Above their bassinets. Can I ever have been
As soft and hesitant as those hands,
Their first tentative grasp of things,
Here in the classroom, or their rampant nights?
I grow weary of trying to persuade them
That the word is a kind of flesh,
That Iseult was nothing without the roses
Of her thighs, the water of Tristan's lips.
O, and the roots of his hair! I am growing old
And find my satisfactions where I can.
Last night, when you spoke to me,
I felt as though my ear were trembling
Like those vases knights kept, rims worn down
By kisses over the gradual dawns . . .
What is it about this light? And why,
When I look up, should I seem to see them
All sitting there naked, laps filled with petals?
I can see the veins branching in their legs,
Blue as the groves of the moon,
Can see how the pores of their skin are cups
Above which tiny flames are floating.
It's all I can do to keep my hands from off myself,
To hold my breasts, my thighs and loamy sex,
As though to protect myself
From such innocence and burning.

Then they are clothed again, the munificence
Of their bodies is once more under wraps.
They yawn. They stretch themselves.
Words fall like evening from their pens.

For the Poets in the Prisons of the Americas

Any one of you has walked along those streets,
Dreaming of weather,
Writing of memory and the sea.

Words for the gulls, you say.
To the six slabs of your cell you whisper:
Not even these lice can speak my name.

I am afraid to do so would only bring you harm,
So you must remain anonymous
Even here in this poem, your sufferings gray

And uniform as a life crammed in a stall.
Here the gray is winter, the ends of afternoon,
When what evening we have sifts down

Between the ridges, a black wasp falls
Into my room and fumbles toward the sill.
Above it burn the same stars

Which hover above the Americas.
This same ghostly moon slivers through your walls,
Filling your sleep with solitudes,

Tides, the silvery dream of wings
Drifting against you with all their small weight.
I have not seen such swaying since summer—

Bees rumpled with pollen, flies blowzy
In the September sun.
And yet nothing like this pure unyielding passion

To enter the night. What does a wasp fear?
What dream does it drop from, out of the attic,
When sleeping means humming

With the whole hidden life of the house?
I sit at my desk, and the silence of the page
Is shattered against the forehead of your walls.

Up here, language has left the body,
Poetry is nothing to fear.
The names of the poets, the things they name,

Nothing but silence and stone.
Better to be the wind. Better to be the sea
Writing its name on all our edges—

Traceries of salt, glints of the moon's descending wings—
For each is its own scar of light,
And each its own signature.

What the Heart Can Bear

He is the first among us not to have died
As the sun comes down on the soft napes
Of the flax, the moon, pale umbel, drifts
Into the sky. The first to learn how little
To expect from the world except the dead
Taste of cobalt, from the body except hair
Falling out in great gouts in the shower,

More naked than any of us have yet to be,
Or he has been since returning like gaunt
Squinting Lazarus, his mouth full of dirt.
What can he believe in anymore?
When he looks into the heavens can he see
Anything other than the Crab Nebula,
Blindly wheeling its arms, who must now

Begin to learn all over again how much
He must forget, how little nakedness
The heart can bear with it into the world?
Is it because the world cares only for its own
Inhuman song that human affection
Has come to seem such a lone, lovely thing?
That I sometimes take myself up, slowly,

In my arms and rock back and forth,
As if to comfort us all—including one
Who is now only dying like the rest of us,
Slowly and in time. He writes to tell me
How those mornings, along the roadsides
Where he walked, he'd find the caked basins
Of rain water fluttering with moths,

Their little flotilla of identical white sails.
He tells me how the body moves
Into such a billowing, aching to come apart.
How the heart does break as the bones
Grow lovely as weeds in late September,
And the body sees how even those things
That fall away keep bringing us ever closer.

Beckian Fritz Goldberg

Beckian Fritz Goldberg is the author of several volumes of poetry, including *Body Betrayer* (Cleveland State University, 1991), *In the Badlands of Desire* (Cleveland State, 1993), and *Never Be the Horse*, winner of the University of Akron Poetry Prize (University of Akron, 1999). Her collection, *Lie Awake Lake*, was awarded the 2004 Field Poetry Prize from Oberlin College Press. She teaches in the Creative Writing Program at Arizona State University.

Lie Awake Lake

We can't get there
by road, by rope, by
wing

by time—
though time would be the way

by boat
by please please

time would be the way

then the reed-quiver
a cloud of gnats
mumbling its hypnotic suggestion

by sleep, sleep
until you say
lift my elbow   straighten
my legs

And I
straightened you in this life
like flowers

but the little water
there was
went to air
where it came from

And all my love for you
came back—
you couldn't take it where
you were going

you'd get halfway there
and then you'd drift
arms by your side

like a clock
plucked…

Wren

Once I fished a wren
from the pool
held it

little volt
in my hand

This I won't forget:

my mother's shoulders

I'm in the backseat
holding my brother's hand

my sister is driving

I don't have to see
anyone's face

the box of ashes
queerly heavy
like metal

like
the soaked sleeve of your sweater

long ago

the way something would rather drown
than trust

the hand that would lift it

Fourth Month

Finally, my father's soul came
to rest in the closet.
This is where you want
the dead—out of sight

and within scolding distance.
By now, it was June.
The grass shrank
and whitened. The sun,

the sun, was out every day
until we thought
it would never go…

Soon the nights would be still
and pointless,
too hot for bedsheets.
You want to sleep in air,
you want to sleep in water.

But what you feel is the sheen
of grief
like a sweat.

My aunt telling my mother
she should bring his ashes home,
to the lake where he was born,

my mother asking me is it all right
to wait—

but dear god who am I?

Story Problem

If Keisha had three million pears and a trainload of apples left Cleveland
at 64 miles per hour and on it was a man who had lost one wife and two
dogs in his current lifetime at 64 miles per hour approaching Euclid then
Ashtabula, the lake wind shimmying and the compartment windows
and each car having ten compartments how much of a wonder is it when
asked to care about all this we fell asleep, we dreamed that love is a form
that comes for us, after Ashtabula, after Conneaut. How many pears does
Keisha want? And what if sometimes in our dreams people changed as
Keisha in the future will be Keith. And if somehow, by the time the train
pulls into Erie, three and one-half apples have disappeared, what of the

water, what of the wind, what of the two dogs, the one wife. What kind
of life is it. A. The man's name is Charlie. B. The pears are Anjou. C. There
is nothing after Ohio. D. A and C. E. All of the Above. F. None of the
Above. Gee, we hope that Keith gets married and has a normal life. We
hope the dogs are in dog-heaven. Though we're only partially awake. And
if at the same time the apples left, a child woke up in the dark of Lorain
like a leaf, hearing the hush at 6 miles per hour, which would stop breath-
ing first? This is at last the essence of the problem as sure as a gardenia.
Which had to enter this story even if through a backdoor.Though most of
us don't want to hear about a story—so think of whisky which also has a
backdoor. This then is a story then about whisky. About fermented pears.
Whatever sure fires exist, and forms come to us. We hope Charlie meets
an attractive widow and gets a puppy. We're not made to understand. The
puppy is small and white and barks a lot. The hell with Lorain. It is white,
white as the soul was invented, its ineffability dispersed into the seconds
at the rate of train windows to grass, but cute—and wriggling—and if the
dog was born on the first day of daylight savings, by which you know
how old are the apples in their train, or you know nothing, still, after all,
or ever will, take a guess. A. Because in infinite time we will be right once.

Leonard Gontarek

Leonard Gontarek has been a cabdriver, movie projectionist, teacher and bookseller. He coordinates Peace/Works: Poets And Writers For Peace. His books include *St. Genevieve Watching over Paris, Van Morrison Can't Find His Feet, Zen for Beginners,* and *Déjà Vu Diner.* He received poetry fellowships from the Pennsylvania Council on the Arts in 1994 and 2004.

Study / White

As an example, the man is angry at autumn.

As an example, the man is upset at the cat.

buries herself in leaves & cries,

carries them back to him like prey.

As an example, a man

sits at a desk in faded admiral clothes,

medals obtained at yard sales,

the voice of despair drowning in him.

The man gets up,

takes a bowl of milk like a small moon

to the cat. As an example, the man's wife

slept with another man. The man

walks over snow crust, chewing down

on a peppermint lifesaver. He wishes

the man's bones would snap like that.

The man rubs the belly

of the cat, hard, the way she likes.

He can see his breath.

Study / Trees

Leaves flare up, kitchen matches

in the permanent trees.

Black flash of pike on Mirror Lake, dropping

like a roll of nickels. I don't want nudes

in paintings. I don't want Beauty through the heart,

small harpoon that opens when pulled out.

I want to break another egg roll with you in moonlight.

Ugly maples, when you're gone.

Study / Crow

Once the weather hits ninety,

I go to the Master, wearing

a paper crown. He knocks it

off & beats it like a rat with

a stick. What he means, I think,

is We should not have

anything that is not

necessary. What he means is Everything

happens underground duplicated by the gods.

On telephone wire, crow.

Farmhouse huge as a hill.

I must not become attached to objects aflame.

Objects within objects I must not make my home.

Sarah Gridley

Sarah Gridley is Assistant Professor of English at Case Western Reserve University and the author of two books of poetry: *Weather Eye Open* (2005) and *Green is the Orator* (2010), both from the University of California Press. Her poems have appeared in various journals, including *Crazyhorse, Denver Quarterly, Gulf Coast, jubilat,* and *New American Poetry.* She is a recipient of an Individual Excellence Award from the Ohio Arts Council and a Creative Workforce Fellowship from the Community Partnership for Arts and Culture.

Posthumous

It is late when the rummage gets underway. The air smells more
of earth than decks. Dockhands brag
to pretty bonnets, cormorants spear at wavy profits.

                    Now for a password

to work at all. For "walnut" to open
a single star.

            I'm done with the worst of cursed and cursing.

                    When the wind stands me up
so I do not fall, I'll forget which psalm
works against which sin.

Work

Nothing to gossip over: white oak shadows, a current

manifolding gold. As was the news

from nowhere: the vegetable dye, the longerwhile

of replication, to weave of the river, *Evenlode.*

There is no place the mourning cloak lifts up.

There is nowhere the question mark doesn't light down.

The tent is on fire

with all you have owned: the known

to be useful, the believed to be beautiful.

The oak lobes are.

The river is. The earth will have us.

Repeat and repeat.

Medieval Physics

Thousands of rulers up
and the wings are a copied motility

and a cabin is for breathing above the earth
and for walking in on elsewhere.

Why not a horse
now that the fields are visible?

The sun is always
circling the story. Like how

you showed me
how the hummingbirds feed:

saying *This is a moat*
                    and pointing

Against the Throne and Monarchy of God

Moon to light the spaces of the glossary. Birdless oak
of folded wings, shadows clotting the moon-green crown.

Meal of a moth, out for the moon.
Meal of a fish and a thorn apple's nectar.

Meal of milk.
Piecemeal.

Moon to light the loophole in mammalian
laws of gravity. Not hand or wing

in the oak. Not *home*:
home in.

Summer Reading

Up in the middle of the yard
is a fishing net being mended in good light. So that even

　　　　　　　the atheist's novel was a place to choose to live.
Bound together for motion in sunshine, the pages felt more
than a few lives long. Their flowers orange

and joyful-yellow, but stuck in dusts
of human traffic, the jewelweed & touch-me-nots

　　　　　　　could release
their contents
at the slightest brush. *It is better—it shall be better with me*

because I have known you.
Can I hope to say it

　　　　　　　in any case? To blossom is thoughtless—
thus we barely have room
for each other.

Summer: the wild carrot umbel went to seed.
Summer: the wild carrot umbel could recite

　　　　　　　the bird nest's negative space. I am not afraid
of the concave shape. These were our common names—
the names for which

we had something in common.

Corrinne Clegg Hales

Corrinne Clegg Hales is the author of three full length poetry collections: *To Make It Right*, winner of the 2010 Autumn House Poetry Prize, *Separate Escapes*, winner of the Richard Snyder Prize from Ashland Poetry Press, and *Underground* from Ahsahta Press. She has also published two chapbooks: *Out of This Place* from March Street Press and *January Fire* from Devil's Millhopper Press. She has received two fellowships from the National Endowment for the Arts and was the winner of the River Styx Poetry Prize for 2000. She teaches in the MFA Program at California State University, Fresno.

The Rich

When she finally got him to agree,
my brother brought the chosen pigeon
to my mother headless, dripping
all over the floor, and dropped it
in the sink. He was twelve,
and didn't want tenderness
messing up his life. His pigeons
nested in the shed out back
above the empty rabbit hutches,
and hadn't been contributing
their fair share. Animals,
my father insisted, are for food
or work or sale. No pets. No feeding
animal mouths before our own.
So our mother kept telling us
how the rich eat squab—how
squab is a delicacy—*squab under glass*—
she'd say, making an elaborate dome shape
with her hands in the air. *And squab is—
believe it or not—just another word
for pigeon.* She'd click her tongue
and shrug whenever she said this
as if the foolish rich had fallen
for some easy-to-see-through scam.
She plucked and gutted and washed
and stuffed, and when she called us
to the table it was sitting there hot
and brown, no bigger than a sparrow,
smack in the middle
of a sea-green Melmac plate,
under a clear glass mixing bowl,

a ragged sprig of spearmint
plopped flat on its breast
and bread crumbs tumbling out
from between its tiny crossed legs.
She was smiling. *The rich*, she said,
pay big bucks for a meal
like this, and when she lifted the glass,
all seven of us gathered around,
imagining we were them—breathing
the abundant odor of onion
and pulling slivers of meat
from the carcass with our fingers.

To Make It Right

Crouched low in my dank pool
of rage, I waited behind
the wooden fence until she walked
through the gate. She was
bigger than me, but slower,
and I sprang up, slamming
deep into her belly with both fists,
over and over with more force
than I believed my body
could produce. She collapsed, hard
and heavy as a wet pair of jeans
might drop from a clothesline, but she didn't
look angry or afraid. She stared at me
with what seemed like awe
before she stopped falling and began
to cry—not loudly, as I expected—
but softly, almost weeping, sitting there
in a pale clump of her mother's
spent daffodils, arms wrapped
around her knees. I could hear
a dog barking in the yard
next door, and someone's car
starting, as if nothing had happened,
and I just stood there, hands hanging
stupidly above her, trembling
with what should have been
shame, wanting her to stand,
to strike back, to make it right.

Forgiven

>   —*for the boy who asked me to pray with him after sex*

I knew what we were going to do
when you down-shifted and turned
onto Millcreek Canyon Road, when you

parked at a gravel turnout overlooking
the hazy sparkle of city lights, when you unrolled
all the windows so we could see

Jupiter and the swollen moon and breathe in
the dampness of dogwood blossoms, when
you cranked the old Rambler's seats back

as far as they would go, when we fell together
into the soft blanket, sighing and humming,
when we let our tongues move into each others'

mouths and ears, when we let our hands slide
under cotton, onto skin. I knew what we were
going to do when you pulled your shirt

off over your head, when I
unbuttoned mine. So, afterward,
when you began to cry

so unexpectedly, covering your face
with your crumpled shirt, asking me why
I let you do it, when you

got down on your knees right there
on the side of the road and asked god
to forgive us for the amazing thing

we'd just done, I pulled my clothes together
and started walking, descending the dark miles
with blouse still flapping open, past other

parked cars and the sweet sounds
of unrepentant lovers inside them, and past
the coldness of the creek and the shadowy

aspens, and I kept moving downward
towards the well-lighted city, where I'd hitch a ride
at the highway, and the goodhearted driver

would take one look as I climbed in—
tucking and buttoning, and smoothing
my hair—and ask what happened, assuming

I'd been, at the least, roughed up
by my date. I do hope you felt forgiven
that night, but I want you to know now

that it's taken all these years
for me to recall the astonishing heat
of your hands on my face and the way

our breathing became a song, how we
could feel our bones pressing right through
our skin, and how we seemed to be

floating, rising, transparent as smoke
for those few fragrant moments
before your prayer.

"Young Nubian Woman"

> *It is a matter of persuading them to pose, which they fear doing...*
> —Pierre Trémaux, 1850s

Her bare feet flat
on stone pavement, she faces
the camera almost naked.
She must be very young,
no hips, no waist, breasts
barely budding on her chest.
This is probably Egypt,
the exhibit note says, and the girl
was brought here as a slave
from central Africa.
She is caught again
at this moment on salted paper
which will give her eternal life
in European galleries
and art books, and keep her
at this age—safe as she will ever be.
It's a kind of seduction, really,
convincing the girl that she won't be
hurt, that she might even like it,
and placing her body just how
he wants it, gently, even tenderly,
and then asking her to be
completely still. Don't move.

This is how I want you
to stay forever. Please
don't move a hair. I wonder
why she complies, what she's
thinking, and I wonder what
the photographer wants me
to see in this girl. I think
of that other photo, a hundred years
later, of a girl about this age
running, screaming, her body
on fire, down a war-pitted road
halfway around the world,
and the four seconds of film
from another war, taken
of a young mother on Saipan
who looked at a camera mounted
on a rifle stock and believed
the photographer aimed to kill her,
or worse, and in fact, he catches her
running towards the cliff
and keeps filming as she throws
her two babies and then
her own panic-driven body
into the sea, and the camera
pans down to the corpse
of a child being battered
in the water and rocks
like dirty laundry. And my own
daughter's slim body at eleven
or twelve, how we wanted
to believe her life
was on the verge of becoming
her own—but I'm looking now
at this African girl, dark hair
chopped into straight lines
framing her face. She stares
into the future, one hand splayed
against the ancient rock wall
behind her. She stiffens,
bracing herself for the long
exposure, and her shadow,
that deformed echo,
slides down the wall.

Barbara Hamby

Barbara Hamby's fourth book of poems, *All Night Lingo Tango*, was published by the University of Pittsburgh Press. Her book of stories, *Lester Higata's 20th Century*, won the Iowa Short Fiction Prize, and she is a Guggenheim Fellow. Hamby teaches at Florida State University and is an inveterate packrat. Her many collections include kimonos, Bakelite bracelets, milagros, 45-rpm records, pre-1965 Barbie dolls, plumeria trees, and nurse novels.

I Beseech Thee, O Yellow Pages

I beseech thee, O Yellow Pages, help me find a number
for Barbara Stanwyck, because I need a tough broad
in my corner right now. She'll pour me a tumbler
of scotch or gin and tell me to buck up, show me the rod
she has hidden in her lingerie drawer. She has a temper,
yeah, but her laugh could take the wax off a cherry-red
Chevy. "Shoot him," she'll say merrily, then scamper
off to screw an insurance company out of another wad
of dough. I'll be left holding the phone or worse, patsy
in another scheme, arrested by Edward G. Robinson
and sent to Sing Sing, while Barbara lives like Gatsby
in Thailand or Tahiti, gambling the night away until the sun
rises in the east, because there are some things a girl can be sure
of, like morning coming after night's inconsolable lure.

The Language of Bees

The language of bees contains 76 distinct words for stinging,
        distinguishes between a prick, puncture,
and mortal wound, elaborates on cause and effect as in a sting
        made to retaliate, irritate, insinuate, infuriate,
incite, rebuke, annoy, nudge, anger, poison, harangue.
        The language of bees has 39 words for queen—
regina apiana, empress of the hive, czarina of nectar,
        maharani of the ovum, sultana of stupor,
principessa of dark desire. The language of bees
        includes 22 words for sunshine, two for rain—
big water and small water, so that a man urinating
        on an azalea bush in the full fuchsia of April
has the linguistic effect of a light shower in September.
        For man, two words—roughly translated—

"hands" and "feet," the first with the imperialistic connotation
        of beekeeper, the second with the delicious
resonance of bareness. All colors are variations on yellow,
        from the exquisite sixteen-syllable word meaning
"diaphanous golden fall," to the dirty ochre of the bitter pollen
        stored in the honeycomb and used by bees for food.

The language of bees is a language of war. For what is peace
        without strife but the boredom of enervating
day-after-day, obese with sweetness, truculent with ennui?
        Attack is delightful to bees, who have hundreds of verbs
embracing strategy, aim, location, velocity: swift, downward swoop
        to stun an antagonist, brazen, kamikaze strike
for no gain but momentum. Yet stealth is essential to bees,
        for they live to consternate their enemies, flying up pant legs,
hovering in grass. No insect is more secretive than the bee,
        for they have two thousand words describing the penetralia
of the hive: octagonal golden chamber of unbearable moistness,
        opaque tabernacle of nectar, sugarplum of polygonal waxy walls.

The language of bees is a language of aeronautics,
        for they have wings—transparent, insubstantial,
black-veined like the fall of an exotic iris.
        For they are tiny dirigibles, aviators
of orchard and field. For they have ambition, cunning,
        and are able to take direct aim.
For they know how to leave the ground, to drift, hover,
        swarm, sail over the tops of trees.

The language of bees is a musical dialect, a full, humming
        congregation of hallelujahs and amens,
at night blue and disconsolate, in the morning bright and bedewed.
        The language of bees contains lavish adjectives
praising the lilting fertility of their queen: fat, red-bottomed
        progenitor of millions, luscious organizer of coitus,
gelatinous distributor of love. The language of bees
        is in the jumble of leaves before rain,
in the quiet night rustle of small animals, for it is eloquent
        and vulgar in the same mouth,
and though its wound is sweet it can be distressing,
        as if words could not hurt or be meant to sting.

Betrothal in B Minor

All women bewail the betrothal of any woman,
beamy-eyed, bedazzled, throwing a fourth finger

about like a marionette. Worse than marriage
in many ways, an engagement, be it moments or millennia,

is a morbid exercise in hope, a mirage, a romance
befuddled by magazine photographs of lips, eyebrows,

brassieres, B-cups, bromides, bimbos bedaubed
with kohl, rouged, bespangled, beaded, beheaded,

really, because a woman loses the brain
she was born with if she believes for a moment

she of all women will escape enslavement of mind,
milk, mooring, the machinations of centuries,

to arrive in a blissful, benign, borderless
Brook Farm where men are uxorious, mooning,

bewitched, besotted, bereft of all beastly,
beer-guzzling qualities. Oh, no, my dear

mademoiselle, marriage is no *déjeuner sur l'herbe*,
no bebop with Little Richard for eternity,

no bedazzled buying spree at Bergdorf or Bendel,
no clinch on the beach with Burt Lancaster.

Although it is sometimes all these things, it is
more often, to quote la Marquise de Merteuil, "War,"

but war against the beastliness within that makes
us want to behave, eat beets, buy beef at the market,

wash with Fab, betray our beautiful minds
tending to the personal hygiene of midgets.

My God, Beelzebub himself could not have manufactured
a more Machiavellian maneuver to bedevil an entire

species than this benighted impulse to replicate
ourselves ad nauseam in the confines of a prison

so perfect, bars are redundant. Even in the Bible
all that begetting and begatting only led to misery,

morbidity, Moses, and murder. I beseech you,
my sisters, let's cease, desist, refrain,

take a breather, but no one can because we are
driven by tiny electrical sparks that bewilder,

befog, beguile, becloud our angelic intellect.
Besieged by hormones, we are stalked by a disease

unnamed, a romantic glaucoma. We are doomed to die,
bespattered and besmirched beneath the dirt,

under the pinks and pansies of domestic domination.
Oh, how I loathe you—perfect curtains, exquisite chairs,

crème brulée of my dreams. Great gods of pyromania,
begrudge not your handmaiden, your fool, the flames

that fall from your fiery sky, for my dress is tattered
and my shoes are different colors, blue and red.

Ode to My 1977 Toyota

Engine like a Singer sewing machine, where have you
            not carried me—to dance class, grocery shopping,
into the heart of darkness and back again? O the fruit
            you've transported—cherries, peaches, blueberries,
watermelons, thousands of Fuji apples—books,
            and all my dark thoughts, the giddy ones, too,
like bottles of champagne popped at the wedding of two people
            who will pass each other on the street as strangers
in twenty years. Ronald Reagan was president when I walked
            into Big Chief Motors and saw you glimmering
on the lot like a slice of broiled mahi mahi or sushi
            without its topknot of tuna. Remember the months
I drove you to work singing "Some Enchanted Evening"?
            Those were scary times. All I thought about
was getting on I-10 with you and not stopping. Would you
            have made it to New Orleans? What would our life
have been like there? I'd forgotten about poetry. Thank God,
            I remembered her. She saved us both. We were young
together. Now we're not. College boys stop us at traffic lights
            and tell me how cool you are. Like an ice cube, I say,
though you've never had air conditioning. Who needed it?
            I would have missed so many smells without you—
confederate jasmine, magnolia blossoms, the briny sigh
            of the Gulf of Mexico, rotting possums scattered
along 319 between Sopchoppy and Panacea. How many holes
            are there in the ballet shoes in your back seat?
How did that pair of men's white loafers end up in your trunk?
            Why do I have so many questions, and why

are the answers like the animals that dart in front of your headlights
            as we drive home from the coast, the Milky Way
strung across the black velvet bowl of the sky like the tiara
            of some impossibly fat empress who rules the universe
but doesn't know if tomorrow is December or Tuesday or June first.

Matthea Harvey

Matthea Harvey is the author of *Sad Little Breathing Machine* (Graywolf, 2004) and *Pity the Bathtub Its Forced Embrace of the Human Form* (Alice James Books, 2000). Her third book of poems, *Modern Life* (Graywolf, 2007) was a finalist for the National Book Critics Circle Award and a *New York Times* Notable Book. Her first children's book, *The Little General and the Giant Snowflake*, illustrated by Elizabeth Zechel, was published by Tin House Books in 2009. Matthea is a contributing editor to *jubilat, Meatpaper* and *BOMB*. She teaches poetry at Sarah Lawrence and lives in Brooklyn.

The Golden Age of Figureheads

First we sloughed off the sailors—when a storm hit we'd lean into it and watch as they slipped into the water. One by one we washed our decks clean, pried their rough fingers from our rudders. Now we can finally go where we want—swooping around archipelagos in packs, zigzagging along the paths the sun and moon make, skimming the Pacific solo. Sometimes we'll peer into the water to catch a glimpse of our old enemies, the anchors, glinting at the bottom of the ocean, the thick ropes that once tethered us to them twisting and turning in the currents like snakes charmed out of their baskets by the song of the sea. We don't mind that our masts are crusted with salt, our rigging grows ragged, our bright paint—reds and golds and greens—has faded so that we're pencil sketches of what we once were. We don't even mind the barnacles that muffle our mouths: after all, we have no common language. The ship with a bird's head wants to squawk with the gulls that forage from its sails, would follow them into the water when they dive for fish if only it could. Her ladyship, who trails sheets of seaweed like floaty green skirts, is lovesick for the sailor who used to stain her lips with wine before each voyage. But there is always the rain. When it falls hard enough we can't tell which way up, which way is down. Then we're like the earth before the equator was invented, like the giant tenor who unbuckles his belt and lets out his one truest note.

If Scissors Aren't the Answer, What's a Doll to Do?

The dotted lines go everywhere. Up the ceiling and around the chandelier. Down the basement steps and straight into the lint tray. In some places the lines are black, like the ones that reframe each framed ancestral photograph on my Wall of Ancestral Photographs. In others they are silvery; hard to see in bright light. I avoid those rooms. I shuffle around in my paper slippers, tiptoe over the envelopes fanning out from the mailslot. I sit in the second-floor window and watch leashes strain between dogs and people; I keep the volume on the stereo low. Sometimes late at night a car—wild, impervious—guns by, swerving in and out of its lane. The next morning, the pansies are re-dotted with dew.

Inside the Good Idea

From the outside it is singular. One wooden horse. Inside ten men sit cross-legged, knees touching. No noun has been invented yet to describe this. They whisper that it would be like sitting in a wine barrel if the curved walls were painted red. The contents are not content. They would like some wine. They quarrel about who gets to sit in the head until finally the smallest man clambers in, promising to send messages back to the belly. He can only look out of one eye at a time. At first there is nothing to report. Black, Dark, The Occasional Star. Then Quiet Footsteps Mixed with Questions. The children are clamoring for it to be brought inside the walls. The head sends back another message which gets caught in the throat: *They are bringing their toy horses to pay their respects to us, brushing their tiny manes, oiling the little wheels. It must be a welcome change from playing war.*

Yona Harvey

Yona Harvey is a swish caught in a net of teeth. She rises in the light of blue curtains & sleeps with one ear open. Maybe she is the water from which she pulls her baby son. Slippery Fish, she once called him. Slippery Fish, her daughter echoed back across the water. Maybe she is the woman closest to the blackboard. Maybe she is the woman wading at the edge of the room. Maybe she has been reading too much Tomaz Salamun. Maybe she is one small word in a noisy sea. Maybe she should speak more of credentials, academic scholarships. But she is afraid you've heard all the best stories. (Hard work, high marks, determination). She should keep better track of her volunteering—carpooling, book sharing, telling the stories of Martin Luther King, Jr. Next year, she'll probably go swimming in Tokyo. Or in Pittsburgh—people wear black & gold there. The rivers take hold & don't let go. The children say: Look! This is Yona Harvey. She buys green lentils from East End Food Co-Op. She prepares dinner, drinks, and works in the city.

To Describe My Body Walking

To describe my body walking I must go back
To my mother's body walking with an aimless switch
In this moment of baptismal snow or abysmal flurry.
There's a shadow of free-fall frenzy & she unhurried
The way snowflakes are unhurried toward transformation
At my living room window. She moves unlabored, she
Will not ask me to invite her in, but she will expect it.
I will open the door to her. She is my mother,
Even if she is made of snow & ice & air & the repetition
Of years & grievances. A means here, a ways there.
She came out of trees surrounding me. I see her cross
Now the creek in her patent leather shoes, their navy
Glimmer like a slick hole I might peer over & fall into,
Against so much snow weighing down the prayerful arms
Of sycamores, which doused the bushes last autumn.
Her little hearse broke down near the exit
That leads to my house. Now she must walk.
She will be tired. I will let her in,
Though she will not ask. She has come so far
Past the mud & twigs, the abandoned nests.
This time of year she can't tell the living from the dead.
The pathway is mostly still except for her moving
With the snow, becoming the snow. Forgiveness?

She is a stamp in it, the tapping of boots
At the porch steps, another cover. Not spring
Or summer. Just her advancing, multiplying—
—falling through branches—there's a flurry of her.

Blessing Blue Crabs

Smiling white teeth, television
    host pleased with her face, her
there-you-have-it filling the screen.
    One last shot of the elegant restaurant
poised a few miles across town, its proud-
    bellied chef & owner, spit-polished silver,
glasses clear enough to ring.
    Goodbye to the women who blessed
the blue crabs with hymns, who undressed
    the trapped bodies from blue-tinted shells,
lifted the meat from its legs, sealed
    flesh for markets, who weren't invited to
sit at the linen-clothed tables of the fine
    restaurant featured on the cooking program,
a "must-stop" for indulgent diners
    passing through the Low country,
who, still in uniform, sang
    stridently in the cannery kitchen,
who spoke barely above whispers to cameras
    stationed outdoors for interviews, against
the backdrop of foamy sea, whimsical sailboats,
    who posed at picnic benches propped for the occasion,
supplied with paper napkins, who sampled
    the chef's famous crab cakes, a cup
of water to wash them down.
    Yes, they are delicious. What else
could they answer without accusation
    of ungratefulness, their dark fingers
shaking away the delicate crumbs?

Discovering Girdles

I don't know what to do with this contraption
of polyester & cotton, troublesome lace. Black,
white, another woman's nude—whatever the color—
its trick is to hide flesh, to constrict the skin
like a bit of truth, a secret buried in the garden
of women's undergarments. A prepubescent girl
signals her mother to quiet, to lower what must be

her first bra, & yes, it's fine & can she go now?
My mother's concerns for me were body odor &
virginity—how to smell like a flower without being plucked.
Robust women filled her church, their stomachs
suffusing the linen of long dresses doused with perfume.
I do not know how to behave, publicly
contemplating these hip huggers that wouldn't matter
to those women, reaching beyond the fitting rooms of Earth.

Raza Ali Hasan

Raza Ali Hasan, author of *Grieving Shias* (Sheep Meadow Press, 2006) and *67 Mogul Miniatures* (Autumn House, 2008), was born in Chittagong, Bangladesh. He grew up in Indonesia and Islamabad, Pakistan, and received his MFA from Syracuse University. His poems have appeared in *AGNI, Shenandoah,* and *Blackbird.* He is a lecturer at the University of Colorado at Boulder.

from *67 Mogul Miniatures*

1
I kept my ear faithfully pinned to the ground
and heard a grand funeral theme—the *thump thump*

of chest beating and calling out to the murdered grandsons,
while a lone bulbul shrieked in my other ear.

Why must I listen, crestfallen like some oriental rose.
Dust be in my mouth, I have a complaint against Allah.

11
It is not easy to draw a still life of a famine.
Pictured from inside a ribcage of hunger

it is a fast moving train carrying grain
elsewhere—where slowness and stillness

still have a place in life, where Cezanne's
"Still Life with Apples" can still fetch a million.

28
Discarded plastic shopping bags blow
into the Desert Garden of Yemen.

The traitorous trade winds have betrayed us.
The price of coffee has collapsed.

Yet Iqbal, the steadfast trader remains, forever wide-eyed.
He sings the tumultuous song of the coffee of commerce.

38
Allah in his mercy and love throws his Koranic rope down
over the rusted, pitted railing, commanding us to hold on tight,

just like our dead parents who tie pieces of string
and rope around their waists, instructing us,

their newly orphaned children, to hold on tight
as they dive under ground, leading the way.

60
"10,000 Iranians prayed at Tehran University last Friday."
Relax, you are in LA. Tartar hordes come and go.

Put your latest Googoosh CD in your latest six-CD changer.
Drive down this freeway. In these dark times, you are

the designated driver and the light coming out of your car's
headlights is that of a bleary, distant star—follow it.

Robert Hass

Robert Hass, former U.S. Poet Laureate and winner of two National Book Critics Circle Awards, is a professor of English at the University of California at Berkeley.

A Story about the Body

The young composer, working that summer at an artist's colony, had watched her for a week. She was Japanese, a painter, almost sixty, and he thought he was in love with her. He loved her work, and her work was like the way she moved her body, used her hands, looked at him directly when she made amused and considered answers to his questions. One night, walking back from a concert, they came to her door and she turned to him and said, "I think you would like to have me. I would like that too, but I must tell you that I have had a double mastectomy," and when he didn't understand, "I've lost both my breasts." The radiance that he had carried around in his belly and chest cavity—like music—withered very quickly, and he made himself look at her when he said, "I'm sorry. I don't think I could." He walked back to his own cabin through the pines, and in the morning he found a small blue bowl on the porch outside his door. It looked to be full of rose petals, but he found when he picked it up that the rose petals were on top; the rest of the bowl—she must have swept them from the corners of her studio—was full of dead bees.

The Apple Trees at Olema

They are walking in the woods along the coast
and in a grassy meadow, wasting, they come upon
two old neglected apple trees. Moss thickened
every bough and the wood of the limbs looked rotten
but the trees were wild with blossom and a green fire
of small new leaves flickered even on the deadest branches.
Blue-eyes, crane's-bills, little Dutchmen
flecked the meadow, and an intricate, leopard-spotted
leaf-green flower whose name they didn't know.
Trout lily, he said; she said, adder's-tongue.
She is shaken by the raw, white, backlit flaring

of the apple blossoms. He is exultant,
as if some thing he felt were verified,
and looks to her to mirror his response.
If it is afternoon, a thin moon of my own dismay
fades like a scar in the sky to the east of them.
He could be knocking wildly at a closed door
in a dream. She thinks, meanwhile, that moss
resembles seaweed drying lightly on a dock.
Torn flesh, it was the repetitive torn flesh
of appetite in the cold white blossoms
that had startled her. Now they seem tender
and where she was repelled she takes the measure
of the trees and lets them in. But he no longer
has the apple trees. This is as sad or happy
as the tide, going out or coming in, at sunset.
The light catching in the spray that spumes up
on the reef is the color of the lesser finch
they notice now flashing dull gold in the light
above the field. They admire the bird together,
it draws them closer, and they start to walk again.
A small boy wanders corridors of a hotel that way.
Behind one door, a maid. Behind another one, a man
in striped pajamas shaving. He holds the number
of his room close to the center of his mind
gravely and delicately, as if it were the key,
and then he wanders among strangers all he wants.

Misery and Splendor

Summoned by conscious recollection, she
would be smiling, they might be in a kitchen talking,
before or after dinner. But they are in this other room,
the window has many small panes, and they are on a couch
embracing. He holds her as tightly
as he can, she buries herself in his body.
Morning, maybe it is evening, light
is flowing through the room. Outside,
the day is slowly succeeded by night,
succeeded by day. The process wobbles wildly
and accelerates: weeks, months, years. The light in the room
does not change, so it is plain what is happening.
They are trying to become one creature,
and something will not have it. They are tender
with each other, afraid
their brief, sharp cries will reconcile them to the moment
when they fall away again. So they rub against each other,
their mouths dry, then wet, then dry.

They feel themselves at the center of a powerful
and baffled will. They feel
they are an almost animal,
washed up on the shore of a world—
or huddled against the gate of a garden—
to which they can't admit they can never be admitted.

Terrance Hayes

Terrance Hayes won the National Book Award for his fourth book of poems, *Lighthead*, published by Penguin. He lives in Pittsburgh with his family, and teaches at Carnegie Mellon University.

The Same City

The rain falling on a night
    in mid-December,
I pull to my father's engine
    wondering how long I'll remember
this. His car is dead. He connects
    jumper-cables to his battery,
then to mine without looking in
    at me & the child. Water beads
on the windshields, the road sign,
    his thin blue coat. I'd get out now,
prove I can stand with him
    in the cold, but he told me to stay
with the infant. I wrap her
    in the blanket staring
for what seems like a long time
    into her open, toothless mouth,
and wish she was mine. I feed her
    an orange softened first in my mouth,
chewed gently until the juice runs
    down my fingers as I squeeze it
into hers. What could any of this matter
    to another man passing on his way
to his family, his radio deafening
    the sound of water & breathing
along all the roads bound to his?
    But to rescue a soul is as close

as anyone comes to God.
    Think of Noah lifting a small black bird
from its nest. Think of a carpenter,
    raising a son that wasn't his.

Let me begin again.
    I want to be holy. In rain
I pull to my father's car
    with my girlfriend's infant.
She was pregnant when we met.
    But we'd make love. We'd make
love below stars & shingles
    while the baby kicked between us.
Perhaps a man whose young child
    bears his face, whose wife waits
as he drives home through rain
    & darkness, perhaps that man
would call me a fool. So what.
    There is one thing I will remember
all my life. It is as small
    & holy as the mouth
of an infant. It is speechless.
    When his car would not stir,
my father climbed in beside us,
    took the orange from my hand,
took the baby in his arms.
    In 1974, this man met my mother
for the first time as I cried or slept
    in the same city that holds us
tonight. If you ever tell my story,
    say that's the year I was born.

        for James L. Hayes

Snow for Wallace Stevens

No one living a snowed-in life
can sleep without a blindfold.
Light is the lion that comes down to drink.
I know *tink and tank and tunk-a-tunk-tunk*
holds nearly the same sound as a bottle.
Drink and drank and drunk-a-drunk-drunk,
light is the lion that comes down.
This song is for *the wise man who avenges
by building his city in snow.*
For his decorations in a nigger cemetery.

How, with pipes of winter
lining his cognition, does someone learn
to bring a sentence to its knees?
Who is not more than his limitations?
Who is not the blood in a wine barrel
and the wine as well? I too, having lost faith
in language, have placed my faith in language.
Thus, I have a capacity for love without
forgiveness. This song is for my foe,
the clean-shaven, gray-suited, gray patron
of Hartford, the emperor of whiteness
blue as a body made of snow.

All the Way Live

"Do all dudes have one big testicle and one little tiny one?"
Hieronymus asked, hiking up his poodle skirt as we staggered
Down Main Street in our getup of wigs and pink bonnets
The night we sprayed NEGROPHOBIA all over the statue of Robert
E. Lee guarding the county courthouse, a symbol of the bondage
We had spent all of our All-the-Way Lives trying to subvert.
Hieronymus's thighs shimmered like the wings of a teenage
Cockroach beneath his skirt as a bullhorn of sheriff verbs
Like *Stop! Freeze!* and *Fire!* outlined us. The town was outraged:
The red-blooded farm boys, the red-eyed bookworms of Harvard,
The housewives and secretaries, even a few liberals hoorayed
When they put us on trial. We were still wearing our lady ward-
Robes, Hieronymus and me, with our rope burns bandaged
And our wigs tilted at the angle of trouble. Everyone was at war
With what it meant to be alive. That's why we refused to be banished,
And why when they set us on fire, there was light at our core.

A Plate of Bones

My silk slick black muscular back-
talking uncle driving me and a school
of fish corpses to church. The sick-eyed
gap-mouthed bass, the kingfish without
kingdom, the silver-thin silver fish—each
dead and separate in a cool bucket. Gilded
and shapely as a necktied Sunday morning,
the fish. *Sit upright*, he said, and I sat up,
riding shotgun looking hard at the road.
He muttered, *Crackers*, as if it was something
swinging from a thin clear wire,
the clump of tiny maggots in a trout's brain,
the flied lazing like the devil's jewelry at our backs.

Last night when the white boy's arm
lassoed his daughter's neck, my uncle
said nothing until they left. I let him feed me
the anger I knew was a birthright,
a plate of bones tin enough to puncture
a lung. But the rods did something in my mouth
I'd heard they killed people for. They went
to a movie and sat quietly and touched
or did not touch in the darkness. My uncle watched
the news with the sound turned down
until she came in, my silk slick black back-
talking cousin, his daughter. He went to work
beating a prayer out of her skin.

Samuel Hazo

Samuel Hazo, Founder and Director of the International Poetry Forum in Pittsburgh, Pennsylvania, is the McAnulty Distinguished Professor Emeritus of English at Duquesne University. His recent books include *Stills* (fiction), *Feather* (drama), and *Spying for God* (essays), as well as *Just Once, A Flight to Elsewhere*, and *The Song of the Horse*, all published by Autumn House Press.

God and Man

After casting the first act, checking sections
of scenery and mastering His rage
because the female lead blundered on page
one, He left the actors to themselves on stage
without a script and fretting for directions.

My Roosevelt Coupé

Coax it, clutch it, kick it
  in the gas was every dawn's
  scenario.
            Then off it bucked,
  backfiring down the block to show
  it minded.
            Each fender gleamed
  a different hue of blue.
Each hubcap chose
  its hill to spin freewheeling
  into traffic.
            I fretted like a spouse
  through chills and overboiling,
  jacked my weekly flats
  and stuffed the spavined seats
  with rags.
            Leaking, the radiator
  healed with swigs of Rinso,
  brake fluid and rainwater.

                        Simonized,
    the hood stuck out like a tramp
    in a tux.
                    All trips were dares.
Journeys were sagas.
                        From Norfolk
    to New York and back,
    I burned eleven quarts
    of oil, seven fuses
    and the horn.
                    One headlight
    dimmed with cataracts.
                        The other
    funneled me one-eyed
    through darker darks than darkness...
O my Roosevelt coupé, my first,
    my Chevrolet of many scars
    and heart attacks, where are you
    now?
                Manhandled, you'd refuse
to budge.
                Stick-shifted
    into low, you'd enigmatically
    reverse.
                Sold finally
    for scrap, you waited on your treads
    while I pocketed thirty
    pieces of unsilver and slunk
    away—Wild Buck Hazo
    abandoning his first and favorite
    mount, unwilling to malinger
    long enough to hear
    the bullet he could never fire.

Toasts for the Lost Lieutenants

For Karl, the Cornell rower,
    who wore the medals he deserved.
For Grogan of Brooklyn, who left
    no memory worth mentioning.
For Foley, who married the Commandant's
    daughter though nothing came of it.
For Clasby, who wanted out,
    and when he could, got out.
For Schoen, who married, stayed in,
    thickened, and retired a colonel.
For Chalfant, who bought a sword
    and dress blues but remained Chalfant.

For Billy Adrian, the best
   of punters, haunted by Korea.
For Nick Christopolos, who kept
   a luger, just in case.
For Soderberg, who taught us
   songs on the hot Sundays.
For Dahlstrom, the tennis king,
   who starched his dungarees erect.
For Jacobson, who followed me
   across the worst of all creeks.
For Laffin and the gun he cracked
   against a rock and left there.
For Nathan Hale, who really was
   descended but shrugged it off.
For Elmore, buried in Yonkers
   five presidents ago.
For Lonnie MacMillan, who spoke
   his Alabamian mind regardless.
For Bremser of Yale, who had it
   and would always have it.
For lean Clyde Lee, who stole
   from Uncle once too often.
For Dewey Ehling and the clarinet
   he kept but never played.
For Lockett of the Sugar Bowl
   champs, and long may he run.
For Lyle Beeler, may he rot
   as an aide to the aide of an aide.
For Joe Buergler, who never
   would pitch in the majors.
For Kerg, who called all women cows
   but married one who wasn't.
For me, who flunked each
   test on weapons but the last.
For Sheridan, who flunked them all,
   then goofed the battle games
   by leaving his position, hiding
   in a pine above the generals'
   latrine until he potted
   every general in sight, thus
   stopping single-handedly the war.

Ballad of a Returnee

He knew he was older and taller.
He saw that the towns were the same.
What made them seem suddenly smaller?
What made him feel somehow to blame

for all that was done to a village
to save a surrounded platoon?
The huts were just booty to pillage
on a hillscape as spare as the moon.

A man with one leg saw him walking
and offered him tea on a mat.
They spent the whole afternoon talking
while his wife cooked the head of a cat.

It wasn't his squad he remembered.
It wasn't the sergeant at Hue
who found his lieutenant dismembered
and buried him there where he lay.

What troubled him most were the places
that once were just places to fight.
He thought of the nightfighters' faces
all blackened to blend with the night.

The whores in their teens were forgotten
and gone were their overnight dates,
and grown were the idly begotten
whose fathers were back in the States.

He never regretted returning.
At least he had lessened his dread.
But the toll that it took for the learning
was 58,000 dead.

He walked in a daze near the water.
He sat all alone on the shore
like a man making peace with the slaughter,
though the price for this peace was war.

Bob Hicok

Bob Hicok's most recent book is *Words for Empty and Words for Full* (University of Pittsburgh Press, 2010). *Animal Soul* was a finalist for the National Book Critics Circle Award.

Solstice: voyeur

I watched the young couple walk into the tall grass and close
the door of summer behind them, their heads floating
on the golden tips, on waves that flock and break like starlings
changing their minds in the middle of changing their minds,
I saw their hips lie down inside those birds, inside the day
of shy midnight, they kissed like waterfalls, like stones
that have traveled a million years to touch, and emerged
hybrid, some of her lips in his words, all of his fists
opened by trust like morning glories, and I smelled green
pouring out of trees into grass, grass into below, I stood
on the moment the earth changes its mind about the sun,
when hiding begins, and raised my hand from the hill
into the shadows behind the lovers, and contemplated
their going with my skin, and listened to the grass
in wind call us home like our mothers before dark.

Bars poetica

This is the story I've tried to tell. Guy
exists. Father mother sister brother.
Oh pretty stars, oh bastard moon
I see you watching me. The trembling
years leading to sex, the trembling sex.
Death as garnish. Death as male lead,
female lead, death as a cast
of thousands. God in, on, as, with,
to, around, because who knows
because. All the while feeling air's

a quilt of tongues, that spaces
between words are more articulate
than words. It's not like you'd hope,
that anyone can make sense.
Look around you, let your ears
breathe deep—almost no one does.
Have another drink. When they throw us out
there's a place down the street
that never closes, and when it does,
we'll climb a fire escape and praise
the genealogy of light. The Big Bang
sounds like what it was, the fucking
that got everything under way.
That love was there from the start
is all I've been trying to say.

1935

for Lester Hicok

He rode in the back with apples and wind.
Rumor was a blast furnace in Battle Creek

needed to be fed. He followed the scent
of work, rode in the back with an ax

and pig. In Battle Creek he'd stand with fifty
or a thousand men. They'd shuffle and smoke,

some would talk while others hid in their hats.
After awhile a man with a clipboard

would ask what he asked and stare as long
as he liked. His nod meant food. He rode

in the back on a coil of chain link fence.
It was warm, shadows popped up from the fields.

In Battle Creek he'd stand. A man would come,
he'd wear a tie and his socks would match.

A furnace needed to be fed, a roof had to rise
over dirt, a pile of steel wanted to move

somewhere else. The rumor was work.
He rode without waving to the men

in other trucks. A rumor was often a lock
on a door. He followed the scent,

rode in the back with apples and wind,
with the tools of his hands and the shadow

of his head running beside the truck.
It got to Battle Creek before he did.

He found other men, their hats,
their cigarettes. He found that their eyes

didn't want him. The furnace was happy
and fat, it didn't need to be fed. Rumor

was a man in Flint had a place and a thing
that needed to be done. He followed the scent,

stuck out his thumb. This is how
my grandfather lived. In the back with a pig.

Cutting edge

I can't be in the avant garde
because I cry when dogs die

in movies. Worse, I sniffle
if they're abandoned or hit

with even the rolled and tepid
discipline of *Newsweek*. My dog

is eight. When I do the math
I get weepy. I see the hole

in the back yard I'll dig,
pet her while imagining

how I'll pet her as the vet
slips the needle in. During

these moments she licks tears
and snot from my face, just

as she took menstrual blood
from my wife's finger

this morning for what it is.
Anyway, sorrow about a dog

looks silly in a beret. It
20 should be plain spoken,

like everything else
I try hard not to say.

Mary Crockett Hill

Mary Crockett Hill has worked as a factory slug, staggeringly bad waitress, incompetent secretary, the person who irons name tags on industrial uniforms, toilet-seat hand model, fundraising spy, freelance writer, history museum director, and college English teacher. Her second book of poetry, *A Theory of Everything*, won the 2008 Autumn House Poetry Prize, selected by Naomi Shihab Nye.

A Theory of Everything

It has something to do with invisible string
rippling out across a universal sunset,
wrapping us up like the perfect brown corded package.

Something to do with the vibration of stars—
how they flicker in tune with each other, humming
    cosmically.
And though I've never seen this reported anywhere

I also believe it has something to do with dogs.
For who else has such capacity to forgive
an entirely other species? Well, yes, God

but I don't mess around with God.
So in my theory, the wet nose of a dog
fits in the space where our heart has been cut out.

And after dogs, the pure yellow of lemons,
the affection small children hold for Band-aids, the urge
to touch a stranger's bald head.

It all has a place in the Theory.
Name it and I will hang it on the clothesline.
Name it, I will chop it up for soup.

What's not to believe, anyway, in a theory
that has room enough for all other theories,
even those that say this Theory is shit?

Sure, the vibration of strings we cannot measure.
And yes, the strings are so fine we haven't
found them yet. One might surmise

this is not about strings, but our desire
for strings. You too are welcome
at this Party of Everything.

Come to my house where
we will speak of aqueducts and whiskers,
we will eat brown bread and touch our feet

under the table. You can tell me
we are not connected, that there is nothing
holding us together.

I will tug your ear and peck you softly on the lips

All about It

He looked like sullied laundry, which is to say
Jeff Clark, which is to say the scrubby field
where Jeff Clark took me when I was 5 and he 13
to teach me, as he put it, how to hump.

Jeff didn't take my clothes off, or his for that matter,
or stick any one of his parts into any one of mine.
He just led me out into the first light of November
where even I suspected we should not have come.

He said, "I bet you don't know anything," and I told him
"I know all about it," and he said, "Show me then."
So I did to him what my brother had described.
It must have looked ridiculous — this thin-boned child

in wrinkled corduroys and mittens, pumping
her intrepid hips against the dawn of 1975.
Perhaps it is wrong for me to smile when thinking on it.
But it is my memory. I'll do with it what I want.

Pantoum for Attachment

My sister the Buddhist says it's my problem.
I say it makes sense I don't want to let go
the hand of my daughter as she sleeps this morning
in the bare room, or the bare room itself for that matter.

I say it makes sense I don't want to let go
—the worn rug, the coffee mug left on the mantle
in the bare room, or the bare room itself for that matter,
the million invisible atoms we're breathing,

the worn rug, the coffee mug left on the mantle,
the half-lit smile she'll make when I wake her,
the million invisible atoms we're breathing—
I want it, of course, I want this touch to become

the half-lit smile she'll make when I wake her,
the nutshell of her small brown head.
I want it, of course, I want this touch to become
enough for the rest of whatever is coming.

The nutshell of her small brown head
turns in her sleep like agreement, cunning
enough for the rest of whatever is coming.
A bird cries morning. Watch as she

turns in her sleep like agreement, cunning,
into a woman in a raincoat by the side of the road.
A bird cries. Morning. Watch as she
(anyone, not my daughter, this other, this vision

of a woman in a raincoat by the side of the road)
walks under the sky as if it were breathing.
Anyone, not my daughter, this other, this vision
I must, my sister says, release. She

walks under the sky as if it were breathing
in all the loose thoughts of a collective sun.
I must, my sister says, release. She
doesn't understand. Why should I let go?

In all the loose thoughts of a collective sun,
where lies the love my grasping mother-love
doesn't understand? Why should I let go
of her tender-boned, still small hand

where lies the love my grasping mother-love
builds a nest to rest in? I would make a sculpture
of her tender-boned, still small hand
—a totem to carry against the future,

a nest to rest in. I would make a sculpture—
the hand of my daughter as she sleeps into morning,
a totem to carry against the future.
My sister the Buddhist says it's my problem.

Young People Today

Apparently they're having sex and eating
non-stop Taco Bell and wearing strange
perfumes and t-shirts that proclaim,
"Hey you! Wanna have my baby?"

And I've considered it and yes I do.
I want that blind white tug
of baby mouth, the pull of milk
as ostentatious as the high note

that a diva won't stop singing.
Looking back, I want more
of sun and field and blanket,
the groundhog who is always

twenty feet away, gnawing
yard greens and pretending
he doesn't see me
so he won't have to run.

In the sense that all pleasures
are at root a threat, I want
a ship that sails into oblivion,
its curtains warbling *tra-la, tra-lee*

and the mercy of horizons
beyond reach. I should stop
to ask what you want.
What is it? Surely

not my baby after all.
I might guess something
between possession and longing
—a folded sheet of paper

made gauzy by the lamplight,
but that would just be
guessing. Instead, let's do this:
hold the quiet of my hand

as we sit and watch the weather
tumble into evening. Perhaps
you'll take out your spent chewing gum
and loll it between your fingers.

Perhaps the sky will open
clamorous petals above us
and what I don't want to look at
will blur in its descent.

Jane Hirshfield

Jane Hirshfield is the author of seven books of poetry, a collection of essays on poems, and three anthologies collecting the work of women poets from the past. *After* (NY: HarperCollins, 2006) was named a "best book of 2006" by *The Washington Post*, *The San Francisco Chronicle*, and England's *Financial Times*, and was shortlisted for England's prestigious T.S. Eliot Award. *Given Sugar, Given Salt* (NY: HarperCollins, 2001) was a finalist for the National Book Critics Circle Award. Her poems appear in *The New Yorker*, *The Atlantic Monthly*, *Poetry, American Poetry Review, Orion, The Georgia Review*, and five editions of *The Best American Poems*. Her new book of poems, *Come, Thief*, was published by Knopf.

First Light Edging Cirrus

10^{25} molecules
are enough
to call woodthrush or apple.

A hummingbird, fewer.
A wristwatch: 10^{24}.

An alphabet's molecules,
tasting of honey, iron, and salt,
cannot be counted—

as some strings, untouched,
sound when a near one is speaking.

As it was when love slipped inside us.
It looked out face to face in every direction.

Then it was inside the tree, the rock, the cloud.

The Supple Deer

The quiet opening
between fence strands
perhaps eighteen inches.

Antlers to hind hooves,
four feet off the ground,
the deer poured through.

No tuft of the coarse white belly hair left behind.

I don't know how a stag turns
into a stream, an arc of water.
I have never felt such accurate envy.

Not of the deer:

To be that porous, to have such largeness pass through me.

Narrowness

Day after day,
my neighbors' cats in the garden.

Each in a distant spot,
like wary planets.

One brindled gray,
one black and white,
one orange.

They remind of the feelings:
how one cannot know another completely.

The way two cats cannot sleep
in one patch of mint-scented shade.

A Hand Is Shaped for What It Holds or Makes

A hand is shaped for what it holds or makes.
Time takes what's handed to it then—warm bread, a stone,
a child whose fingers touch the page to keep her place.

Beloved, grown old separately, your face
shows me the changes on my own.
I see the histories it holds, the argument it makes

against the thresh of trees, the racing clouds, the race
of birds and sky birds always lose:
        the lines have ranged, but not the cheek's strong bone.
My fingers touching there recall that place.

Once we were one. Then what time did, and hands, erased
us from the future we had owned.
For some, the future holds what hands release, not make.

We made a bridge. We walked it. Laced
night's sounds with passion.
Owls' pennywhistles, after, took our place.

Wasps leave their nest. Wind takes the papery case.
Our wooden house, less easily undone,
now houses others. A life is shaped by what it holds or makes.
I make these words for what they can't replace.

Perishable, It Said

Perishable, it said on the plastic container,
and below, in different ink,
the date to be used by, the last teaspoon consumed.

I found myself looking:
now at the back of each hand,
now inside the knees,
now turning over each foot to look at the sole.

Then at the leaves of the young tomato plants,
then at the arguing jays.

Under the wooden table and lifted stones, looking.
Coffee cups, olives, cheeses,
hunger , sorrow, fears—
these too would certainly vanish, without knowing when.

How suddenly then
the strange happiness took me,
like a man with strong hands and strong mouth,
inside what hour with its perishing perfumes and clashings.

Tony Hoagland

Tony Hoagland has published four books of poems: *Sweet Ruin, Donkey Gospel, What Narcissism Means to Me,* and *Unincorporated Persons in the Late Honda Dynasty.* He teaches at the University of Houston and in the Warren Wilson low-residency MFA program and has received grants from the NEA and the Guggenheim Foundation.

The News

The big country beat the little country up
like a schoolyard bully,
so an even bigger country stepped in
and knocked it on its ass to make it nice,
which reminds me of my Uncle Bob's
                    philosophy of parenting.

It's August, I'm sitting on the porch swing,
touching the sores inside my mouth
with the tip of my tongue, watching the sun
go down in the west like a sinking ship,
from which a flood of sticky orange bleeds out.

It's the hour of meatloaf perfume emanating from the houses.
It's the season of Little League practice
and atonal high school band rehearsals.
You can't buy a beach umbrella in the stores till next year.
The summer beauty pageants are all over,
and no one I know won the swimsuit competition.

This year illness just flirted with me,
picking me up and putting me down
like a cat with a ball of yarn,
so I walked among the living like a tourist,
and I wore my health
like a borrowed shirt,
knowing I would probably have to give it back.

There are the terrible things that happen to you
and the terrible things that you yourself make happen,
like George, who bought a little red sportscar
for his favorite niece
            to smash her life to pieces in.

And the girl on the radio sings,
You know what I'm talking about. *Bawhoop, awhoop.*

This year it seems like everyone is getting tattoos—
sharks and Chinese characters,
hummingbirds and musical notes—
but the tattoo I would like to get
is of a fist and a rose.

But I can't tell how they will fit together on my shoulder:
If the rose is inside the fist, it will be crushed or hidden;
if the fist is closed,—as a fist by definition is,—
it cannot reach out and touch the rose.

Yet the only tattoo I want
is of a fist and rose, together.
Fist, that helps you survive.
Rose, without which
                    you have no reason to.

Suicide Song

But now I am afraid I know too much to kill myself
Though I would still like to jump off a high bridge

At midnight, or paddle a kayak out to sea
Until I turn into a speck, or wear a necktie made of knotted rope

But people would squirm, it would hurt them in some way,
And I am too knowledgeable now to hurt people imprecisely.

No longer do I live by the law of me,
No longer having the excuse of youth or craziness,

And dying you know shows a serious ingratitude
For sunsets and beehive hairdos and the precious green corrugated

Pickles they place at the edge of your plate.
Killing yourself is wasteful, like spilling oil

At sea or not recycling all the kisses you've been given,
And anyway, who has clothes nice enough to be caught dead in?

Not me. You stay alive you stupid asshole
Because you haven't been excused.

You haven't finished though it takes a mule
To chew this food.

It is a stone, it is an inconvenience, it is an innocence,
And I turn against it like a record

Turns against the needle
That makes it play.

Phone Call

Maybe I overdid it
when I called my father an enemy of humanity.
That might have been a little strongly put,
a slight overexaggeration,

an immoderate description of the person
who at that moment, two thousand miles away,
holding the telephone receiver six inches from his ear,
must have regretted paying for my therapy.

What I meant was that my father
was an enemy of *my* humanity
and what I meant behind that
was that my father was split
into two people, one of them

living deep inside of me
like a bad king or an incurable disease—
blighting my crops,
striking down my herds,
poisoning my wells— the other
standing in another time zone,
in a kitchen in Wyoming,
with bad knees and white hair sprouting from his ears.

I don't want to scream forever,
I don't want to live without proportion
like some kind of infection from the past,

so I have to remember the second father,
the one whose tv dinner is getting cold
while he holds the phone in his left hand
and stares blankly out the window

where just now the sun is going down
and the last fingertips of sunlight
are withdrawing from the hills
they once touched like a child.

Two Trains

Then there was that song called "Two Trains Running,"
a Mississippi blues they play on late-night radio,
that program after midnight called FM in the AM,
—well, I always thought it was about *trains*.

Then somebody told me it was about what a man and woman do
under the covers of their bed, moving back and forth
like slow pistons in a shiny black locomotive,
the rods and valves trying to stay coordinated

long enough that they will "get to the station"
at the same time. And one of the trains
goes out of sight into the mountain tunnel,
but when they break back into the light

the other train has somehow pulled ahead,
the two trains running like that, side by side,
first one and then the other, with the fierce white
bursts of smoke puffing from their stacks,
into a sky so sharp and blue you want to die.

So then for a long time I thought the song was about sex.

But then Mack told me that all train songs
are really about Jesus, about how the second train
is shadowing the first, so He walks in your footsteps
and He watches you from behind, He is running with you,

He is your brakeman and your engineer,
your coolant and your coal,
and He will catch you when you fall,
and when you stall He will push you through
the darkest mountain valley, up the steepest hill,

and the rough *chuff chuff* of His fingers on the washboard
and the harmonica *woo woo* is the long soul cry by which He
pulls you through the bloody tunnel of the world.
So then I thought the two trains song was a gospel song.

Then I quit my job in Santa Fe and Sharon drove
her spike heel through my heart
and I got twelve years older and Dean moved away,
and now I think the song might be about good-byes—

because we are not even in the same time zone,
or moving at the same speed, or perhaps even
headed towards the same destination—
forgodsakes, we are not even trains!

What grief it is to love some people like your own
blood, and then to see them simply disappear;
to feel time bearing us away
                one boxcar at a time.

And sometimes, sitting in my chair
I can feel the absence stretching out in all directions—
like the deaf, defoliated silence
just after a train has thundered past the platform,

just before the mindless birds begin to chirp again
—and the wildflowers that grow beside the tracks
wobble wildly on their little stems,
                then gradually grow still and stand

motherless and vertical in the middle of everything.

Marie Howe

Marie Howe lives in New York City and is the author of *The Good Thief*, *What the Living Do*, and *The Kingdom of Ordinary Time*.

What the Living Do

Johnny, the kitchen sink has been clogged for days, some utensil probably
    fell down there.
And the Drano won't work but smells dangerous, and the crusty dishes
    have piled up

waiting for the plumber I still haven't called. This is the everyday we
    spoke of.
It's winter again: the sky's a deep headstrong blue, and the sunlight
    pours through

the open living room windows because the heat's on too high in here, and
    I can't turn it off.
For weeks now, driving, or dropping a bag of groceries in the street,
    the bag breaking,

I've been thinking: This is what the living do. And yesterday, hurrying
    along those
wobbly bricks in the Cambridge sidewalk, spilling my coffee down my
    wrist and sleeve,

I thought it again, and again later, when buying a hairbrush: This is it.
Parking. Slamming the car door shut in the cold. What you called
    that yearning.

What you finally gave up. We want the spring to come and the winter to
    pass. We want
whoever to call or not call, a letter, a kiss—we want more and more and
    then more of it.

But there are moments, walking, when I catch a glimpse of myself in the
    window glass,
say, the window of the corner video store, and I'm gripped by a cherishing
    so deep

for my own blowing hair, chapped face, and unbuttoned coat that I'm
    speechless:
I am living, I remember you.

Practicing

I want to write a love poem for the girls I kissed in seventh grade,
a song for what we did on the floor in the basement

of somebody's parents' house, a hymn for what we didn't say but thought:
That feels good or *I like that*, when we learned how to open each other's
    mouths

how to move our tongues to make somebody moan. We called it
    practicing, and
one was the boy, and we paired off—maybe six or eight girls—and
    turned out

the lights and kissed and kissed until we were stoned on kisses, and
    lifted our
nightgowns or let the straps drop, and, Now you be the boy:

concrete floor, sleeping bag or couch, playroom, game room, train
    room, laundry.
Linda's basement was like a boat with booths and portholes

instead of windows. Gloria's father had a bar downstairs with stools
    that spun,
plush carpeting. We kissed each other's throats.

We sucked each other's breasts, and we left marks, and never spoke of it
    upstairs
outdoors, in daylight, not once. We did it, and it was

practicing, and slept, sprawled so our legs still locked or crossed, a hand
    still lost
in someone's hair. . . and we grew up and hardly mentioned who

the first kiss really was—a girl like us, still sticky with the moisturizer we'd
shared in the bathroom. I want to write a song

for that thick silence in the dark, and the first pure thrill of unreluctant
    desire,
just before we made ourselves stop.

The Copper Beech

Immense, entirely itself,
it wore that yard like a dress,

with limbs low enough for me to enter it
and climb the crooked ladder to where

I could lean against the trunk and practice being alone.

One day, I heard the sound before I saw it, rain fell
darkening the sidewalk.

Sitting close to the center, not very high in the branches,
I heard it hitting the high leaves, and I was happy,

watching it happen without it happening to me.

Gray Jacobik

Gray Jacobik's book, *The Double Task* (University of Massachusetts Press, 1998), received The Juniper Prize. *The Surface of Last Scattering* (Texas Review Press, 1999) won the X. J. Kennedy Poetry Prize. *Brave Disguises* (University of Pittsburgh Press, 2002) won the AWP Poetry Series Award. Her most recent book is *Little Boy Blue: A Memoir in Verse* (CavanKerry Press, 2011.)

The Tapeworm

It rushes out of you the way Magritte's train engine
rushes out of a fireplace; something
illogical and fast, the long freight of embarrassing
incident coupled to fear. Groceries left at the checkout
because a roommate took your cash, a car wasting
without repairs, the dog saved by a vet
you can't pay, so can't bring home. The ugly humiliating
chewed-up rag of it. Deadweight of trinkets
bought to console that don't console. How you can't get
enough of what you don't really want,
yet in the make-do, grab. Recompense that's supposed
to stave off— what?— the flush of shame
that stipples your neck. Two babies asleep on blankets
on a cold linoleum floor, no furniture,
no food in the fridge, none on shelves— the quick hysteria
of suppose. Suppose you borrow?
Suppose you take. . . ? But worse is the man who
promises work and delivers rape,
though he throws two twenties at you afterwards
that feed you a week. The gut-wrack of
can't-afford, primal yelp that keeps you swallowing hard.
Credit bureaus, bill collectors, taxes, bank.
The old stumble-and-fall-down, temp awhile, whore
awhile, give The Man his due. And here,
at last, you shit it out: the blind-eyed parasite who
bloodies you, the sharp-toothed gnawing
worm of desperation.

Skirts

Women spin and dance in skirts, sleep and wake
in them sometimes, ascend and descend stairs.
Some have walked into the sea in skirts,

which is like tossing a skirt over a man's head,
or pressing his face against the tent of one.
Some woman, maybe wearing a velvet skirt,
has embraced another woman—so that one skirt brushes
against another. Women wash and wring and hang
skirts up to dry, spray them, iron them, hem them,
slip them over slips, over tights. Once, I confess,
I owned six black ones: rayon, wool, gabardine,
linen, cotton, silk. The wind can blow the bulk of a skirt
between a woman's legs, or wrap her in
a twist, or billow underneath so skirls of wind touch
faintly, delightfully. Some women hear skirts
murmuring or sighing, conversing with the flesh
they cover. But most skirts drape in silence, the silence
of slow snow falling, or the hushed liquid glide
of a woman's body through a sunlit pool, the sweet
descent to sleep, or passion, or passion's nemesis,
ennui. A woman's spirit lengthens or widens in a skirt,
magnified by cloth and cut and her stride through
the quickened space. If instead a woman wears
a tight skirt, she feels containment and its
amplification— reduction's power to suggest.
Right now my favorite is a crimpy cinnabar silk
I twist into wrinkles to dry. I wear it walking in
the evenings. I vanish as its folds enfold the sky.

The 750 Hands

> Mar de lagrimas (Sea of Tears)
> —Osvoldo Yero

Each is cast in porcelain, fired, glazed a shade
of blue or greenish-blue, some left hands,
but mostly right, and each is the hand
of a Cuban artist. Some left during
the great flight of the mid-sixties
and the lesser flights of the seventies
and eighties. And some, forced to work
in mines and canefields, stayed in their
homeland. The hands hang a dozen deep,
a great wave on a long wall, each turned
slightly, thumb up, palm exposed.
From the side we see fingernails,
knuckles, knotted ridges of arteries,
scars of accidents and toil. Inert and cold,
signaling from stony depths, disembodied
yet overarching, as if each lived more
in the sky than in the flesh, more in

the sea than on the shore; the hands
of its people, the sky and sea that hold Cuba.
Each man or woman kept a hand in plaster
long enough to form a mold, each mold
received the poured clay, the glaze, the fire,
filling the void of absence with existence—
*I lived through sorrowful times and made art
with this hand.* Nothing can stop
a hand from finding what it needs.
Nothing can stop the maker.

Mark Jarman

Mark Jarman's latest collections are *Epistles* and *Bone Fires: New and Selected Poems* (Sarabande, 2007, 2011). His collection, *Questions for Ecclesiastes* (Story Line Press, 1997), won the Lenore Marshall Poetry Prize for 1998. He teaches at Vanderbilt University.

Butterflies under Persimmon

I heard a woman
   State once that because
He peered so closely

At a stream of ants
   On the damp, naked
Limb of a fruit tree,

She fell for her husband.
   She wanted to be studied
With that attention,

To fascinate as if
   She were another species,
Whose willingness to be

Looked at lovingly
   Was her defense, to be
Like a phenomenon

Among leaves, a body
   That would make him leave
His body in the act of loving,

Beautifully engrossed.
   I can't remember what
She looked like. I never met

The husband. But leaning close
     To the newly dropped
Persimmon in the wet grass,

And the huddle of four
     Or five hungry satyrs,
Drab at first glance, the dull

Brown of age spots, flitting
     Away in too many
Directions, too quickly

To count exactly, small
     As they are, in the shade
At the tree's base; leaning

Out of the sunlight, as if
     I could take part in the feast there,
Where, mid-September,

The persimmons drop,
     So ripe and taut a touch
Can break the skin;

Leaning close enough
     To trouble the eye-spotted
Satyrs, no bigger than

Eyelids, and the fritillaries,
     Their calmer companions,
Like floating shreds of fire,

Whose feet have organs
     Of taste that make their tongues
Uncoil in reflex with

Goodness underfoot,
     I thought of that woman's
Lover, there on my belly

In sun and shadow,
     And wished I could be like that.

In the Tube

They beat the edge
  Of the dawn light,
     The pearly pre-glow

Right at their heels,
  The three boys
    Carrying the fourth

Rolled in a sheet.
  They all had taken
    Something the night

Before in a beach
  House and this one
    Drowned in his sleep.

They acted quickly,
  These instinctive
    Athletes who cross

The faces of tons
  Of crushing water
    Which refrain

From curling over
  And burying them
    Alive because they

Are nimble, quick,
  Tuned to the wit
    Of their survivors'

Bodies. They hurried
  From the running car
    And laid their friend

Like a Sunday paper
  On his parents' doorstep,
    And drove off to

The place where the sharp
  New light would score
    The wave crests and they

Would ride below them,
  Dodging the onrush.

The Wind

Worrying about the children I kept waiting
  To be relieved and walked to the gallery
On a frigid morning in the nation's capital.
  Great clouds of vapor smoking from the street-vents

Unraveled the long stone views of public buildings.
　　And small among them, private and insistent,
My fretting was a nightmare nakedness,
　　Which must be obvious but no one sees.
I'd come to town on business. It was finished.
　　I had a little time and stalked through rooms
Of likenesses and paint that still looked wet
　　On the old masters and the younger masters.
I looked around, wanting to be changed,
　　And passed the pictures as if they were stalled traffic
And I had chosen to get out and walk.
　　Then faced the modest painting by Vallotton,
"The Wind," in the East Wing, and walked on,
　　And then returned and stood before it, feeling
A southern breeze begin, hearing a hymn,
　　"Breathe on me, breath of God." Eight trees were bending
From right to left across the picture plane.
　　So wind-altered I couldn't give them names,
They bowed away yet faced what made them bow.
　　The undergrowth beneath them caught the sunlight
And handled it with fronds of yellow shining.
　　We were looking up from the floor of Paradise—
I saw that suddenly— and God was calling,
　　Warming the cool of the day with his vast breath.
The trees, his angels, pointed where he was looking.
　　It wasn't clear if we had fallen yet.
But if we had, this green half-kneeling stir,
　　In which things rooted and inevitable were swaying,
Might soothe his wrath and make him think again.
　　The sympathetic magic of the paint
Was like a prayer sent both from the past,
　　A gift from the dead artist, and from the future,
Vaulting the barrier of all that had been done
　　And fixed forever, bathing the judged world
In a wish to soften harshness, everything leaning.
　　This wind, painted by Felix Vallotton,
In 1910, somewhere in France, conveyed
　　Counsel like a draft of medicine.
And in that counsel, drawn over my anger,
　　So that it passed through every leaf of it,
(For anger is what I felt, a cloudy ire
　　At children who were ceasing to be children)
Came what I had to do. The picture said,
　　"Forgive them. And let them live their lives."

Astragaloi

We know there must be consciousness in things,
        In bits of gravel pecked up by a hen
To grind inside her crop, and spider silk
        Just as it hardens stickily in air,
And even those things paralyzed in place,
        The wall brick, the hat peg, the steel beam
Inside the skyscraper, and lost, forgotten,
        And buried in ancient tombs, the toys and games.
Those starry jacks, those knucklebones of glass
        Meant for the dead to play with, toss and catch
Back of the hand and read the patterns of,
        Diversions to beguile the endless time,
Never to be picked up again . . . They're thinking,
        Surely, all of them. They are lost in thought.

Honorée Fanonne Jeffers

Honorée Fanonne Jeffers is the author of two books of poetry, *The Gospel of Barbecue* (Kent State, 2000), which was chosen by Lucille Clifton as the winner of the 1999 Wick Poetry Prize, and *Outlandish Blues* (Wesleyan, 2003). A native Southerner, she now lives in Oklahoma.

Confederate Pride Day at Bama (Tuscaloosa, 1994)

The first time, my liberal white friends try
to prepare me. I might feel ashamed when I hear
rebel yells, see the too familiar flag waving.
You know they're going to sing the song, don't you?

The fraternity boys dressed in gray uniforms,
marching boldly around the yard, then coming home to black
maids, their heads tied up in bright handkerchiefs.

Faces greased to perfection once a year. *Can you believe
they make those women dress up like mammies?*
Southern meals prepared with eye-rolling care.
You should stage a protest. For me or my mama?

Come day, go day, God sends Sunday and I see those
sisters at the grocery store buying food every week.
We smile and sometimes meet each other's gaze.

Nod.
At the very least, write a letter. Some kinds of anger
need screaming. Some kinds just worry the gut
like a meal of unwashed greens, peas picked

too early from the field. Or a dark woman, her brow
wrapped in red, smiling to herself, then hawking
and spitting her seasoning into a Dixie cooking pot.

Don't Know What Love Is

My mother can't recall the exact
infamous year but Mama does know
that she and her friends were teenagers
when they sneaked out to an official joint
in the middle of the woods to listen
to Dinah Washington sing their favorite
love song. They wanted to dance together
so close they'd be standing behind
each other but Mama says, *Dinah showed*
up late and acted ugly and on top of
that she didn't want to sing the song.
This is supposed to be the story of Mama's
blues and how she threw good money
after bad but this is South Georgia
and Dinah's standing in high heels on a Jim
Crow stage two feet off the ground.
She's sniffing the perfume of homemade
cigarettes, chitlin plates, hair grease one
grade above Vaseline and the premature
funk wafting up from the rowdy kids
with no home training. Can't even pee
straight much less recognize a silver lamé
dress. All they know to do is demand
one song because they risked a certain
butt-whipping to be in this joint, in these woods.
Dinah won't sing it, though.
She just won't sing the song.
I'm an evil gal, she hollers out instead.
Don't you bother with me!

Hagar to Sarai

Don't give me nothing in
exchange for a beating
in my belly, sore nipples
way after the sucking is gone.
Don't thank me for my body,
a fine drinking skin
turned inside out for you.
Don't thank me for the back
that don't break from Abram's weight.
I know what you need— a baby's
wail in the morning,
smile on your man's face,
his loins full of much obliged.

I know what you need;
don't give me your grief
to help this thing along.
I know how emptiness feels.
Woman, I know how
to make my own tears.

Ilya Kaminsky

Ilya Kaminsky was born in Odessa, Ukraine. He is author of the chapbook *Musica Humana* (Chapiteau, 2002) and a full-length collection of poems, *Dancing in Odessa* (Tupelo, 2004). He is the co-editor of *The Ecco Anthology of International Poetry* (HarperCollins, 2010) and also the editor and primary translator of *This Lamentable City: Poems of Polina Barskova* (Tupelo, 2010). He teaches at San Diego State University and in the New England College MFA Program in Poetry.

In Praise of Laughter

Where days bend and straighten
in a city that belongs to no nation
but all the nations of wind,

she spoke the speech of poplar trees—
her ears trembling as she spoke, my Aunt Rose
composed odes to barbershops, drugstores.

Her soul walking on two feet, the soul or no soul, a child's allowance,
she loved street musicians and knew
that my grandfather composed lectures on the supply

and demand of clouds in our country:
the State declared him an enemy of the people.
He ran after a train with tomatoes in his coat

and danced naked on the table in front of our house—
he was shot, and my grandmother raped
by the public prosecutor, who stuck his pen in her vagina,

the pen which signed people off for twenty years.
But in the secret history of anger—*one man's silence
lives in the bodies of others*—as we dance to keep from falling,

between the doctor and the prosecutor:
my family, the people of Odessa,
women with huge breasts, old men naive and childlike,

all our words, heaps of burning feathers
that rise and rise with each retelling.

Aunt Rose

In a soldier's uniform, in wooden shoes, she danced
at either end of day, my Aunt Rose.
Her husband rescued a pregnant woman

from the burning house—he heard laughter,
each day's own little artillery—in that fire
he burnt his genitals. My Aunt Rose

took other people's children—she clicked her tongue as they cried
and August pulled curtains evening after evening.
I saw her, chalk between her fingers,

she wrote lessons on an empty blackboard,
her hand moved and the board remained empty.
We lived in a city by the sea but there was

another city at the bottom of the sea
and only local children believed in its existence.
She believed them. She hung her husband's

picture on a wall in her apartment. Each month
on a different wall. I now see her with that picture, hammer
in her left hand, nail in her mouth.

From her mouth, a smell of wild garlic—
she moves toward me in her pajamas
arguing with me and with herself.

The evenings are my evidence, this evening
in which she dips her hands up to her elbows,
the evening is asleep inside her shoulder—her shoulder

rounded by sleep.

My Mother's Tango

I see her windows open in the rain, laundry in the windows—
she rides a wild pony for my birthday,
a white pony on the seventh floor.

"And where will we keep it?" "On the balcony!"
the pony neighing on the balcony for nine weeks.
At the center of my life: my mother dances,

yes here, as in childhood, my mother
asks to describe the stages of my happiness—
she speaks of soups, she is of their telling;

between the regiments of saucers and towels,
she moves so fast—she is motionless,
opening and closing doors.

But what was happiness? A pony on the balcony!
My mother's past, a cloak she wore on her shoulder.
I draw an axis through the afternoon

to see her, sixty, courting a foreign language—
young, not young—my mother
gallops a pony on the seventh floor.

She becomes a stranger and acts herself, opens
what is shut, shuts what is open.

Brigit Kelly

Brigit Kelly's third book of poems, *The Orchard*, was published by BOA Editions, Ltd., in 2004. She currently teaches in the creative writing program at the University of Illinois.

Black Swan

I told the boy I found him under a bush.
What was the harm? I told him he was sleeping
And that a black swan slept beside him,
The swan's feathers hot, the scent of the hot feathers
And of the bush's hot white flowers
As rank and sweet as the stewed milk of a goat.
The bush was in a strange garden, a place
So old it seemed to exist outside of time.
In one spot, great stone steps leading nowhere.
In another, statues of horsemen posting giant stone horses
Along a high wall. And here, were triangular beds
Of flowers flush with red flowers. And there,
Circular beds flush with white. And in every bush
And bed flew small birds and the cries of small birds.
I told the boy I looked for him a long time
And when I found him I watched him sleeping,
His arm around the swan's moist neck,
The swan's head tucked fast behind the boy's back,
The feathered breast and the bare breast breathing as one,
And then very swiftly and without making a sound,
So that I would not wake the sleeping bird,
I picked the boy up and slipped him into my belly,
The way one might slip something stolen
Into a purse. And brought him here....
And so it was. And so it was. A child with skin
So white it was not like the skin of a boy at all,
But like the skin of a newborn rabbit, or like the skin
Of a lily, pulseless and thin. And a giant bird
With burning feathers. And beyond them both
A pond of incredible blackness, overarched

With ancient trees and patterned with shifting shades,
The small wind in the branches making a sound
Like the knocking of a thousand wooden bells....
Things of such beauty. But still I might
Have forgotten, had not the boy, who stands now
To my waist, his hair a cap of shining feathers,
Come to me today weeping because some older boys
Had taunted him and torn his new coat,
Had he not, when I bent my head to his head,
Said softly, but with great anger, "I wish I had never
Been born. I wish I were back under the bush,"
Which made the old garden rise up again,
Shadowed and more strange. Small birds
Running fast and the grapple of chill coming on.
There was the pond, half-circled with trees. And there
The flowerless bush. But there was no swan.
There was no black swan. And beneath
The sound of the wind, I could hear, dark and low,
The giant stone hooves of the horses,
Striking and striking the hardening ground.

The Dragon

The bees came out of the junipers, two small swarms
The size of melons; and golden, too, like melons,
They hung next to each other, at the height of a deer's breast,
Above the wet black compost. And because
The light was very bright it was hard to see them,
And harder still to see what hung between them.
A snake hung between them. The bees held up a snake,
Lifting each side of his narrow neck, just below
The pointed head, and in this way, very slowly
They carried the snake through the garden,
The snake's long body hanging down, its tail dragging
The ground, as if the creature were a criminal
Being escorted to execution or a child king
To the throne. I kept thinking the snake
Might be a hose, held by two ghostly hands,
But the snake was a snake, his body green as the grass
His tail divided, his skin oiled, the way the male member
Is oiled by the female's juices, the greenness overbright,
The bees gold, the winged serpent moving silently
Through the air. There was something deadly in it,
Or already dead. Something beyond the report
Of beauty. I laid my face against my arm, and there
It stayed for the length of time it takes two swarms
Of bees to carry a snake through a wide garden,
Past a sleeping swan, past the dead roses nailed

To the wall, past the small pond. And when
I looked up the bees and the snake were gone,
But the garden smelled of broken fruit, and across
The grass a shadow lay for which there was no source,
A narrow plinth dividing the garden, and the air
Was like the air after a fire, or the air before a storm,
Ungodly still, but full of dark shapes turning.

Elegy

Wind buffs the waterstained stone cupids and shakes
Old rain from the pines' low branches, small change
Spilling over the graves the years have smashed
With a hammer—*forget this, forget that, leave no
Stone unturned.* The grass grows high, sweet-smelling,
Many-footed, ever-running. No one tends it. No
One comes....*And where am I now?*....Is this a beginning,
A middle, or an end?....Before I knew you I stood
In this place. Now I forsake the past as I knew it
To feed you into it. But that is not right. You step
Into it. I *find* you here, in the shifting grass,
In the late light, as if you had always been here.
Behind you two torn black cedars flame white
Against the darkening fields....If you turn to me,
Quiet man? If you turn? If I speak softly?
If I say, *Take off, take off your glasses....Let me see
Your sightless eyes?....I will be beautiful then....*
Look, the heart moves as the moths do, scuttering
Like a child's thoughts above this broken stone
And that. And I lie down. I lie down in the long grass,
Something I am not given to doing, and I feel
The weight of your hand on my belly, and the wind
Parts the grasses, and the distance spills through—
The glassy fields, the black black earth, the pale air
Streaming headlong toward the abbey's far stones
And streaming back again....The drowned scent of lilacs
By the abbey, it is a drug. It drives one senseless.
It drives one blind. You can cup the enormous lilac cones
In your hands—ripened, weightless, and taut—
And it is like holding someone's heart in your hands,
Or holding a cloud of moths. I lift them up, my hands.
Grave man, bend toward me. Lay your face....*here*....
Rest....I took the stalks of the dead wisteria
From the glass jar propped against the open grave
And put in the shell-shaped wildflowers
I picked along the road. I cannot name them.
Bread and butter, perhaps. I am not good

With names. But nameless you walked toward me
And I knew you, a swelling in the heart,
A silence in the heart, the wild wind-blown grass
Burning—as the sun falls below the earth—
Brighter than a bed of lilies struck by snow.

Susan Kelly-DeWitt

Susan Kelly-DeWitt is the author of *The Fortunate Islands* (Marick Press, 2008) as well as a number of chapbooks—most recently, *Cassiopeia Above the Banyan Tree, Poems About Hawaii* (Rattlesnake Press, 2007). She has won a number of awards for her work, including a Wallace Stegner Fellowship, and her poetry has also been featured on "Writer's Almanac" and "Verse Daily." Currently an instructor for the University of California Davis Extension, she lives in Sacramento, California, where she is also an exhibiting visual artist and a resurrected book reviewer.

Egrets at Bolinas Lagoon

They looked like callas or tulips
you could gather with a fist

or white amaryllis
you could snip from their shimmering
place in the world

you could slip from their stems
with sharp scissors

but they were toiling
the salt under-veins, tunneling
the weedy caverns

with yellow pickaxes,
hunting up
a shining nugget
of flesh.

I thought of Van Gogh again:
"Making progress is like miner's work."

The birds that glowed like headlamps
were transformed by those alchemical
words, into painters and poets.

That same night
I woke nauseous, in a sweat,
with all the old worries.

Pomegranates

My mother, gray bird
beside a white bowl
of pomegranates.

They flare
against her face,
creating an odd
            balance.

She is retelling the family
myths. In this one, her mouth
is cut and bleeding, her teeth
pop out like seeds.

It is winter.
My father is King
of the Underworld.

"My whole mouth,"
she explains, drawing open
her lower lip, exposing the hidden
scars, "was pulp."

I memorize exactly, word
for word:

*He was quick
and strong, his punch
like a boxer's.*

*We'd been married
only six months, still newlyweds . . .*

as I pluck a pomegranate
from the bowl, hack it

open, place

a single blood
red seed on my tongue.

Apple Blossoms

One evening in winter
when nothing has been enough,
when the days are too short,

the nights too long
and cheerless, the secret
and docile buds of the apple

blossoms begin their quick
ascent to light. Night
after interminable night

the sugars pucker and swell
into green slips, green
silks. And just as you find

yourself at the end
of winter's long, cold
rope, the blossoms open

like pink thimbles
and that black dollop
of shine called

bumblebee stumbles in.

Crossing the Mojave at Night

This is how we outran
the word *Fugitive*:

The needle climbed
the glowing dial of digits,

the tires lifted off
to become night air

as my father topped
ninety.

The warrant
at his back scratched

its head, flashed
its bloody reds

and began the slow
wail that followed us

across three states.
The swollen vein

at his temple grew
tough as pipeweed.

Jane Kenyon

During her lifetime Jane Kenyon published four books of poetry—*Constance* (1993), *Let Evening Come* (1990), *The Boat of Quiet Hours* (1986), and *From Room to Room* (1978)—and a book of translation, *Twenty Poems of Anna Akhmatova* (1985). In December 1993 she and her husband Donald Hall were the subject of an Emmy Award-winning Bill Moyers documentary, "A Life Together." At the time of her death from leukemia, in April 1995, Kenyon was New Hampshire's poet laureate. *Otherwise: New and Selected Poems*, was released in 1996 by Graywolf Press.

Prognosis

I walked alone in the chill of dawn
while my mind leapt, as the teachers

of detachment say, like a drunken
monkey. Then a gray shape, an owl,

passed overhead. An owl is not
like a crow. A crow makes convivial

chuckings as it flies,
but the owl flew well beyond me

before I heard it coming, and when it
settled, the bough did not sway.

Happiness

There's just no accounting for happiness,
or the way it turns up like a prodigal
who comes back to the dust at your feet
having squandered a fortune far away.

And how can you not forgive?
You make a feast in honor of what
was lost, and take from its place the finest
garment, which you saved for an occasion
you could not imagine, and you weep night and day
to know that you were not abandoned,
that happiness saved its most extreme form
for you alone.

No, happiness is the uncle you never
knew about, who flies a single-engine plane
onto the grassy landing strip, hitchhikes
into town, and inquires at every door
until he finds you asleep midafternoon
as you so often are during the unmerciful
hours of your despair.

It comes to the monk in his cell.
It comes to the woman sweeping the street
with a birch broom, to the child
whose mother has passed out from drink.
It comes to the lover, to the dog chewing
a sock, to the pusher, to the basket maker,
and to the clerk stacking cans of carrots
in the night.
                    It even comes to the boulder
in the perpetual shade of pine barrens,
to rain falling on the open sea,
to the wineglass, weary of holding wine.

Eating the Cookies

The cousin from Maine, knowing
about her diverticulitis, left out the nuts,
so the cookies weren't entirely to my taste,
but they were good enough; yes, good enough.

Each time I emptied a drawer or shelf
I permitted myself to eat one.
I cleared the closet of silk caftans
that slipped easily from clattering hangers,
and from the bureau I took her nightgowns
and sweaters, financial documents
neatly cinctured in long gray envelopes,
and the hairnets and peppermints she'd tucked among
Lucite frames abounding with great-grandchildren,
solemn in their Christmas finery.

Finally the drawers were empty,
the bags full, and the largest cookie,
which I had saved for last, lay
solitary in the tin with a nimbus
of crumbs around it. There would be no more
parcels from Portland. I took it up
and sniffed it, and before eating it,
pressed it against my forehead, because
it seemed like the next thing to do.

Pharaoh

"The future ain't what it used to be,"
said the sage of the New York Yankees
as he pounded his mitt, releasing
the red dust of the infield
into the harshly illuminated evening air.

Big hands. Men with big hands
make things happen. The surgeon,
when I asked how big your tumor was,
held forth his substantial fist
with its globed class ring.

Home again, we live as charily as strangers.
Things are off: Touch rankles, food
is not good. Even the kindness of friends
turns burdensome; their flowers sadden
us, so many and so fair.

I woke in the night to see your
diminished bulk lying beside me—
you on your back, like a sarcophagus
as your feet held up the covers....
The things you might need in the next
life surrounded you— your comb and glasses,
water, a book and a pen.

Maurice Kilwein Guevara

Maurice Kilwein Guevara was born in 1961 in Belencito, Colombia. He is the author of *Postmortem, Poems of the River Spirit*, and *Autobiography of So-and-so*. He was the first person of Latino descent ever to be elected President of the Association of Writers and Writing Programs (AWP). He is currently Professor of English at the University of Wisconsin, Milwaukee.

Doña Josefina Counsels Doña Concepción before Entering Sears

Conchita debemos to speak totalmente in English
cuando we go into Sears okay   Por qué
Porque didn't you hear lo que pasó   It say
on the eleven o'clock news anoche que two robbers
was caught in Sears and now this is the part
I'm not completely segura que I got everything
porque channel 2 tiene tú sabes that big fat guy
that's hard to understand porque his nose sit on his lip
like a elefante pues the point es que the robbers the police say
was two young men pretty big y one have a hairy face
and the other is calvo that's right he's baldy and okay
believe me qué barbaridad porque Hairy Face
and Mister Baldy goes right into the underwear department
takes all the money from the caja yeah uh-huh the cash register
and mira Mister Baldy goes to this poor Italian woman that I
guess would be like us sixty o sixty-five who is the section
of the back-support brassieres and he makes her put a big bra
over her head para que she can't see nothing and kneel
like she talking to God to save her poor life
y other things horrible pero the point como dije
es que there was two of them and both was speaking Spanish
y por eso is a good thing Conchita so the people at Sears
don't confuse us with Hairy and Baldy that we speak English only
okay ready
                    Oh what a nice day to be aquí en Sears Miss Conception

Fast Forward

I marry, I divorce, I put three quarters in a parking meter in Milwaukee, it's the next year, then the end of spring four years later, and now I'm married to the woman whose reflection I saw in the dark blue window of a classroom. We move to the foothills of the Alleghenies, to a farm house owned by a deaf couple. There are clouds and a blue sky, milking cows. The old man always has a hammer and a can of nails he rattles; when the windows are open you can hear him and the old woman screaming at each other. My new wife complains about the rusty water. She's thirty and urgent, I want to make a baby too, one night I mount her on the hard kitchen floor. Three weeks later her period comes heavier than the months before. By fall, still barren, we both start to see them: The blurred Amish woman in dark bonnet by the landing, the streak of the infant in her arms, the x-ray fingers of the baby, the ghost mop luminous in the corner by the starry window.

How Grammar School Is Changing

In the early years all of the teachers were Nouns. They were very strict Nouns. They wore black robes that reached to the floor and had a fondness for caning the palms of your hands. In the beginning there was very little light; then a window was placed in the east wall of the school. The first Verb to enter the classroom through our new and only window was a Be. It was yellow and black and buzzed by my ear. One day Be walked vertically up the world map from Santiago to Santa Marta and stopped to smell the salt water. Thinking twice, it flew up to Florida and was eyeing Orange County when my mean third grade Noun squashed Be with her big white reader. She said, "We only need one river in this town," which didn't make any sense. It wasn't long, however, before more stuff started coming in through the windows (there were now four) and through the new fire doors and down the chimney: Adjectives with big, bright, yellow and orange, polka-dot bow ties; Adverbs who yodeled longingly for their homeland; a Pronoun who wore cornrows with green ribbons (I confess I had my first crush on She); a family of Silver Brackets; Question Marks and Periods snowed down the chimney; and, finally, the Invisible Etceteras—pranksters that they are—started moaning sweet nothings in my Noun's ear, which made her grin a little, thank God. By the time I was in the fifth grade, after a vicious fight with the village elders, the principal had hired Dr. Miguel de Sustantivo to make the school bilingual: *y tú sabes lo que pasó después: vinieron las familias Adjetivo y Pronombre y Verbo y más y más*....But yesterday a new little someone came from far, far away who sits sad all alone at lunch. Does anyone know a few words in Vietnamese? I would like to say Good Morning.

Elizabeth Kirschner

Elizabeth Kirschner has published five books of poetry: *Twenty Colors, Postal Routes, Slow Risen Among the Smoke Trees, Surrender to Light*, and *My Life as a Doll* (Autumn House, 2008). She teaches at Fairfield University, studies with the Boston Ballet, and has collaborated with many composers. A cycle of her poems set to Robert Schumann's "Dichterliebe" premiered in Vienna in 2005 and was released on a CD by Albany Records. She lives on the coast of Maine.

from *My Life as a Doll*

Why do I love the winter garden so?
Is it because I hear the dirge

of dirt, elegy of vanquished blossoms?
Whatever emerges at season's end

comes from a harrowing heaven: yesterday,
I believed I was a wooden woman

with a wooden heart the wolves
would tear apart. I jerked

about like a marionette with
tangled strings—slash of claws, teeth

sinking in to rip the flesh off
my wooden bones. When I was four

years old, my mother pummeled
the back of my head with a baseball bat.

I remember the pain. I remember
hitting the floor like a scarecrow

that was a heap of broken straw.
This is why I love the winter garden so:

energy of enigma. Icy blossoms.

Once Mother came
into my room reeking of gin.
I curled deep in the half-
shell of myself waiting for her blows.

Instead, she walked over
to my bed, climbed on top
of me and passed out.
I thought she was dying.
I thought she was drowning me
with her liquor-sodden
breath. Beneath her,

I felt like a blank blur,
a smudge on the face of time,
an unraveling penumbra.
In the bin of halted dreams,
my breath became shorter and
shorter while her drool
trickled across my face as if it were
tears. She was the tearless one—

I cried for her, about her,
in her, but she responded
with moth-eaten words, drunken
slurs that made the whole
house tipsy. Her body
was a boat full of June
snow falling incessantly,
insanely from incumbent clouds.

While boys milked my breasts until
they were empty, I longed to be donned

in a habit. I wanted to float down cloistered
corridors like a black butterfly whose scales

were relics stolen from Mary. I wanted to marry
a martyr, I wanted to be a saint, but

my lips were rubbed raw by too many kisses
from boys who took and took—suffering would be

my salvation, my one way ticket to a heaven
full of copulating angels—they loved a good fuck

and I dreamed of dreaming in their lascivious arms.
There I would get pregnant with a baby angel

and I would mother her tenderly while my own mother
lay drunk on the sofa, smoking a cigarette

like a tiny flare that signaled her heartbeat.
Soon, soon I would be a centerfold saint

she would kneel before praying a prayer that sounded
like curses—o glory be the day I condemned her

to the hell she belonged in—it was a zoo,
it had a cage and I had the key.

    In the psych ward, I remained
    a dust-baby. One breath
    would blow me into the four corners
    of the wind. I clutched

    my baby picture and my son's
    favorite teddy bear. Lions
    walked out of walls. Howler monkeys
    screamed their cries of grief.

    It was all wave and wavering.
    I watched the river from my window—
    it was the color of mother-of-pearl
    and the snow died in it.

    I fell to my knees while remembering
    how much my mother loved
    the dogwood blossoms:
    each was a pink velvet boat.

    I was ready to be castaway,
    but in what dark harbor
    would I be utterly human
    which is to say, hardly begun?

While my words become blooming elegies,
God pries me open like a clam shell

full of snot and pearls, snot and pearls.
My heart is a sweet tooth addicted

to darkness, the frightening dark full of
scabs and scales. Who will bring me back

when I disappear in the hidey-hole
of my brain with a voice that says:

touch-me-not, love-me-not? This
is when my name breaks down into

bitter dust tumbling like a tumbleweed
in catacombs of the dead. There

my mother greets me with a teeny-
weenie kiss that blisters my lips.

Go in to go under, go in to plunder
was the motto of her blankedy-blank

life. O tour-de-force of living tears—
what holds me together? Cord of water?

Slipknot of air? Downward motion
has no magic potion and there's sparkly stuff

in my head letting out thousands of tiny
shocks. In the cave of my childhood,

I made a little music: *mouse-music,
mouse-music* and once the sound of a cricket

buried in flames. The Kyrie of its cry
never retires, nor do I. I was

a grey-haired child, had a wizened
face, bones full of hot wires.

Damage is done when love is undone
and I'm a bouquet of burnt matches,

an ashen petal fallen from a loony-
tunes moon. Stomp, smudge, chalk

me into cinders and I will rise like
a genie out of a bottle of destitute dreams.

My scent is offal, seared grass
and dirt drenched with the blood of

the war dead. Why must there be
warring between heaven and earth,

dead Mother and me? The kiss of peace
has been smeared into blear

and white doves have bloodied their feathers
in hell's red bile of dew. I can be scraped

from the bottom of God's shoe, my scars
are pregnant with pain and I am a bloody stew.

Dressed in mole's clothes, I dig
past my open grave with raggedy paws

till I'm blinded with blinding light
that scorches the blackened wick

of my blackened soul, my masterpiece.

Romella Kitchens

Romella Kitchens' most recent collection is *Hip Hop Warrior* published by *Main Street Rag*. Her work has also been published in *Van Gogh's Ear, 5AM, MEAT, Caprice, The California Quarterly*, and two Autumn House anthologies: *Joyful Noise: An Anthology Of American Spiritual Poetry* and *The Working Poet: 75 Writing Exercises And A Poetry Anthology*. She began as a literary writer and then branched out to performance poetry.

The Reflected Face of the Sea

We went to the Sylvia Beach Hotel
in Newport that summer
seals sunned themselves on the rocks
the air was hard
with the smells of the fish cannery

Life seemed sane

O Mary, won't you remember me this way?

*

I found a nickel on the pier
it disappeared in a squint of sunlight

I saw old men in tattered jackets
who had nowhere to go
I disliked their weakness
but understood their pain
everyone gets worked over
now and then

It's the seventh inning, no runs, you're up
to bat   nothing but strikes so far
all the time

*

Newport made me want to lie down, cover myself
with sand and weep

The ocean was unsettled that year
the ocean kept throwing up its fists

I wanted to sit near it
make a friend of it

You can make love to the Atlantic
it folds you in its arms
your breath quickens

*

Far from the beach
men line up at the door to the soup kitchen
the line snaps like a cobra's tail
they bring terror to hunger
their bodies jangle at the notion of food

*

If I could be certain I would return
I would go to the sea naked
I would swim in the sea naked

Maybe it's the African in me
that longs for your face, Sea
maybe you were my husband
many lives ago

If even one man loves me
he will bring this poem to you
read it loud enough
to crest over your waves
and create a shiver of adoration

Foundling I was   my boat dashed in the darkness
O ship-wrecked sea, I am in pieces without you

*

At night I lie in bed and hear your sound
the passion of life seems solely and wildly
in your waves

My heart drums for you
primal, forceful

Naked I would go to you like an untainted Eve
find pleasure in you
and you in me

O Ancient One   O Rebirth,
Keeper of the Trident
you know I understand
your rages and rested waves

*

I walked the city streets
looking for faces like my own
I wasn't lonely but knew
I had to go home

There was a hummingbird I missed
who might come to my window
and mourn me

And I knew
the long tapering fingers of loneliness
would touch me if I didn't twist out of its vines

At a bar, a thick and malevolent woman called me ugly
said I didn't deserve to be with my man
who's white   I said   *don't you know?*
sometimes ugly women get the best men?

I didn't let her bother me
I was just a visitor in the shitpile of her life

*

I'm not a constant smoker
but I'm thinking about death today
and old vices come upon me like rain

I make coffee   good fresh coffee
and think about times when I could barely afford it

Nicotine rushes to my brain
rain keeps falling down on itself tripping
on my skin

The coffee kisses my lips
green pears drop into the dark palm of the earth

Florida

I was in Florida with relatives
I kept looking off the back porch
into the darkness of the sandy unknown
the bottles strung on my aunt's lemon tree

stirred in the breeze   their glass was green
and brown and clear   I wondered why
we couldn't see the demons
they were supposed to catch

I didn't like Florida   we went in midsummer
and it was hot   my father and sister
had a fight in the front yard of my aunt's house
she wanted to return to college early

so he took out a pocket knife and threatened
to cut her throat   she left anyway
I packed my suitcase   love or no love
I wanted to be anywhere else

but the spirits in the house were kind
you could feel the love of dead relatives
brushing your shoulder   the house
is a Chinese restaurant now

and all the money from the sale is gone
that summer I watched lemons fall
from the bottle tree   I heard
             a dark frog cry

Ted Kooser

Former United States Poet Laureate Ted Kooser is a retired life insurance executive who lives on acreage near the village of Garland, Nebraska, with his wife, Kathleen Rutledge. Kooser has received a great deal of recognition for his poetry, including the Hugo Prize from *Poetry Northwest*, the Kunitz Prize from Columbia, the Boatwright Prize from *Shenandoah*, as well as two National Endowment writing fellowships. He is the author of eight full-length collections of poetry, nine chapbooks and special editions, several books of prose, and *Braided Creek*, a poetry collaboration with Jim Harrison.

Selecting a Reader

First, I would have her be beautiful,
and walking carefully up on my poetry
at the loneliest moment of an afternoon,
her hair still damp at the neck
from washing it. She should be wearing
a raincoat, an old one, dirty
from not having money enough for the cleaners.
She will take out her glasses, and there
in the bookstore, she will thumb
over my poems, then put the book back
up on its shelf. She will say to herself,
"For that kind of money, I can get
my raincoat cleaned." And she will.

Geronimo's Mirror

That flash from a distant hillside,
that firefly in the blue shadows of rock—
that's Geronimo's mirror.
After all of these years, he's up there
still trying to warn us
that the soldiers are coming.
He sees them riding along the horizon
in an endless line,
sees them dipping down into the valley
rider by rider.
His mirror of tin, cupped in his palm,
says they're nearer now.
It says he can hear the black rock

sounding under their hooves,
can smell the sharp smoke of dust in the air.
Now he can hear their dark voices,
the old voices of horses,
and the talk that is leather's.
And now they are climbing the hill,
that holy hill that is Geronimo's,
but he is not afraid.
His mirror is warning the others,
and we are the others.

Old Soldiers' Home

On benches in front of the Old Soldiers' Home,
the old soldiers unwrap the pale brown packages
of their hands, folding the fingers back
and looking inside, then closing them up again
and gazing off across the grounds,
safe with the secret.

Laundry

A pink house trailer,
scuffed and rusted, sunken
in weeds. On the line,

five pale blue workshirts
up to their elbows
in raspberry canes—

a good, clean crew
of pickers, out early,
sleeves wet with dew,

and near them, a pair
of bright yellow panties
urging them on.

Nancy Krygowski

Nancy Krygowski's first book of poems, *Velocity*, was chosen by Gerald Stern for the Agnes Lynch Starrett Prize from the University of Pittsburgh Press. She is co-founder and Assistant Artistic Director of the Gist Street Reading Series and an adult literacy instructor. She lives on a hilltop in Pittsburgh.

The Bus Comes, the Girl Gets On

The famous linguist Walter Ong
says to subordinate—
because, if, since—

is a sign of a literate
culture, and I think I know
what he means:

Since the sun didn't rise today,
night walked on
in its thick black shoes.
Or,
If night walks on
in its thick black shoes,
there will be no bus,
there is no girl.

See what I can do?
Take the things of the world
and put them in an orderly order:

Since the sun rises, the birds sing.

And,
If the birds sing, the sun will rise,
the bus will come.

And,
Because the crows are angry,
yelling in their man-of-the-house way,

the sun rises,
a rifle
in her delicate hands,
crosshairs curtaining
her one good eye.

Like every morning.

Walter Ong talks sentences—
and though he loves how,
in the morning, light becomes pink
as his imaginary wife's slippers,
as swirling and red as the grenadine
in last night's drink,

and though he would never cage
a bird,
I wonder if even he sometimes forgets
the trickiness in deciding
who or what

gets control,
and
the complex beauty
of and and and.

Heaven, as We Know It

My dead sister and I
are walking down the street.
She is here because
I am lonely and she understands
and because
this woman with the most beautiful breasts
just walked by,
and no one else,
not even this friend
who hasn't died yet
and who is walking with us,
can understand what I mean
when I say,
Her breasts are so beautiful.
I wish this street
were the desert in winter at sunset
and we were lying down
talking about the most perfect foods
we have ever eaten,
and that is simply all.

I love these beautiful things.
I love putting words together.
And I love all this listening,
which isn't just in my head,
which is heaven.

Maxine Kumin

Maxine Kumin's 17th poetry collection, *Where I Live: New and Selected Poems 1990–2010*, was published by Norton. Her awards include the Pulitzer and Ruth Lilly Poetry Prizes; Poet Laureate of New Hampshire, 1989-1994; and Consultant in Poetry to the Library of Congress, 1980-81. She and her husband live on a farm in Warner, NH.

Jack

How pleasant the yellow butter
melting on white kernels, the meniscus
of red wine that coats the insides of our goblets

where we sit with sturdy friends as old as we are
after shucking the garden's last Silver Queen
and setting husks and stalks aside for the horses

the last two of our lives, still noble to look upon:
our first foal, now a bossy mare of 28
which calibrates to 84 in people years

and my chestnut gelding, not exactly a youngster
at 22. Every year, the end of summer
lazy and golden, invites grief and regret:

suddenly it's 1980, winter buffets us,
winds strike like cruelty out of Dickens. Somehow
we have seven horses for six stalls. One of them,

a big-nosed roan gelding, calm as a president's portrait
lives in the rectangle that leads to the stalls. We call it
the motel lobby. Wise old campaigner, he dunks his

hay in the water bucket to soften it, then visits the others
who hang their heads over their dutch doors. Sometimes
he sprawls out flat to nap in his commodious quarters.

That spring, in the bustle of grooming
and riding and shoeing, I remember I let him go
to a neighbor I thought was a friend, and the following

fall she sold him down the river. I meant to
but never did go looking for him, to buy him back
and now my old guilt is flooding this twilit table

my guilt is ghosting the candles that pale us to skeletons
the ones we must all become in an as yet unspecified order.
Oh Jack, tethered in what rough stall alone

did you remember that one good winter?

Family Reunion

The week in August you come home,
adult, professional, aloof,
we roast and carve the fatted calf
— in our case home-grown pig, the chine
garlicked and crisped, the applesauce
hand-pressed. Hand-pressed the greengage wine.

Nothing is cost-effective here.
The peas, the beets, the lettuces
hand sown, are raised to stand apart.
The electric fence ticks like the slow heart
of something we fed and bedded for a year,
then killed with kindness's one bullet
and paid Jake Mott to do the butchering.

In winter we lure the birds with suet,
thaw lungs and kidneys for the cat.
Darlings, it's all a circle from the ring
of wire that keeps the raccoons from the corn
to the gouged pine table that we lounge around,
distressed before any of you was born.

Benign and dozy from our gluttonies,
the candles down to stubs, defenses down,
love leaking out unguarded the way
juice dribbles from the fence when grounded
by grass stalks or a forgotten hoe,
how eloquent, how beautiful you seem!

Wearing our gestures, how wise you grow,
ballooning to overfill our space,
the almost-parents of your parents now.
So briefly having you back to measure us
is harder than having let you go.

February

First waking to the gray
of linsey-woolsey cloth
the vivid spotted dogs
the red-fox cattle and
the meeker-colored horses
flattened in snow fog

first waking into gray
flecked with common cock-
crow unfolding the same
chilblain-bruised feet
the old shoulder ache
Mama every day

remembering how you won
the death you wished for
the death you sidled up to
remembering how

like a child in late afternoon
drained from the jubilant sledding
you were content to coast
the run-out to a stop

booted and capped in the barn
joy enters where I haul
a hay bale by its binding string
and with my free hand pull
your easy death along.

On Being Asked to Write a Poem
in Memory of Anne Sexton

The elk discards his antlers every spring.
They rebud, they grow, they are growing

an inch a day to form a rococo rack
with a five-foot spread even as we speak:

cartilage at first, covered with velvet;
bendable, tender gristle, yet

destined to ossify, the velvet sloughed off,
hanging in tatters from alders and scrub growth.

No matter how hardened it seems there was pain.
Blood on the snow from rubbing, rubbing, rubbing.

What a heavy candelabrum to be borne
forth, each year more elaborately turned:

the special issues, the prizes in her name.
Above the mantel the late elk's antlers gleam.

Dorianne Laux

Dorianne Laux's most recent collections are *Facts About the Moon* and *The Book of Men*. She is also co-author, with Kim Addonizio, of *The Poet's Companion: A Guide to the Pleasures of Writing Poetry*. Laux is an Associate Professor and works in the University of Oregon's Creative Writing Program.

Pearl

> *She was a headlong assault, a hysterical discharge,*
> *an act of total extermination.*
> ——Myra Friedman, *Buried Alive: The Biography of Janis Joplin*

She was nothing much, this plain-faced girl from Texas,
this moonfaced child who opened her mouth
to the gravel pit churning in her belly, acne-faced
daughter of Leadbelly, Bessie, Otis, and the booze-
filled moon, child of the honky-tonk bar-talk crowd
who cackled like a bird of prey, velvet cape blown
open in the Monterey wind, ringed fingers fisted
at her throat, howling the slagheap up and out
into the sawdusted air. Barefaced, mouth warped
and wailing like giving birth, like being eaten alive
from the inside, or crooning like the first child
abandoned by God, trying to woo him back,
down on her knees and pleading for a second chance.
When she sang she danced a stand-in-place dance,
one foot stamping at that fire, that bed of coals;
one leg locked at the knee and quivering, the other
pumping its oil-rig rhythm, her bony hip jigging
so the beaded belt slapped her thigh.
Didn't she give it to us? So loud so hard so furious,
hurling heat-seeking balls of lightning
down the long human aisles, her voice crashing
into us— sonic booms to the heart— this little white girl
who showed us what it was like to die
for love, to jump right up and die for it night after
drumbeaten night, going down shrieking— hair
feathered, frayed, eyes glazed, addicted to the song—
a one-woman let me show you how it's done, how it is,
where it goes when you can't hold it in anymore.
Child of everything gone wrong, gone bad, gone down,
gone. Girl with the girlish breasts and woman hips,
thick-necked, sweat misting her upper lip, hooded eyes
raining a wild blue light, hands reaching out

to the ocean we made, all that anguish and longing
swelling and rising at her feet. Didn't she burn
herself up for us, shaking us alive? That child,
that girl, that rawboned woman, stranded
in a storm on a blackened stage like a house
on fire.

Family Stories

I had a boyfriend who told me stories about his family,
how an argument once ended when his father
seized a lit birthday cake in both hands
and hurled it out a second-story window. That,
I thought, was what a normal family was like: anger
sent out across the sill, landing like a gift
to decorate the sidewalk below. In mine
it was fists and direct hits to the solar plexus,
and nobody ever forgave anyone. But I believed
the people in his stories really loved one another,
even when they yelled and shoved their feet
through cabinet doors or held a chair like a bottle
of cheap champagne, christening the wall,
rungs exploding from their holes.
I said it sounded harmless, the pomp and fury
of the passionate. He said it was a curse
being born Italian and Catholic and when he
looked from that window what he saw was the moment
rudely crushed. But all I could see was a gorgeous
three-layer cake gliding like a battered ship
down the sidewalk, the smoking candles broken, sunk
deep in the icing, a few still burning.

Twilight

My daughter set whatever had begun
to wither or rot on the rail
of the backyard deck. Pear, apple, over-ripe
banana, in October a pumpkin
that by August had gone to dust.
She took photos of the process: pear
with its belly bruised, weekly
growing more squat, the dark spot spreading.
Orange caving in at the navel.
Banana skins tanning like animal hides.
As their outsides grew tough,
their insides grew moist— a crack in the crust
and the dank pudding spewed out.
Pear neck at half-mast, pear bottom black,

pear neck sunk into the drooped shoulders of pear.
She observed and recorded the progress, watched
the realm of the solid transmute and dissolve,
documenting the musk-fragrant, incremental
descent, its delectable inevitability.
She delighted in her entropic world
with complete abandon— never expressing
repulsion or remorse, only taking
her deliberate daily photos: pumpkin
with its knifed hat tipped jauntily
above carved eyes, pumpkin sinking sweetly
into its own orange face, buckling, breaking,
sweating in sunlight, mold webbed and glowing
through a triangle nose, the punched-out smile
a grimace slipping down its furred chin.
When did she become disinterested, distracted
by her life? Where to go? What to do?
Did her socks match? One day she left
her dark harvest behind and walked
to the rink where her skate blades
skimmed the ice, inscribing girlish circles
on the blue skirl of the deserted rink.
Or she lingered at the stalls until twilight,
brushing down her favorite horse, sugar
cubes in her pockets, an apple in her purse.
She actually had a purse. Filled to the clasp
with the evidence of her life: lip gloss,
stubby pencils and colored pens, a little book
she wrote in faithfully, archiving last
names that began with A on the A page,
B's on the B, a billfold with money
and a photo ID, her own face gazing out
through the tiny plastic window.
She stared back at herself like any ordinary girl,
not a girl obsessed with ruin and collapse
who stalked her backyard with a camera.
Something else had caught her eye.
See her lift the tawny jewel
to his whiskered lips, her hand level,
her fingers flat and quivering. Look
at the gratitude in her face
when he takes the first dangerous bite.

Dust

Someone spoke to me last night,
told me the truth. Just a few words,
but I recognized it.

I knew I should make myself get up,
write it down, but it was late,
and I was exhausted from working
all day in the garden, moving rocks.
Now, I remember only the flavor—
not like food, sweet or sharp.
More like a fine powder, like dust.
And I wasn't elated or frightened,
but simply rapt, aware.
That's how it is sometimes—
God comes to your window,
all bright light and black wings,
and you're just too tired to open it.

Sydney Lea

Sydney Lea is the author of a novel, *A Place in Mind*, two collections of outdoor essays, *Hunting the Whole Way Home* and *A Little Wildness*, and eight volumes of poetry, the most recent of which is *Ghost Pain*. His previous volume, *Pursuit of a Wound*, was a finalist for the 2001 Pulitzer Prize.

The Vanishing

> *... you are like graves which are not seen, and men*
> *walk over them without knowing it.*
> —Luke, 11:44

We all insist ever since that we knew he'd end up a corpse.
He had no skill, or rather will, to temper whatever
he chose to say, and there was something anyway
that got on your nerves before he so much as opened his mouth.
His uncombed hair, a sort of bronze not found in nature —
even that would strike you as insult. Give him a drink
and there'd be things much worse to make you clench your teeth.
Though he came from central Europe somewhere, his English was pure,
except that he clung to and flaunted his accent. He used a *v*
for *w*, just for example, in this or that word, which seemed
a way for him to stress his status as an alien
in every sense of the term. He got into jam after jam.
It appeared a sort of mission. Blame the booze, I'd reckon:
why else, to mention one case, insult a mammoth marine,
call him a *half-ass, chickenshit pansy*? No broken bones
that time, but a slew of stitches. The cops sent the leatherneck home
without so much as a reprimand as soon as he told them
what had been said and by whom. The guy was a mooch, a bum.
He wrecked friends' cars and homes and tried to seduce their wives.
He'd never apologize, and so in the end he didn't
have a friend. One day he disappeared completely,
never again to be found. Of course there wasn't a man
or woman to insist on a thorough search. I knew him myself,
but I certainly didn't go to the law. He was nothing to me.
And yet that categorical vanishing lends to the wind
along our local river an eloquence after dark

it never had before. What it may be eloquent of
I'm not ready or able to say, nor can I tell you why
that edgy articulation should echo in the sirens
of cruiser or ambulance, of birds that cry in the night
and even ones that sing by day, like phoebe or dove.

Ars Vitae

for Ted Leeson

All I've said—I made it up, including the Things that Really Happened.
Outside my window now, above the autumn pond I've conjured,
two dapper kingfishers start to flit as I dream them,

and in morning fog the trees of October show brightly because just now
    I've imagined
a sun so sharp it could make you bleed. Once—*think* of the number!—
seven lithe otters led me and my brother

downstream as we two fished the mighty Missouri. That's a memory of
    Montana,
which is "not a place," as I'm reminded by a favorite western writer,
"but the name of a place." There are dogs I've treasured, quick

and lost, and horses and songs, and people, living and gone—
    although in fact
they're only what I've concocted from a life of talk. And yet whatever
I've talked about is fact. It must be true

or else I only had some maps, I had no place. Nor did I know
old woodsmen or their stories, to choose an example, but only read
a book or two. I had nothing. I never knew

a soul, a thing. I made up the eagle I saw today as he stooped to the neck
of a Canada goose. I made up the goose, which collapsed at the river's edge,
which I also devised. She fell close by, as dead

as if I'd shot her myself as I paddled. I intended to stop and watch that eagle,
whose tail still showed dark stripes, which means I'd made him into a
    young one:
I'd stop with an eye to beholding another dive

from a blighted elm that leaned at what I'd construed as just the proper
    angle.
But I kept on moving northward, fabricating the umber and mauve
leaves that floated upriver, counter to reason,

beside my gliding wisp of canoe. I invented the leaves so I could conceive
that backwash of eddy, and feel it move me—like many of my visions,
including those of Things that Really Happened—

as if my up were down, and my progress that fluent, easy, at least for
    moments.

Fathomless

I remember that store, and the nasty redneck whose stink
seemed a challenge to everyone in it. The scene
is decades old, but I'm still confused that no one
took up the challenge — including me, though I liked
an occasional fight back then. The prospect of pain

meant less to me once, I guess. An aneurysm
had just killed my brother, so the pain I'm talking about
was my body's. I breathed up another pain that day.
I checked the man's beat pickup; why would he want them,
those skunks knee-deep in its bed? I left the lot

still more confused, my sweet retriever shivering
on the seat beside me. The godawful smell still clung
to the dog's wet coat, and my own. There'd be no more hikes
for us that morning: rain had arrived, bone-chilling.
If you killed a skunk, why would you keep the thing?

To kill some time, I stopped at The Jackpot View.
We've always called it that. Five mountaintops bled
into mists to my east in New Hampshire. The sudden squalls
spilled leaves on the woods-floor's pall of nondescript hue.
Now he was dead. Now my brother was dead.

I can't define any God, but only this morning,
I caught a whiff of road-killed skunk and thought
I could speak of Him or Her or It as surely
as I could tell you the slightest thing concerning
the man I'm remembering now, the one who shot

or trapped or clubbed those miserable reeking creatures.
The smallest enigmas we ever encounter remain
as hard to explain as all the epical ones.
I've failed for years to fathom the death of my brother;
but it's just as hard to understand why a scene

in an old Vermont store should linger like dead-skunk odor,
which if you've been tainted lately comes back to scent you
whenever a rain blows in—or like some pains,
which you may have thought you'd gotten over forever,
but which at some odd prompting come back and haunt you

Li-Young Lee

Li-Young Lee was born in Jakarta, Indonesia, in 1957. He is the author of *Book of My Nights, Rose, The City in Which I Love You*, and *Behind My Eyes*. He has also written an autobiography, *The Winged Seed*. He lives in Chicago with his wife and children.

The Hammock

When I lay my head in my mother's lap
I think how day hides the stars,
the way I lay hidden once, waiting
inside my mother's singing to herself. And I remember
how she carried me on her back
between home and the kindergarten,
once each morning and once each afternoon.

I don't know what my mother's thinking.

When my son lays his head in my lap, I wonder:
Do his father's kisses keep his father's worries
from becoming his? I think, *Dear God*, and remember
there are stars we haven't heard from yet:
They have so far to arrive. *Amen*,
I think, and I feel almost comforted.

I've no idea what my child is thinking.

Between two unknowns, I live my life.
Between my mother's hopes, older than I am
by coming before me, and my child's wishes, older than I am
by outliving me. And what's it like?
Is it a door, and good-bye on either side?
A window, and eternity on either side?
Yes, and a little singing between two great rests.

Words for Worry

Another word for *father* is *worry*.

Worry boils the water
for tea in the middle of the night.

Worry trimmed the child's nails before
singing him to sleep.

Another word for *son* is *delight*,
another word, *hidden*.

And another is *One-Who-Goes-Away*.
Yet another, *One-Who-Returns*.

So many words for son:
He-Who-Dreams-for-All-Our-Sakes.
His-Play-Vouchsafes-Our-Winter-Share.
His-Dispersal-Wins-the-Birds.

But only one word for *father*.
And sometimes a man is both.
Which is to say sometimes a man
manifests mysteries beyond
his own understanding.

For instance, being the one and the many,
and the loneliness of either. Or

the living light we see by, we never see. Or

the sole word weighs
heavy as a various name.

And sleepless worry folds the laundry for tomorrow.
Tired worry wakes the child for school.

Orphan worry writes the note he hides
in the child's bag.
It begins, *Dear Firefly*….

Praise Them

The birds don't alter space.
They reveal it. The sky
never fills with any
leftover flying. They leave
nothing to trace. It is our own
astonishment collects
in chill air. Be glad.
They equal their due
moment never begging,
and enter ours

without parting day. See
how three birds in a winter tree
make the tree barer.
Two fly away, and new rooms
open in December.
Give up what you guessed
about a whirring heart, the little
beaks and claws, their constant hunger.
We're the nervous ones.
If even one of our violent number
could be gentle
long enough that one of them
found it safe inside
our finally untroubled and untroubling gaze,
who wouldn't hear
what singing completes us?

Julia Levine

Julia Levine's poetry collections include *Ditch-tender, Ask*—winner of the Tampa Review Prize, and *Practicing for Heaven*, which won the 1998 Anhinga Prize for Poetry, as well as a bronze medal from *Foreword* magazine. She received her Ph.D. from University of California at Berkeley in clinical psychology. She lives and works in Davis, where she continues to be obsessed with trauma, memory, and the wild.

Vigil

Now the geese are crying for the falling year.

Adrift and on fire, flickers return from the blue hills.
Moths tear open the fierce green lawn

like directions to the next world, tattered into bits,
shredded handfuls thrown up to sun.

Remember last Halloween, when our neighbor called
the animals and archangels, one by one, across his doorway

and in they came, to his wife's hospital bed, frightened
but obedient, while he lifted their hands into hers.

Some things need to know they can still be touched.
Some things astonish us with the deeper names

of what was never meant to be
like the dream my child had of your guitar,

so certain that you'd brought the music back,
that she woke and padded down the hallway

to find me, here, alone, sewing her black cape and gown,
listening to the strange lantern of the geese

passing on . . .

My Gemini

Because she is waiting to be lifted
out of the silence of my unremembered life,
nothing can rinse her from what I carry
or how I travel these fields,
watching magpies scatter arrows into the sky,
and always knowing she slipped apart
from what was once seamless,
so that something of me, though torn,

would keep on arriving. Ahead of me
combines are spinning knives
deep into the ground,
leaving combs of threshed hay
to argue for a world that cuts everywhere.

This is how she wants me to walk,
steady and awake, into all that dies
before it can return, the last leaves
whispering further and further into silence,
these thistles bony with light,
and only the ravens black enough
to spill over with such a thin sun.

She wants me to touch it all,
knees bent in asters,
my fingers rattling petals,
remembering the months
she wrapped my mittened hand
back around the spoon, urging me to dig
down to the tiny locket
netted in the roots of our sugar maple.

She wants me to know even darkness
will speak if you listen, that each hidden word
asks to come to light,
that someday my body will call for her
to step back in.

Until then, she says,
we are practicing for heaven,
and this is how you get there,
the ladder built rung by rung
with the truth of whatever happens.

Nights on Lake Michigan

Downstairs, bitter voices wolved my door
and listening pulled the terror closer

until my room swelled with grim animals
stalking the forest around our cabin:

porcupines rasping bark off porch railings,
bats spitting darkness across the sleeping elms.

What child could have made another dream
from the bones of that cabin? At my window,
the lake soured into blackness. No moon yet.
If only I could have seen a path winding into morning

the way our rolling dock would stretch into the lake,
away from where my parents simmered in lounge chairs,

my mother tying up laces on three pairs of shoes,
my father devouring journals of disease,

his ear tuned to the peculiar music of the body's
pipes and strings. A path that would have led away

to where water held me as if my weight were sweet
and the underwater sand were rice paper

printed with tiny shells; away to where the wind rose up
as if someone called from the further shore,

whitecaps repeating my lost name. If only night
had been a smaller lake I could swim across,

where nightjars gently celloed in the rushes,
and sleep was how the silence borrowed me.

Fontanelle

1.

Stranded in that clockless month of her arrival,
I listen to our neighbor sawing down back doors,
and rock her, tiny fists of breath uncurling,
while the details of each afternoon are revealed:
that still hour before the mailman crosses the street
to unlock his grey tomb of letters, or after school,
children looking for a game to start, and finally
scarlet lights weeding the horizon,
when the men silence their tools and only darkness
bangs out across the empty lots. Now the homeless women

are shaking olives from roadside trees, black pellets
raining down on their plastic bonnets
as this room gathers us into the heart of the house.
Torn up from sleep,
without a memory of dreams, all that will remain
in the essential loneliness before dawn,
is blue milk running from my body
and the violence of her genderless desire
clamping down on my skin.

2.

And then as I stare mutely out the window
at the shut door of the world, there is a night of weather,
trails of light scarring blackness, pelting whip of rain
rattling the fenceline. As giant conifers
crack and fall in the cemetery, the dead around us
unable to hold onto that last tangled handful of roots,
I begin my journey through each child's room,
knowing I am not tending their fear, but my own,
that I will never again travel far enough away
to be injured, to feel wilderness jar against me.
I count the miles between lightning and thunder
as the distance narrows and then widens in retreat.
And when I return to summon you up from sleep,
how desperately I want that brief moment of overlap:
when what was seen can finally be felt, that brilliant flash
when the self finally marries what it was
with what it has become.

3.

As she begins to arrive within her body,
I dare touch the fontanelle,
a vein visibly pulsing under that taut canvas,
tiny plates of skull still undone. Outside,
empty songs of the builders' hammers
flush a handful of crows into the sky. All winter
between rains searing streets into rivers,
sandbags packed around the sewer's roaring throat,
workmen waited inside steamy cabs of their trucks
to forge that blue carbon into a neighborhood.
Now when I take her out among the dark scars
of newly rolled streets, sidewalks not yet lined
with chalk drawings or paired initials,
her eyes without vocabulary,
a hare bounds out ahead of us,
dark-tipped ears sliding between wall guides
of new houses that stand open, without secrets,
a forest of forms not yet fully seen:
the world just before it can be known.

Miriam Levine

Miriam Levine is the author of three poetry collections, including *The Dark Opens* (Autumn House Poetry Prize 2007); *In Paterson*, a novel; *Devotion: A Memoir*, and *A Guide to Writers' Homes in New England*. Her poems have appeared in numerous magazines and The Pushcart Prize anthology. A recipient of a National Endowment for the Arts fellowship and grants from the Massachusetts Artists Foundation, she lives in Massachusetts and Florida.

Candlewood

for Julia

We go into dark and dark opens.
Boats tipped with light and moon on the water.
There is no difference between the tree and the shadow of the tree.
There is no space between light and the wave coming shoreward.
No break between the voice and the word.
There is no difference between your breath and your dear life.
There is no end of you.

Staying In

I kiss the rain for washing away choices.

Why rush out to listen to another writer
when I can watch the horizon disappear?

Sun, rain, day, night—
any way—
the line between ocean and sky doesn't exist.

A white-out storm brings down birds and blows supple palms seaward.

I'll bend too.

There's enough wind to rip flags and knock
the yoke from my shoulders.

1

5 MIRIAM LEVINE

I've done enough chores to last a lifetime.
My scrubbed blouse hangs dripping from the rack,
my soaked socks slung over the rail.

An enormous palm frond floats in the flooded gutter.

I have no job except to praise.

Surfer at Wellfleet
for Helen

Where does he get
the patience to wait through the twilight, rocking
on his stomach in the break and surge,
head to the side, as if he were sleeping? It's freezing
in the afterglow when he finally rises on his one long ride home.

Aaron's Retreat

My uncle knew I wasn't a child
when he held out his arms to dance,
but he jerked back stiff
as if my breasts could kill.
The creases of his formal trousers grazed
my nylon-sheathed legs. My hair frosted
with his whiskey breath, our black shoes, pointed
as fox-headed stoles, his body gone,
except for cold, expert, guiding hands.
Sealed into my tight skin
I kept on going, and neither of us stumbled.
Though I was dizzy when he spun me
I knew it would pass.
His hands were as steady as when
he drove home drunk through the dark.
He could ease his silver Chrysler
up the narrow driveway, without a scratch,
though his face was white as ash, right eye
swollen closed, as if cut by the loose lace
of a boxer's glove. Ulcers burned through
thin skin along his shinbones. He held me
so far away from his ruin I thought
he was fine, both of us were,
but tonight, lost on a strange road,
when I slow down,
let every speeding car pass,
each pair of stinging headlights die,

and my oval mirror turn black
as I breathe in relief,
ahead only the beam of my own lights,
I remember how Aaron would leave the main road
and drive into the hills to dry out in a monastery.
The monks would lead him to his small cell
and he would lie down on the stiff sheet
and wait in the dark to come back to himself.

Philip Levine

Philip Levine now divides his time between Fresno and Brooklyn. His collections *Ashes* and *What Work Is* both won the National Book Award. *The Simple Truth* won the Pulitzer Prize. His best book, *One for the Rose*, won nothing.

The Wandering Poets

As they return from their pilgrimage,
footsore and disgusted, only a few
wear jackets and ties. As usual
Gerald is the most emphatic: he stands
at the corner of Broadway and Spring
and demands that an angel descend
from heaven carrying a glass of tea,
sugared with a little lemon and milk—
not a big deal when you consider
how far he's come without the least thanks.
It's early April—poetry month—at the center
of the known world; somewhere tulips
nudge their way heavenward, forsythias
blaze until you have to look away.
How did we come to despise this life?
Somewhere an axe falls, somewhere a boy
hurls a rock, somewhere the answer
is waiting curled in the brown leaves
of a mountain oak. Gerald has fallen
to the sidewalk and the lunch crowds
step carefully over him; the lesser writers
scurry toward their cars or descend
into the subway to make their appointments.
It's so quiet only you hear the poem
he's polished all his life, delivered on
a froth of blood and meaning nothing.

The Gatekeeper's Children

This is the house of the very rich.
You can tell because it's taken all
the colors and left only the spaces

between colors where the absence
of rage and hunger survives. If you could
get close you could touch the embers
of red, the tiny beaks of yellow,
that jab back, the sacred blue that mimics
the color of heaven. Behind the house
the children digging in the flower beds
have been out there since dawn waiting
to be called in for hot chocolate or tea
or the remnants of meals. No one can see
them, even though children are meant
to be seen, and these are good kids
who go on working in silence.
They're called the gatekeeper's children,
though there is no gate nor—of course—
any gatekeeper, but if there were
these would be his, the seven of them,
heads bowed, knifing the earth. Is that rain,
snow or what smearing their vision?
Remember, in the beginning they agreed
to accept a sky that answered nothing,
they agreed to lower their eyes, to accept
the gifts the hard ground hoarded.
Even though they were only children
they agreed to draw no more breath
than fire requires and yet never to burn.

Words on the Wind

Ford, River Rouge

I'd walk up the hill through wild grasses
rich with milkweed and flags and make a nest
in the place I'd tamped down over the days
of decent weather. The view was something
terrifying and never the same:
when the wind blew from the west I smelled
the smoke of simple earth becoming steel,
of burned rubber, or what I thought was flesh.
On calm days the great plumes rose straight up
to insult the thousand nostrils of God.
I was twenty-four and had no use
for the God of my fathers who chose them
for slaughter or worse, no use for any
God except the one I still harbor
in the deepest organs, the one we call
the heart or soul, terms that meant nothing.

Yet in spite of that words came on the wind
as I sat cross-legged drinking chocolate milk.
Can you imagine God speaking to you
on a hill top in Dearborn, where no kikes
or niggers were allowed, where the wind
came in waves through the wild grasses
that had the courage to thrive? How I yearned
for the character of weeds and grass
that seemed more mysterious and grand
than the words the wind scattered through air
so fetid I smelled sweet. Noon, May 12,
1952. I wrote it on a calendar
at home and later threw the thing away.
You want those words, you who still believe,
who think the exact words are essential
to your salvation or whatever
it is you pray for? I'll take you there
on a spring day of wind and low gray sky,
a Dearborn day. We'll bring two quarts
of chocolate milk and little store-bought
pies, apple, cherry, or pineapple,
each worse than the other, and find the nest
of fifty years ago, and maybe we'll smoke
as all young men did, and lean back
into the flattened grass, and rest our heads
on the cold ground while we add our own
exhalations to the exquisite chaos
of the air, and commune with whomever.

1934

You might hear that after dark in towns
like Detroit packs of wild dogs took over
the streets. I was there. It never happened.
In the old country before the Great War,
my people were merchants and butchers,
and then the killings drove the family
first to England, then Canada, then here.
My father's brother had a shoe repair shop
for a time on Brush Street; he'd learned
the trade from his father back in Kiev.
My mother's family was in junk. The men
were huge, thick chested, with long arms
and great scarred hands. My uncle Leo
could embrace a barrel of scrap metal,
laugh out his huge laugh, and lift it up

just for the joy. His wife, Rebecca,
let her hair grow out in great wiry tangles
and carried her little fists like hammers.
Late summer Sundays we'd drive out
to the country and pick armloads
of sweet corn, boil them in sugar,
and eat and eat until we couldn't.
Can you believe those people would let
dogs take what was theirs, would cross
an ocean and a continent to let
anyone or anything dictate?
After dark these same men would drink
out on the front steps. The neighbors claimed
they howled at the moon. Another lie.
Sometimes they told stories of life
back in Russia, stories I half-believed,
of magic escapes and revenge killings,
of the gorgeous Ukrainian girls they had.
One night they tore up the lawn wrestling, until
Leo triumphed, Leo in his vested suit,
gray and sweat-stained. My uncle Josef
was different; tall and slender, he'd
come into the family through marriage
here in Michigan. A pensive, gentle man,
when stray dogs came to the back door
of the shoe shop he'd let them in, even
feed them. Their owners, he told me,
barely had enough to feed themselves.
Uncle Josef would take a battered pair
of work shoes and cut the soles off
with a hooked cobbler's knife and then,
drawing one nail at a time from his mouth,
pound on a new sole. He'd pry off
the heel and do the same. I was just a kid,
seven at most, and never tired of watching
how at the polishing wheel the leather
took on its color and began to glow.
Once he made a knife for me, complete
with a little scabbard that looped
around my belt. The black handle, too,
was leather, taken from a boot no one
reclaimed. He pounded and shaped it
until it felt like stone. Whenever you're
scared, he told me, just rub the handle
three times and nothing bad can happen.

Larry Levis

Larry Levis, who died in 1996, wrote six books of poetry: *Wrecking Crew, The Afterlife, The Dollmaker's Ghost, Winter Stars, The Widening Spell of the Leaves,* and *Elegy. The Selected Levis: Selected and with an Afterword by David St. John* was published by the University of Pittsburgh Press in 2000.

The Poet at Seventeen

My youth? I hear it mostly in the long, volleying
Echoes of billiards in the pool halls where
I spent it all, extravagantly, believing
My delicate touch on a cue would last for years.

Outside the vineyards vanished under rain,
And the trees held still or seemed to hold their breath
When the men I worked with, pruning orchards, sang
Their lost songs: *Amapola; La Paloma;*

Jalisco, No Te Rajes—the corny tunes
Their sons would just as soon forget, at recess,
Where they lounged apart in small groups of their own.
Still, even when they laughed, they laughed in Spanish.

I hated high school then, & on weekends drove
A tractor through the widowed fields. It was so boring
I memorized poems above the engine's monotone.
Sometimes whole days slipped past without my noticing,
And birds of all kinds flew in front of me then.
I learned to tell them apart by their empty squabblings,
The slightest change in plumage, or the inflection
Of a call. And why not admit it? I was happy

Then. I believed in no one. I had the kind
Of solitude the world usually allows
Only to kings & criminals who are extinct,
Who disdain this world, & who rot, corrupt & shallow

As fields I disced: I turned up the same gray
Earth for years. Still, the land made a glum raisin
Each autumn, & made that little hell of days—
The vines must have seemed like cages to the Mexicans

Who were paid seven cents a tray for the grapes
They picked. Inside the vines it was hot, & spiders
Strummed their emptiness. Black widows, Daddy Longlegs.
The vine canes whipped our faces. None of us cared.

And the girls I tried to talk to after class
Sailed by, then each night lay enthroned in my bed,
With nothing on but the jewels of their embarrassment.
Eyes, lips, dreams. No one. The sky & the road.

A life like that? It seemed to go on forever—
Reading poems in school, then driving a stuttering tractor
Warm afternoons, then billiards on blue October
Nights. The thick stars. But mostly now I remember

The trees, wearing their mysterious yellow sullenness
Like party dresses. And parties I didn't attend.
And then the first ice hung like spider lattices
Or the embroideries of Great Aunt No One,

And then the first dark entering the trees—
And inside, the adults with their cocktails before dinner,
The way they always seemed afraid of something,
And sat so rigidly, although the land was theirs.

My Story in a Late Style of Fire

Whenever I listen to Billie Holiday, I am reminded
That I, too, was once banished from New York City.
Not because of drugs or because I was interesting enough
For any wan, overworked patrolman to worry about—
His expression usually a great, gauzy spiderweb of bewilderment
Over his face—I was banished from New York City by a woman.
Sometimes, after we had stopped laughing, I would look
At her & see a cold note of sorrow or puzzlement go
Over her face as if someone else were there, behind it,
Not laughing at all. We were, I think, "in love." No, I'm sure.
If my house burned down tomorrow morning, & if I & my wife
And son stood looking on at the flames, & if, then,
Someone stepped out of the crowd of bystanders
And said to me: "Didn't you once know…?" *No*. But if
One of the flames, rising up in the scherzo of fire, turned
All the windows blank with light, & if that flame could speak,
And if it said to me: "You loved her, didn't you?" I'd answer,
Hands in my pockets, "Yes." And then I'd let fire & misfortune
Overwhelm my life. Sometimes, remembering those days,
I watch a warm, dry wind bothering a whole line of elms
And maples along a street in this neighborhood until

They're all moving at once, until I feel just like them,
Trembling & in unison. None of this matters now,
But I never felt alone all that year, & if I had sorrows,
I also had laughter, the affliction of angels & children.
Which can set a whole house on fire if you'd let it. And even then
You might still laugh to see all of your belongings set you free
In one long choiring of flames that sang only to you—
Either because no one else could hear them, or because
No one else wanted to. And, mostly, because they know.
They know such music cannot last, & that it would
Tear them apart if they listened. In those days,
I was, in fact, already married, just as I am now,
Although to another woman. And that day I could have stayed
In New York. I had friends there. I could have strayed
Up Lexington Avenue, or down to Third, & caught a faint
Glistening of the sea between the buildings. But all I wanted
Was to hold her all morning, until her body was, again,
A bright field, or until we both reached some thicket
As if at the end of a lane, or at the end of all desire,
And where we could, therefore, be alone again, & make
Some dignity out of loneliness. As, mostly, people cannot do.
Billie Holiday, whose life was shorter & more humiliating
Than my own, would have understood all this, if only
Because even in her late addiction & her bloodstream's
Hallelujahs, she, too, sang often of some affair, or someone
Gone, & therefore permanent. And sometimes she sang for
Nothing, even then, & it isn't anyone's business, if she did.
That morning, when *she* asked me to leave, wearing only
The apricot tinted, fraying chemise, I wanted to stay.
But I also wanted to go, to lose her suddenly, almost
For no reason, & certainly without any explanation.
I remember looking down at a pair of singular tracks
Made in a light snow the night before, at how they were
Gradually effacing themselves beneath the tires
Of the morning traffic, & thinking that my only other choice
Was fire, ashes, abandonment, solitude. All of which happened
Anyway, & soon after, & by divorce. I know this isn't much.
But I wanted to explain this life to you, even if
I had to become, over the years, someone else to do it.
You have to think of me what you think of me. I had
To live my life, even its late, florid style. Before
You judge this, think of her. Then think of fire,
Its laughter, the music of splintering beams & glass,
The flames reaching through the second story of a house
Almost as if to—mistakenly—rescue someone who
Left you years ago. It is so American, fire. So like us,
Its desolation. And its eventual, brief triumph.

Ada Limón

Born in California, Ada Limón received her MFA in Creative Writing-Poetry from New York University. Her first book, *lucky wreck*, won the 2005 Autumn House Poetry Prize. Her second book, *This Big Fake World*, won the Pearl Poetry Prize. Her third book, *Sharks in the Rivers*, was published by Milkweed Editions in 2010. She has received fellowships from the Provincetown Fine Arts Work Center, the New York Foundation for the Arts, and won the Chicago Literary Award for poetry.

Selecting Things for Vagueness

I want to know some things
for certain, and other things
for vague. Have some vague idea
of where you are, not an address,
no train stop, no telephone,
no relative, no neighbor, no local,
no highway blah blah blah, no turnpike,
no regional, no county, no watershed,
no school district, no supermarket,
no tributary, no mailbox, no corner,
no state bird, no "as the crow flies,"
'cause what I'd do when I find you,
well mister, this I know for certain.

The Lost Glove

does not miss the flesh of your left palm,
instead it is content in its bed of grass and
garbage. You, also, do not miss the glove.

You watched it go. On the way to the bar
you passed it. Old Red found it once,
brought it in. You looked away

into the bottled mirror, which was not
away at all, but rather, back at
you, all the while it pointed, the rips in the seams

opening like one thousand mouths. No,
it does not want you back. It wants people to
know who sits on the bar stool is a liar,

an absentee landlord, and how you forgot,
how the goldfish forgets she's already eaten
and goes on drinking her air. You felt the

fingerprint of something, but not the finger,
almost a pleasant pressure, walking backwards
through a door, until, the leather wet with April,

the inside rotted out like a body, it found its way
to the curb and became all things dismissed,
the anger blistering in the throat, the handcuff

of obligation and it lay there, in the daylight
saying, *Do not forget what I accuse you of,* saying,
do not forget that You are the you in this poem.

Centerfold

Crouched in the corner of the barn,
we sat with the cedar chest splayed,
and the magazines laid out in perfect
piles. I was the first to reach the
centerfold and together we stared.
These women, these giantesses,
folded over couches, on bear rugs,
or steel bars, their bodies so slick
they could slip through the pages
and then through your fingers.
One, in particular, was my favorite,
with her left leg perched on a ballet bar and her
hair piled around her shoulders,
I thought she must be famous.
I thought how lovely it would be to
be her, to be naked all the time,
and dancing.

The Firemen Are Dancing

I am running my finger through the rough knotted hole
on the edge of the stained, oak, bar table.

It looks like it could be an eyehole and I think it
would be the scariest thing in the world if I were an ant,

a hole where the bottom drops out, just like that, on to the floor.

I don't want to drink tonight, or if I do, I want to drink a lot, enough
to lie down on the ash blackened floor and watch everything through
the eyehole.

Everyone is talking about parties, the vice cop keeps looking
at the guy we call Red and that's fine by me
because I don't like him, never have.

O and the firemen are dancing. My favorite part is how
they are dancing so close.

One is pulling the other to his hip and one with the hat is laughing
and tossing his head back as if they were seventeen or, even, as if they
were alone.

And it's okay that I don't have a specific *you* right now and it's okay
that I'm not sure who this *you* I am speaking to is anymore.

The firemen are dancing and one of them has leaned his head on the
other's blue shoulder and the ones at the window are singing
and watching with big, lovely, fireman smiles.

And it's okay that you weren't here to see it, I'm going to tell you
all about it. Even if you never ask, I will.

Anne Marie Macari

Anne Marie Macari has published three books of poetry, most recently *She Heads into the Wilderness* (Autumn House Press, 2008). In 2000 her book *Ivory Cradle* won the APR/Honickman first book prize for poetry, chosen by Robert Creeley, and was followed by *Gloryland* (Alice James Books, 2005). Also winner of the James Dickey prize for poetry from *Five Points* magazine, Macari is director of the Drew University Low-Residency Program in Poetry. She has three sons; and she currently lives in the Delaware River town of Lambertville, New Jersey, with her long-time companion, Gerald Stern.

Earth Elegy

By the time it fell, the tree was already part rot,
eaten by termites and ants,

stained with rain and urine, colonized. For years
I watched from my kitchen

as it ungathered in leaves and needles,

bleached, dissolving, though I hardly noticed
how the slow orgy

of weather took it season after season
into the pelvic

trench of dirt, and I got used to seeing it
pointing down the hill

like a giant's fibrous arm
soft with fungus.

We'd kick it to see the wood crumble, see
the insects, horrible kinds,

writhe out of its cracks. And once I read that our air
is full of life we can't see

and thought of the sky falling with the falling tree,

and disintegrating with the tree, a company
of beings, billions,

dying as we were dying and other beings driving
through the debris

and living off it—the dining and dead together,
unseen, spinning and tilted

like us on our axis, pitched toward some
ever-place

of crashing trees, ravenous creatures,
the dirt lit

with their living-dying backbones.

Praying Mantis

The praying mantis rests on
my green towel near
the open window, each distinct part
like a child's wooden toy.

My son carries it to the sill overlooking
the yard. The mantis moves gently
like a creature in love,
though I have seen one devour

a grasshopper slowly—grasshopper
half in, half out, of its mouth—
stick arms lifted up
to its mandibles. Maybe grace

is what we do without hatred.
Grace doesn't need us.
It is silent as the mantis, head bowed
and mouth moving as if

it wanted for nothing as it waits
to impale an insect—
even a hummingbird—with the spines
of its forelegs. The first chill

of September settles around
the house, which for this moment
is the house grace made, in which
for this moment we have

no hatred for each other, only
a constant hunger
that is our way of moving
through the world. O mantis,

Christ child. Your six legs
a cradle: inside
your long thorax,
your abdomen, rocking.

Steller's Sea Cow

Even as they killed them
to extinction, the sea cows
drifted and swam in arctic waters
unafraid of the stranded men.

In the sea cows' parables it was foretold
that extinction comes
into the mind before the body,
a kingdom of oblivion

to swim toward, like the last
passenger pigeon perched
in a zoo, forgetting how
to fly, or a sea cow

slaughtered and dragged to shore, the last
of its kind in the frozen strait—
toothless, spearless,
as the day it was made

but too big to hide. Now they are
parables of themselves
floating in the bloodstreams of humans
who don't even know

they are haunted, followed by sea cows
who watch them as clouds
watch the ocean where the creatures
lived, or by passenger pigeons

who fly into memory, zigzagging
overhead like invisible
schools of fish. *Come children,*
the great mammals whisper,

find yourselves in the family
of man among the giants
of history. And she who writes
about the lost sea cow,

tell her the air she moves in
is singed with extinction.
We are waiting. Remember how
we turned the other cheek?

The world is never
alone, it was never alone.

Sunbathing

Once, when I was twenty-one, a hundred students
naked around a lake,

and in loathing I let myself be free and lay
on my towel, breasts

to the sun, swam that way, and squatted
and dried, and looked

to see whose body was better, whose worse,
whose gathered

like cotton under the skin, who sagged,
strutted, stared down.

For comfort I thought, *they're frightening,*
who love themselves,

diving, splashing, swimming up to the men,
their breasts floating.

What the sun did to my tender skin that day
I don't want to remember.

Even fish have their scales, animals fur,

not just this small arrow-shaped patch of hair
pointing toward the hidden bulb,

hollowed ground of lost Eden, where the tree waits
to respring, and the fruit

to drop at my feet.

In time I understood what I was made for.
Knew how long the bulb

could wait underground before it split
into flower,

how later it would rot and when I'd die
I'd taste the ground-up

mineral of petal and stem, the well
of mucous and blood,

and come to see I had loved this body

without knowing it, and it had loved me—

body and spirit—small, floating—
how we sometimes moved

as one, unclothed in the moist air.

Gary Margolis

Gary Margolis is Director of Counseling and Associate Professor of English (part-time) at Middlebury College. A former staff member at the Bread Loaf and University of Vermont Writers' Conferences, his most recent book of poems is *Below the Falls* (Addison Press, 2010). He was awarded the first annual Sam Dietzel Award by St. Michael's College for mental health practice in Vermont.

Self-Portrait in the Garden, 1847

Hippolyte Bayard (1801-1886) rests his arm
On the wooden barrel as if he were leaning
On the body of a grand piano. He's placed
A vase and tilted flower pot beside him
And leaned a ladder against a trellis, as aware
Of the large tin watering can he's put to
His right, as he is of himself, looking out
To something he made that doesn't know
It's a camera. Surely, he believes he'll be
Perceived, if not known, by someone like me,
Who's thinking of who might read this
One day hoeing the garden, mulched in hay
And scraps of paper, drafts of poems
And bits of letters. The curator suggests

He could have surrounded himself with swords
And a fountain or stood in front of a ministry,
Instead of the things of his life he gathered
From a shed next to his neighbor's cottage.
Bayard appears to be a man unafraid of not
Being remembered, arranged this way because
He knew he could see himself and eventually be
Seen looking out through time in the theater
Of his vest and waistcoat, dress shirt and necktie,
Posed and imposing himself in this row
Of things, like a sweet and bitter weed.

Lincoln on the Battlefield of Antietam, October 3, 1862

From a Brady photograph

Oh, my president, tall as a tent-pole,
Standing next to McClellan and Pinkerton,
All top hat and long coat, at attention,
It seems like, trying to be still enough,
To be taken, shot, by Gardner the Scot,
Brady's assistant, trying not to move
More than the wind in the unknown leaves
Or the bodies in front of him, which lay dead
Long enough not to blur.

The Burning Bush of Basketball

It's just God dressed up
as Michael Jordan.
—Larry Bird, 1986

He was everywhere at once—
        driving past Bird and dunking,
stepping into three-point land
        and getting nothing but net,
bulling into the lane in traffic
        and hooking up what some call
garbage. Nearly everything
        he shot went in, from almost
anywhere on the court. And high
        above courtside, even Johnny
Most, the voice of the Celtics—
        no one more biased than he—
with his voice-box of gravel,
        sang praises, sang praises.
Nothing worked to stop him—
        double-teams or triple-teams,
not the illegal zone defense,
        for which they were warned and hit
with a technical. The wall of
        Parrish, Walton and McHale
he went through or around;
        the smooth defensive glove
of Johnson he took off;
        and the pesky, adolescent rage
of Ainge he blessed with a smile
        and a hoop. The great Bird,
with all of his blonde points,
        played as if he were watching,

as if the basket and basketball
    combined into a burning bush,
all fire, all voice. Everyone
    inside the Garden, and at home
outside the Garden, watched what
    no one had ever done before.
Jordan went to the well of the basket
    and drew up bucket after bucket
to which the final number 63
    was added to his playoff name
in the line score, in the team totals
    (still not enough to win)
for which we sang praise that Sunday
    God was a bull from Chicago, winning
us over, burning the parquet floor.

On the Way to the Sitter's

I could take you by the orchards
    and still skirt the duster's spray.
That way's shortest and we could
    watch apples weigh down their
branches with their own sweet weight.
    I'd say the apples grew partly
because of the rain and wait to tell you
    the biting spray tells each fruit
how red to turn and when it's time
    to drop into a Jamaican's hand.
I could take you another way,
    past the church and Longey's store,
by the roadside houses that display
    their home-made sales. I'd ask if you
saw the sign for freezer lamb, its hand-
    painted sheep grazing next to their
shepherd's address, saw the work
    clothes swaying from our neighbor's
lines like chicory when the wind
    from a truck or the wind drives by.
I could take you the way you ask for,
    which is always just out-of-the-way,
past the house with paper lanterns
    strung and every car the owners drove
still kept next to the white machines
    that worked for them. Here,
by the way, they raise a pair of baby bulls
    in a pen with hay and water. I do say
each of you, my girl and boy, could take
    one for a walk, steering your bull

with the hair of a willow switch.
      This is nearly the way the young
oxherder tamed his ox
      in the six drawings Jitoku drew
of love inside of mind. I think of him
      each time I go this way so we can stop
and pick an overhanging, roadside
      MacIntosh to rub the spray from,
we can see our faces curving on
      its skin, before we disappear by biting in.

William Matthews

William Matthews is the author of a dozen books of poetry, essays, and translations. He won the National Book Critics' Circle Award for *Time & Money* (Houghton Mifflin, 1995), has been the recipient of fellowships from the Guggenheim and Ingram Merrill foundations, and in April 1997 was awarded the Ruth Lilly Prize. At the time of his death in 1997, he was a professor of English and director of the writing program at the College of the City University of New York.

The Cloister

The last light of a July evening drained
into the streets below. My love and I had hard
things to say and hear, and we sat over
wine, faltering, picking our words carefully.

The afternoon before I had lain across
my bed and my cat leapt up to lie
alongside me, purring and slowly
growing dozy. By this ritual I could

clear some clutter from my baroque brain.
And into that brief vacancy the image
of a horse cantered, coming straight to me,
and I knew it brought hard talk and hurt

and fear. How did we do? A medium job,
which is well above average. But because
she had opened her heart to me as far
as she did, I saw her fierce privacy,

like a gnarled, luxuriant tree all hung
with disappointments, and I knew
that to love her I must love the tree
and the nothing it cares for me.

Housecooling

Those ashes shimmering dully in the fireplace,
like tarnished fish scales? I swept them out.
Those tiny tumbleweeds of dust that stalled
against a penny or a paperclip under the bed?
I lay along the grain of the floorboards
and stared each pill into the vacuum's mouth.
I loved that house and I was moving out.

What do you want to do when you grow up?
they asked, and I never said, *I want to haunt
a house.* But I grew pale. The way cops "lift"
fingerprints, that's how I touched the house.
The way one of my sons would stand in front
of me and say, *I'm outta here,* and he would mean
it, his crisp, heart-creasing husk delivering

a kind of telegram from wherever the rest of him
had gone—that's how I laved and scoured
and patrolled the house, and how I made my small
withdrawals and made my wan way outta there.
And then I was gone. I took what I could.
Each smudge I left, each slur, each whorl, I left
for love, but love of what I cannot say.

Mingus at The Showplace

I was miserable, of course, for I was seventeen,
and so I swung into action and wrote a poem,

and it was miserable, for that was how I thought
poetry worked: you digested experience and shat

literature. It was 1960 at The Showplace, long since
defunct, on West 4th St., and I sat at the bar,

casting beer money from a thin reel of ones,
the kid in the city, big ears like a puppy.

And I knew Mingus was a genius. I knew two
other things, but as it happened they were wrong.

So I made him look at the poem.
"There's a lot of that going around," he said,

and Sweet Baby Jesus he was right. He glowered
at me but he didn't look as if he thought

bad poems were dangerous, the way some poets do.
If they were baseball executives they'd plot

to destroy sandlots everywhere so that the game
could be saved from children. Of course later

that night he fired his pianist in mid-number
and flurried him from the stand.

"We've suffered a diminuendo in personnel,"
he explained, and the band played on.

A Night at the Opera

"The tenor's too fat," the beautiful young
woman complains, "and the soprano
dowdy and old." But what if Otello's
not black, if Rigoletto's hump lists,
if airy Gilda and her entourage
of flesh outweigh the cello section?

In fairy tales, the prince has a good heart,
and so as an outward and visible
sign of an inward, invisible grace,
his face is not creased, nor are his limbs gnarled.
Our tenor holds in his liver-spotted
hands the soprano's broad, burgeoning face.

Their combined age is ninety-seven; there's
spittle in both pinches of her mouth;
a vein in his temple twitches like a worm.
Their faces are a foot apart. His eyes
widen with fear as he climbs to the high
B-flat he'll have to hit and hold for five

dire seconds. And then they'll stay in their stalled
hug for as long as we applaud. Franco
Corelli once bit Birgit Nilsson's ear
in just such a command embrace because
he felt she'd upstaged him. Their costumes weigh
fifteen pounds apiece; they're poached in sweat

and smell like fermenting pigs; their voices rise
and twine not from beauty, nor from the lack
of it, but from the hope for accuracy
and passion, both. They have to hit the note
and the emotion, both, with the one poor
arrow of the voice. Beauty's for amateurs.

Jo McDougall

Jo McDougall grew up on a rice farm in the Arkansas Delta. Her books include *Dirt* and *Satisfied with Havoc*, both published by Autumn House, and *Daddy's Money*, a memoir published by the University of Arkansas. She has taught at universities in Arkansas, Louisiana, and Kansas. Recipient of a John Ciardi Fellowship, fellowships to The MacDowell Colony, and awards from the DeWitt Wallace/Reader's Digest foundation and the Academy of American Poets, she was also the 2000 winner of Arkansas' Porter Prize.

Telling Time

My son and I walk away
from his sister's day-old grave.
Our backs to the sun,
the forward pitch of our shadows
tells us the time.
By sweetest accident
he inclines
his shadow, touching mine.

Dirt

Its arrogance will break your heart.
Two weeks ago
we had to coax it
into taking her body.
Today,
after a light rain,
I see it hasn't bothered
to conceal its seams.

Why I Get Up Each Day

Tomorrow, maybe, or today
sunlight will discover one red leaf.
The sound will shatter crystal.

Summer

Every summer when I was a child,
I visited my grandmother's farm.
We didn't say much to each other,
listening to voices:
the far bark of a dog,
from somewhere, thunder,
the easy complaint
of the porch swing.

When it rains,
quickening old ashes in the fireplace,
I want to go back,
to the house that was,
the people that were,
the chores, the horses, the cat.

But what if I could?
What if someone,
glancing up from a sewing machine or a plow,
should see me there?

The Good Hand

After a stroke of luck, my son's left hand
and arm lie lifeless. He has to remind
them, wherever he goes, to come along.
With the good hand he gives his old, strong

handshake, pulls on his shoes, adjusts his braces,
cooks, turns pages, touches the bored faces
of three dogs, struggles with rubber bands,
writes checks, drives a tractor, harrows and plants.

He caresses the hair of his two boys and his wife
and often takes with his good hand, my hand
or touches my shoulder when I sigh or laugh
over some loss we both can understand.

Waiting Room

I see you here most every day. How are you?
The coffee's gone. I've asked the desk for more
but I guess they're overworked and underpaid.
The nurses try. They've sure been good to us.
Who do you have here? I'm so sorry.

He's young, your son, isn't he, for that to happen?
Our son's here, too. He's not doing good. It's AIDS.
That was my husband that just left. He hates
for me to talk to anyone about Tommy.
Lord, it's expensive, having somebody here.
We're staying in our son's trailer. I'm afraid
he'll never go back to it. He's failed a lot
these last few days. How's your son? Well.
I'm so sorry. I'll be praying for him.

We live two hundred miles away. The driving
back and forth, we can't afford it. But even
staying in the trailer, you've got to eat,
and groceries are out of sight. We're getting too old
to drive in traffic. My husband doesn't do good
in places like this— the waiting, you know. Of course
you do. Does your son have children? Well,
there's no explaining these things. We take what comes.

I'm just thankful we can be here with Tommy.
You can't just walk away. Some do, you know.
Some of our friends said we ought to put
our son right out in the street. They would. My husband's
taking this real hard. He's aged ten years.
We've gone through nearly all our savings. I'm sure
you've noticed I'm missing some front teeth. Now,
I guess, I'll never get my partial plate.

I wish I could go buy me a new dress.
Might cheer Tommy up. He takes it hard
when I leave. All we can do is be here.
You can't just walk away. Remember, hon,
we're all right where we're supposed to be.
That's what I tell my husband. Here he is.

Herschel, come and meet someone. Her son
is in here, too. I simply can't believe
that traffic. I've lived my whole life in this state
and never been, not once, in this city.
We had our boy late, a good baby,
never any trouble at all. You have to go?

God bless. One day at a time, that's what I say.
Will you be here tomorrow? If there's a miracle,
we'll have hot coffee. But I wouldn't hold my breath.

Cancer

It eased under the door
like a mouse.
We scarcely noticed.
Then the scuttling.
Then the high squeak
that shattered the house.

Tempting the Muse

Tilt your head provocatively,
round your vowels,
make a place for him
in the cleavage of your breasts.
Hope for the best.
What you'll get is anybody's guess.

Once, I pulled out all the stops
and a pickpocket wandered in,
reeking of booze and need;
and once, Death,
who apologized for getting the wrong house
and went on his way—
but not before his eyes,
red as a red snapper's,
undid every button of my dress.

Luck

In the middle of phoning in an order
to Spiegel,
a woman discovers
she's been struck dumb.
When the doctors tell her there is no cure,
she smiles. If she could, she would tell them
her joy.
She remembers a time when she was a child,
pinning towels on the line
in the white and sparkling silence of
the farm.

What We Need

It is just as well we do not see,
in the shadows behind the hasty tent
of the Allen Brothers Greatest Show,

Lola the Lion Tamer and the Great Valdini
in Nikes and jeans
sharing a tired cigarette
before she girds her wrists with glistening amulets
and snaps the tigers into rage,
before he adjusts the glimmering cummerbund
and makes from air
the white and trembling doves, the pair.

Jane Mead

Jane Mead's most recent book is *The Usable Field* (Alice James, 2008). She is the recipient of grants and awards from the Whiting, Lannan, and Guggenheim Foundations. She farms in northern California.

Concerning That Prayer I Cannot Make

Jesus, I am cruelly lonely
and I do not know what I have done
nor do I suspect that you will answer me.

And, what is more, I have spent
these bare months bargaining
with my soul as if I could make her
promise to love me when now it seems
that what I meant when I said "soul"
was that the river reflects
the railway bridge just as the sky
says it should—it speaks that language.

I do not know who you are.

I come here every day
to be beneath this bridge,
to sit beside this river,
so I *must* have seen the way
the clouds just slide
under the rusty arch—
without snagging on the bolts,
how they are borne along on the dark water—
I must have noticed their fluent speed
and also how that tattered blue T-shirt
remains snagged on the crown
of the mostly sunk dead tree
despite the current's constant pulling.
Yes, somewhere in my mind there must
be the image of a sky blue T-shirt, caught,
and the white islands of ice flying by

and the light clouds flying slowly
under the bridge, though today the river's
fully melted. I must have seen.

But I did not see.

I am not equal to my longing.
Somewhere there should be a place
the exact shape of my emptiness—
there should be a place
responsible for taking one back.
The river, of course, has no mercy—
it just lifts the dead fish
toward the sea.

Of course, of course.

What I *meant* when I said "soul"
was that there should be a place.

On the far bank the warehouse lights
blink red, then green, and all the yellow
machines with their rusted scoops and lifts
sit under a thin layer of sunny frost.

And look—
my own palm—
there, slowly rocking.
It is *my* pale palm—
palm where a black pebble
is turning and turning.

    Listen—
    all you bare trees
    burrs
    brambles
    pile of twigs
    red and green lights flashing
    muddy bottle shards
    shoe half buried—listen

    listen, I am holy.

Passing a Truck Full of Chickens
at Night on Highway Eighty

What struck me first was their panic.

Some were pulled by the wind from moving
to the ends of the stacked cages,
some had their heads blown through the bars—

and could not get them in again.
Some hung there like that—dead—
their own feathers blowing, clotting

in their faces. Then
I saw the one that made me slow some—
I lingered there beside her for five miles.

She had pushed her head through the space
between bars—to get a better view.
She had the look of a dog in the back

of a pickup, that eager look of a dog
who knows she's being taken along.
She craned her neck.

She looked around, watched me, then
strained to see over the car—strained
to see what happened beyond.

That is the chicken I want to be.

W.S. Merwin

United States Poet Laureate W.S. Merwin was born in New York City in 1927. From 1949 to 1951 he worked as a tutor in France, Mallorca, and Portugal; for several years afterward he made the greater part of his living by translating from French, Spanish, Latin, and Portuguese. Merwin has authored dozens of books of poetry and prose. His many awards include the Pulitzer Prize in Poetry for *The Shadow Of Sirius* and the National Book Award in Poetry for *Migration: New and Selected Poems*. W.S. Merwin has lived in Hawaii since 1976.

No

Out at the end of the street in the cemetery
the tombstones stared across the wheeling shadows
of tombstones while the names and dates wept on
in full daylight and behind them were the hill
sheared off two rusted tracks under a black
iron gate led up out of pure darkness
and the unbroken sound of pure darkness
that went on all the time under everything
not breathing beneath the sounds of breathing
but no they said it was not the entrance
to the underworld or anything like that
in fact all the houses along the street
had been paid for by what had come from there
in the days of the negatives of the pictures

To Paula in Late Spring

Let me imagine that we will come again
when we want to and it will be spring
we will be no older than we ever were
the worn griefs will have eased like the early cloud
through which the morning slowly comes to itself
and the ancient defenses against the dead
will be done with and left to the dead at last
the light will be as it is now in the garden
that we have made here these years together
of our long evenings and astonishment

Blueberries After Dark

So this is the way the night tastes
one at a time
not early or late

my mother told me
that I was not afraid of the dark
and when I looked it was true

how did she know
so long ago

with her father dead
almost before she could remember
and her mother following him
not long after
and then her grandmother
who had brought her up
and a little later
her only brother
and then her firstborn
gone as soon
as he was born
she knew

The Song of the Trolleys

It was one of the carols
of summer and I knew that
even when all the leaves
were falling through it as it passed
and when frost crusted the tracks
as soon as they had stopped ringing
summer stayed on in that song
going again the whole way
out of sight to the river
under the hill and hissing
when it had to stop
then humming to itself
while it waited until
it could start again
out of an echo warning
once more with a clang of its bell
I could hear it coming
from far summers that I
had never known
long before I could see it
swinging its head

to its own tune on its way
and hardly arrived before it
was going and its singing
receding with its growing
smaller until it was gone
into sounds that resound
only when they have come to silence
the voices of morning stars
and the notes that once rose
out of the throats of women
from cold mountain villages
at the fringe of the forest
calling over the melting
snow to the spirits asleep
in the green heart of the woods
Wake now it is time again

The Pinnacle

Both of us understood
what a privilege it was
to be out for a walk
with each other
we could tell from our different
heights that this
kind of thing happened
so rarely that it might
not come around again
from me to be allowed
even before I
had started school
to go out for a walk
with Miss Giles
who had just retired
from being a teacher all her life

she was beautiful
in her camel hair coat
that seemed like the autumn leaves
our walk was her idea
we liked listening to each other
her voice was soft and sure
and we went our favorite way
the first time just in case
it was the only time
even though it might be too far
we went all the way
up the Palisades to the place

we called the pinnacle
with its park at the cliff's edge
overlooking the river
it was already a secret
the pinnacle
as we were walking back
when the time was later
than we realized
and in fact no one
seemed to know where we had been
even when she told them
no one had heard of the pinnacle

and then where did she go

Little Soul

after Hadrian

Little soul little stray
little drifter
now where will you stay
all pale and all alone
after the way
you used to make fun of things

Recognitions

Stories come to us like new senses

a wave and an ash tree were sisters
they had been separated since they were children
but they went on believing in each other
though each was sure that the other must be lost
they cherished traits of themselves that they thought of
as family resemblances features they held in common
the sheen of the wave fluttered in remembrance
of the undersides of the leaves of the ash tree
in the summer air and the limbs of the ash tree
recalled the wave as the breeze lifted it
and they wrote to each other every day
without knowing where to send the letters
some of which have come to light only now
revealing in their old but familiar language
a view of the world we could not have guessed at

but that we always wanted to believe

The Odds

His first winter in that city
after years in the north a friend
wrote to me of how people there
were dealing with the cold
he told me that crews
were digging up the avenue
down at the corner all day
the men keeping a fire going
in an old oil drum with holes
down the sides and feeding it whatever
turned up and he had been watching
two men by the barrel with three
gloves between them passing one
glove back and forth
while they stamped their feet
and he had tried to tell whether
it was a right or a left glove.

Judson Mitcham

Judson Mitcham is the author of three collections of poems, *Somewhere in Ecclesiastes* (University of Missouri, 1991), and *This April Day* (Anhinga, 2003), as well as two novels, both from the University of Georgia Press: *The Sweet Everlasting* (1996) and *Sabbath Creek* (2004). He lives in Macon, GA, with his wife, Jean.

Surrender

We were ordinary men,
unable to embrace each other fully—
to bury a face in the other man's neck,
to rock like drunks in the doorway, saying
goodbye. It was always a handshake
and maybe that sideways hug,
with an arm around the shoulders.
                              In the hospital
you couldn't understand, didn't know me,
tried to overturn the rack by the bed, tear
the needles from your arm; searched everywhere,
underneath the sheets and the pillow,
for your clothes, *going home*; grew frightened
when confused by the purpose of a spoon, angry
when you couldn't even urinate—failing
to hit the plastic bottle, till I held you.
If I leaned down close
when the baffled agitation started up,
and I smoothed back your hair, or I kissed you
on the forehead or the cheek, whispered "Daddy,"
you'd throw your arms around me.

There's a way a man turns to a woman,
so his lips just barely graze hers, yet in this,
there is everything that follows, each detail
of forgetting where they are.
And today, I am trembling with desire, wild
for the years, when my lips feel yours, cool

as gold. One kiss for the infinite
particulars of love, to tell you this:

I will be with you there, in the darkness.

The Multitude

The woman in the airplane wanted
to talk about Christ. I did not.
I raised my magazine. She continued, saying Christ
promised heaven to the thief
who believed while nailed to the cross.
The clouds looked solid far beneath. She began
the story of her life, and I stopped her
as politely as I could, saying please, right now,
I'd simply like to read. And for a while,
she did keep quiet, then she asked
if I'd ever really given Christ a chance, so I tried
telling her a joke, chose the one
about the Pope and Richard Nixon in a rowboat.
She discovered nothing funny in the story.
Jesus fed the multitude, she said.
I looked around to find an empty seat.
There wasn't one. She asked me if I knew
about the sower and the seed; about Zaccheus;
Legion and the swine; Mary Magdalene;
Lazarus; the rich young ruler. And I did,
I knew about them all. I told her yes,
sweet Jesus; got the stewardess
to bring another bourbon; tried to buy
the missionary one, but she declined.
And when the plane set down,
I'd escaped up the aisle, made the door,
and started walking fast toward the baggage claim,
when I saw them, all at once, on the concourse:
thousands I would never see again, who'd remain
nothing in my life, who would never have names;
and I realized I'd entertained—strangely,
and for no good reason I could see—
the hope of someone waiting there
who loved me.

History of Rain

What if every prayer for rain brought it down?
What if prayer made drunks quit the bars, numbers hit,
the right girl smile, shirts tumble from the dryer
fully ironed? What if God

required no more than a word? Every spot
of cancer would dissolve like peppermint,
every heart pump blood through arteries as clean
as drinking straws then. All grief would be gone,

all reverence and wonder. But if rain
should fall only once in a thousand years, rare
as a comet, if for fifty generations
there was never that sweet hint of metal in the air

until late one April afternoon
when the dust began to swirl above the ballfield,
and the first big drops fell, popping in the dirt,
and sudden as a thought, great gray-white sheets

steamed on the asphalt, fought with the pines,
would we all not walk out trying to believe
our place in the history of rain? We'd be there
for the shining of the world:

the weeds made gaudy with the quicksilver breeze;
the rainbows floating over black-glass streets;
each cupped thing bright with its blessing; and long
afterwards, a noise like praise, the rain

still falling in the trees.

Writing

But prayer was not enough, after all, for my father.
His last two brothers died five weeks apart.
He couldn't get to sleep, had no appetite, sat
staring. Though he prayed,
he could find no peace until he tried
to write about his brothers, tell a story
for each one: Perry's long travail
with the steamfitters' union, which he worked for;
and Harvey—here the handwriting changes,
he bears down—Harvey loved his children.

I discovered those few sheets of paper
as I looked through my father's old Bible
on the morning of his funeral. The others
in the family had seen them long ago;
they had all known the story,
and they told me I had not, most probably, because
I am a writer,

and my father was embarrassed by his effort. Yet
who has seen him as I can: risen

in the middle of the night, bending over
the paper, working close
to the heart of all greatness, he is so lost.

Marilyn Nelson

Marilyn Nelson is a three-time National Book Award Finalist and the author of many acclaimed books for young people and adults, including *Carver: A Life in Poems*, and *A Wreath for Emmett Till*. Since 2003, she has opened her home in the Connecticut countryside to other poets, especially those belonging to underrepresented groups, as Soul Mountain Retreat.

Egyptian Blue

From red clay spotted on a hillside
Carver came up with a quadruple-
oxidized pigment the blue
of a royal mummy's innermost windings,
an Egyptian blue
no artist or scientist had duplicated
since the days of old King Tut.
It's the bluest blue,
bluer than lapis.
Paint factories and manufacturers
of artists' materials
begged him for the formula,
offering the top floor of Fort Knox.
He sent it
for the cost of the two-cent stamp
it cost him to mail it.

It's an indescribable blue.
You see it every day
on everything from shutters
to a child-sized flowered dress.
We've learned to live with it
without loving it, as if it were
something ordinary,
that blue the world sought
for five thousand years.
Look around with me: There it is
in the folder on my desk,
in my close-up photo of a fairy tern,
in the thumbtacks in my corkboard
holding up photos, poems, quotes, prayers,
a beaded ancestral goddess juju doll
(it's the blue of the scarab in her hand).

It's the blue of that dictionary
of American Regional English,
of the box of eighty standard envelopes,
the blue of that dress waiting to be ironed,
the blue of sky in that Guatemalan cross,
it's the blue of the Black Madonna's veil.

Bedside Reading

for St. Mark's Episcopal, Good Friday 1999

In his careful welter of dried leaves and seeds,
soil samples, quartz pebbles, notes-to-myself, letters,
on Dr. Carver's bedside table
next to his pocket watch,
folded in Aunt Mariah's Bible:
the Bill of Sale.
Seven hundred dollars
for a thirteen-year-old girl named Mary.

He moves it from passage
to favorite passage.
Fifteen cents
for every day she had lived.
Three hundred fifty dollars
for each son.
No charge
for two stillborn daughters
buried out there with the Carvers' child.

This new incandescent light makes
his evening's reading unwaveringly easy,
if he remembers to wipe his spectacles.
He turns to the blossoming story
of Abraham's dumbstruck luck,
of Isaac's pure trust in his father's wisdom.
Seven hundred dollars for all of her future.
He shakes his head.

    When the ram bleats from the thicket,
        Isaac...   like me...   understands
    the only things you can ever
      really...   trust...
    are...
        the natural order...
            ...and the Creator's love...
      spiraling...
    out of chaos...

Dr. Carver smoothes the page
and closes the book
on his only link with his mother.

He folds the wings of his spectacles
and bows his head for a minute.
Placing the Bible on the table
he forgets again at first, and blows at the light.
Then he lies back dreaming as the bulb cools.

Cafeteria Food

*Iowa State College of Agriculture
and Mechanic Arts, 1891*

Even when you've been living on
wild mushrooms, hickory nuts,
occasional banquet leftovers sneaked
out of the hotel kitchen by a colored cook,
and weeds; even when you know it feeds you,
mind and body, keeps you going
through the gauntlet
of whispered assault
as you wait in line;
even when it's free
except for the pride
you have to pay by eating
alone in the basement,
hot meat or chicken and potatoes
and fresh baked bread and buttery
vegetables; even when there's dessert;
even when you can count on it day after day;
even when it's good,
it's bad.

Dave Newman

Dave Newman lives in Trafford, Pennsylvania. He's worked as a truck driver, a book store manager, an air filter salesman, and a college teacher. He is the author of the novel *Please Don't Shoot Anyone Tonight* (World Parade Books) and numerous poetry chapbooks.

The God in Walt Whitman

Whitman said, "In the faces of men and women I see God."
I believe that, and because of that, I see God in the face
of Walt Whitman, the only poet, ever, who wanted to be praised
so he could get down on his knees and worship with the people.
When the Civil War broke out, he left his home in Brooklyn,
traveled to DC and volunteered in a hospital for three years.
When his little brother, George Washington Whitman,
was wounded in battle, Walt immediately rushed into
the field to find and care for him. Back at the hospital,
he spent most of his salary on gifts, candy, and tobacco,
giving soldiers the love and attention they so desperately needed.
That's the god in Whitman, and that's why his writing
is greater than his writing. He saw the blood and the bones.
"Death is nothing here," he wrote in a diary, meaning of course,
"Death is everything here." He couldn't leave his tent in the morning
to shave without seeing the corpses piled up on stretchers.
His refusal to turn away—that's the God in Whitman, too.
And that's why you don't scan his poems for meter.
That's why rhyme is useless. That's why I believe it when
he said, "What a devil thou art, Poverty!" Or, better yet, this:
"Stand up for the stupid and crazy." Or, my favorite: "I feel I am
of them—I belong to those convicts and prostitutes myself,
and henceforth I will not deny them— for how can I deny myself?"
It's the god in Whitman that saves us all, and it scares the weak.
The Critic in London didn't see the God in Whitman, and the guy who
reviewed the first edition of *Leaves of Grass* said, "Whitman is
acquainted with art, as a hog is with mathematics." I'm not going to

tell you the critic's name. But you know Walt Whitman now, or are
remembering him again, and all of us here know now we have something
good to do, so let's do it, and if that doesn't work, let's do it again.

9/11

Jean said, "A plane just crashed into
one of the Towers," and I said, "Oh yeah,"
and smiled. Jean was 73 and a little batty.
She worked as a cashier at a newsstand
at the Pittsburgh airport, and I was dropping
off my paperwork in the backroom.
I managed a bookstore owned by
the same company, and I was working
sixty hours a week, commuting
eighty miles round trip, and, basically,
dying. Once a week, sometimes twice,
my wife would say, "Do you understand
that I'm having a nervous breakdown?"
We had a little son, nine months old,
who my wife was afraid of. He was
a beautiful baby, already on the verge
of speech, and I barely knew him.
He wouldn't sleep through the night.
He screamed almost all the time.
None of my wife's friends
wanted to be friends with her
now that she had a screaming baby.
My wife's mother was sick again.
All those lovely people who promised
to babysit for us fell from our lives
like tree branches under a chainsaw.
I understood why my wife was having
a nervous breakdown, but there was nothing
I could do, and if she me told about it three
times in one week, I'd say, "Honestly, sweetie,
could you please shut the fuck up for a change?"

After I dropped off my paperwork and came
back out from the office and into the store,
Jean said, "Another plane just crashed into
the second Tower, and the Pentagon, too."
Jean didn't seem so batty now. Word was
spreading through the airport: terrorists.
Were we next? I'm not sure I even cared.

They shut down the airport, and we were gone
by noon. The parkway was empty, downtown

Pittsburgh like a ghost town as I cruised through
the tunnels like a bullet in the barrel of a gun.

Nobody was at the house when I got home,
so I watched TV for a minute and took a nap.
Maybe the world was ending. Maybe not.
I hadn't had a nap in months, and when my wife
came home, I loved her, and wanted, more than
anything, for her to be happy and unburdened.
I thought about how much I loved my country,
and how unbelievably awful I felt for those
people crushed in the Towers, and the news
kept showing video of a man jumping from
a window, choosing to free-fall to his death,
rather than the smoke or fire inside the building.

I went to eat with my wife and son
at a cheap steakhouse up the road.
I fed my son black beans from my chili,
and he laughed and smiled and smashed
crackers into his face, and didn't scream once.
We took our time eating. We didn't rush home.
I started to think how I probably wouldn't have to
work the next day, and I started to feel good
about the world, my world, small as it was.
The weekend before, I'd worked sixteen hours
in one day, slept three hours, and did it again.
This was not uncommon. It was expected.
There was no way the airport, even one
in Pittsburgh, was going to be open
the day after two planes piloted
by religious nutballs did an impersonation
of a nuclear weapon on America's great city.
I'm not saying I would have wished death
on anyone, but, in the face of tragedy,
I was able to celebrate my own small victory.
That night, we hired a sitter, and I drank
beer in a bar with my wife, and it was sad,
but, more than that, it was fun, and we were
happy to be out together, timeless, and in love.

Bo Diddley

for Bob Pajich

I wish I could get that hambone beat on the page—
do you know what I'm talking about? One loud guitar
played clean, three chords, an electric bass, drums,

and those barbed wire lyrics that go, "I know you
don't love me no more, I'm a sixty-minute man,
tombstone hand and a graveyard mind, rattlesnake."
Who do you love? All we wanted in Ohio was to get
fucked up. Drunk but not drunk enough, we raced
Route 7, north to south, south to north, looking
for a bar, looking for anything really, everything.
I know it doesn't matter now, but it goddamn did then.
The backbeat, I mean, those rhythm and blues bullets
fired at the bullseye of the hips, hips, not the heart,
not the head, the hips, where it all starts, always.
We had Bo Diddley on ten, and sang "Pills," every word,
and only turned down the volume long enough to hear
the gravel crunch under our tires. There was a light on
in the bar, but the door was locked. It was just past two.
Two o'clock, dry. One minute til, drunk. I hate laws.
What a goddamn pain to be thirsty for a beer and stuck
outside kicking stones. We pulled back on Route 7,
The volume up. You can lose the rhythm and find it again,
but if it doesn't come back, you die. You die stumbling.
A critic once said, "Bo Diddley has the only famous
maracas player in the world." We don't dance enough.
There's music, more than enough for all of us,
and yet it's quiet all the time. I like the sound
of my own heart. I like your heart, too, the way
it races at all the right moments and sings.
We were in Ohio. Drunk. We wanted to be famous.

Naomi Shihab Nye

Naomi Shihab Nye grew up in St. Louis, Jerusa-
lem, and San Antonio, where she now lives. Her
poetry books include *19 Varieties of Gazelle* (a Na-
tional Book Award finalist), *Fuel, Red Suitcase*, and
Words Under the Words. She also writes children's
books, essays, novels for teens, and short stories,
and has edited eight poetry anthologies including
This Same Sky and *What Have You Lost?*

Sure

Today you rain on me from every corner of the sky.
Softly vanishing hair, a tiny tea set from Mexico
perched on a shelf with the life-size cups.

I remember knotting my braid on your bed,
ten months into your silence.
Someone said you were unreachable,
we could chatter and you wouldn't know.
You raised yourself on magnificent dying elbows
to speak one line,
"Don't— be— so— sure."
The room was stunned.
Lying back on your pillow, you smiled at me.
No one else saw it.
Later they even denied they heard.

All your life, never mind.
It hurts, but never mind.
You fed me corn from cans, stirring busily.
I lined up the salt shakers on your table.
We were proud of each other for nothing.
You, because I finished my meal.
Me, because you wore a flowered dress.
Life was a tablet of small reasons.
"That's that," you'd say, pushing back your chair.
"And now let's go see if the bakery has a cake."

Today, as I knelt to spell a word for a boy,
it was your old floor under me,
cool sections of black and white tile,
I'd lie on my belly tracing their sides.
St. Louis, movies sold popcorn,

baby lions born in zoos,
the newspapers would never find us.

One moth lighting on the sink
in a dark apartment years ago.
You point, should I catch it?
Oh, never mind.
A million motions later, I open my hand,
and it is there.

Lunch in Nablus City Park

When you lunch in a town which has recently known war
under a calm slate sky mirroring none of it,
certain words feel impossible in the mouth.
Casualty: too casual, it must be changed.
A short man stacks mounds of pita bread
on each end of the table, muttering
something about more to come.
Plump birds landing on park benches
surely had their eyes closed recently,
must have seen nothing of weapons or blockades.
When the woman across from you whispers
I don't think we can take it anymore
and you say there are people praying for her
in the mountains of Himalaya and she says
Lady, it is not enough, then what?

A plate of cigar-shaped meatballs, dish of tomato,
friends dipping bread—
I will not marry till there is true love, says one,
throwing back her cascade of perfumed hair.
He says the University of Texas seems remote to him
as Mars, and last month he stayed in his house
for 26 days. He will not leave, he refuses to leave.
In the market they are selling
men's shoes with air vents, a beggar displays
the giant scab of leg he must drag from alley to alley,
and students gather to discuss what constitutes
genuine protest.

In summers, this cafe is full.
Today only our table sends laughter into the trees.
What cannot be answered checkers the tablecloth
between the squares of white and red.
Where do the souls of hills hide
when there is shooting in the valleys?
What makes a man with a gun seem bigger
than a man with almonds? How can there be war

and the next day eating, a man stacking plates
on the curl of his arm, a table of people
toasting one another in languages of grace:
for you who came so far;
for you who held out, wearing a black scarf
to signify grief;
for you who believe true love can find you
amidst this atlas of tears linking one town
to its own memory of mortar,
when it was still a dream to be built
and people moved here, believing,
and someone with sky and birds in his heart
said this would be a good place for a park.

Dusk

where is the name no one answered to
gone off to live by itself
beneath the pine trees separating the houses
without a friend or a bed
without a father to tell it stories
how hard was the path it walked on
all those years belonging to none
of our struggles drifting under
the calendar page elusive as
residue   when someone said
how have you been   it was
strangely that name that tried
to answer

Swerve

The dog Rosie who comes home
after 9 days with something darker
in her eyes will not be able to say, exactly,
where she went and what she saw.
But the summer shifts into
another key for all who searched for her.
Now we know how many mournful dogs
sprawl exhausted in dirt on streets called Riddle
and Labor, on the back curve by the ancient brewery,
how many empty houses, wreckages, broken shelves,
cushionless sofas, lonely tracks,
and the stunning folds of fat
on two shirtless brothers
who sat on the tail of their truck.
They watched blankly as we circled
their block. How many bony cats,

smashed bottles…and the man
in a white apron who burst forth
as I coaxed his dog to take
a closer look at it, does he keep it near him
in the kitchen now? Under the swirling fan,
thinking I have my eye on it, as the unwanted dogs
limp down to the river,
panting, and their next night looms.

Famous

The river is famous to the fish.

The loud voice is famous to silence,
which knew it would inherit the earth
before anybody said so.

The cat sleeping on the fence
is famous to the birds
watching him from the birdhouse.

The tear is famous, briefly, to the cheek.

The idea you carry close to your bosom
is famous to your bosom.

The boot is famous to the earth,
more famous than the dress shoe,
which is famous only to floors.

The bent photograph is famous to the one who carries it
and not at all famous to the one who is pictured.

I want to be famous to shuffling men
who smile while crossing streets,
sticky children in grocery lines,
famous as the one who smiled back.

I want to be famous in the way a pulley is famous,
or a buttonhole, not because it did anything spectacular,
but because it never forgot what it could do.

Ed Ochester

Ed Ochester is the editor of the Pitt Poetry Series, and a founding editor of the literary magazine *5 AM*. A professor emeritus at the University of Pittsburgh and a core faculty member of the Bennington College MFA Writing Seminars, Ochester has won many awards, including most recently the George Garrett Award from the Association of Writers & Writing Programs. Of his many books of poetry, *Snow White Horses* and *Unreconstructed* were published by Autumn House.

Changing the Name to Ochester

When other grandpas came to Ellis Island
the Immigration people asked "Name?"
and they said "Sergius Bronislaus Jygsywglywcz"
and the officer said "ok, from now on your name's
Sarge Jerko," and Sarge trundled off to the Lower East Side
with a lead cross and a sausage wrapped in a hair shirt
and shared a tiny ill-lit room with eight *Landleute*
and next to a pot of boiling diapers began to carve
yo-yos to peddle on the street and forty years later
was Sarge Jerko, Inc., the Yo-Yo King,
but my grandfather who was born in this country
(no one living knows anything about *his* parents)
and was an engineer for Con Edison
when he married the immigrant girl
Katherina Humrich who everybody said
was once very pretty but when I knew her
had a tight bun, thin German lips
and a nose which came to her chin;
her major pleasures were trips to Coney Island
with friends and frightening little children
by jumping out from behind curtains, after which
she cackled hilariously. This is all I know for certain
about my grandfather: 1) his name was Olshevski,
and he changed it shortly after his marriage,
when they were living in an Irish neighborhood,
2) while working at Con Ed he bought a yacht
my grandmother said, but my mother said "Mom,
it was just a boat," 3) he left Katherina
ater the fourth son was born, and she lived
im a tiny apartment on Chauncy Street
which smelled, even when I was eight,
like boiled diapers, 4) he was reported
to be handsome and have "a roving eye,"

5) my father and his brothers
all of whom are dead now
refused to go to his funeral
and never spoke of him.

Ths is a poem about forgiving Grandpa
for my not knowing him. And father, if you're
reading over my shoulder, I don't forget how
you had three cents spending money a week
and gave two cents to the church, or how
Uncle George, the baby who was everybody's
darling, couldn't go to college because he had
to work to support the family like everybody else
and how he became a fire chief in the City of New York,
and how Uncle Will, before he died of cancer,
became an advisor to LaGuardia and made a bundle
by being appointed trustee of orphans' estates,
or how Uncle Frank, driving his battery truck
once was stopped by Will and LaGuardia in their big car
and they chatted, and Uncle Frank—my favorite uncle,
neither Olshevski nor Ochester—still talks
about how his partner Paddy kept saying
"Bejasus, it was the Mayor,"
or how because you had to support your brothers
you couldn't marry till 30
and were engaged for eight years to my mother
who to this day loves you because you did
what you had to do, and how you built your business
going door-to-door selling insurance on Chauncy Street
and Myrtle Avenue till late at night, arguing and collecting
quarters and dimes from people who lived in tiny apartments
smelling of boiled diapers.
Nearly twenty years since your death, father,
and long ago I've forgiven you, and I think
you did love me really, and who am I, who was born
as you said "with everything," to condemn
your bitterness toward your father who left you
as you said "with nothing"?

I don't believe in original sin.
I believe if we're strong enough and gather our powers
we could work it out: no petty human misery,
no windrows of the dead slaughtered
in suicide charges, no hearts shrunken
and blackened like meat spitted
and held too long to the fire.
But what everybody knows

is enough to make you laugh
and to break your heart.
Grandpa, forty years after your death,
by the power vested in me as the oldest
living Ochester in the direct line I hereby
forgive you. And though you died,
my mother says, penniless and alone
with no one to talk to
I hope that when you abandoned your family
you lived well. I hope you sailed your 15-foot
yacht out into Long Island Sound
with a pretty woman on board and a bottle
of plum brandy. I hope that when the huge yacht
with "Jerko II" on the stern sailed by
you looked up and said "honey,
you'll be sailing one like that some day"
and that she giggled and said "yeah,
hon, gimme a kiss" and afterwards tilted
the bottle, and that the sun was shining
on the Sound, and that you enjoyed
the bitter smell of the brine and
the brilliance of the white scud and
that when you made love that night
it was good and lasted
a long, long time.

Fred Astaire

The secret of his popularity was
that he looked like a bus driver
who could dance. In my teens
I hated his movies, and told my Aunt Carrie
they were corny and "unrealistic"
but she just laughed and said "you go
to his movies because they *ain't* realistic,"
Aunt Carrie who worked as a file clerk
and spent an hour each way on the subway
commuting. And later, if I'd been honest,
I would have realized that's why I loved
Dickens and Keats, his "Grecian Urn," and
doesn't Fred look a bit like Carlos Williams
who also talks plain without ornament just
like Astaire when he's singing? A critic said
he had "an unspectacular voice" and lacked
"the vocal technique of a trained singer" but
had great respect for the lyrics and "immaculate
timing," so that even Mel Torme called him,

as a jazz singer, "the greatest bar none,"
and how wonderful that the man who danced
with Ginger Rogers and Rita Hayworth and Judy
Garland and worked with the Gershwins,
Ira and George, and Noel Coward
was "really" named Frederick Austerlitz,
the son of an immigrant, and that when he took
his first screen test some moron—probably
an early critic of Williams, too—reported to his boss:
"can't act, can't sing, balding, can dance
a little."
                    No wonder Carrie loved him
as she shuttled underground in New York
where nearly everyone if they worked
their asses off 40-plus a week got "enough
to live on" and, like most Americans,
lived on dreams.

Monroeville, PA

One day a kid yelled
"Hey Asshole!"
and everybody on the street
turned around

Retired Miners

In Dr. Capelletti's office,
crippled and wheezing:

"If any guy   tells you
he got rich   through hard work
ask him   whose?"

The Canaries in Uncle Arthur's Basement

In the white house in Rutherford
the ancient upright piano never worked
and the icy kitchen smelled of Spic and Span.
Aunt Lizzie's pumpkin pie turned out green
and no one ate it but me and I did
because it was the green of the back porch.
That was the Thanksgiving it rained and I first thought
of rain as tears, because Aunt Lizzie was in tears
because Arthur came home from the soccer game drunk
and because he missed dinner brought a potted plant

for each female relative, and walked around the table
kissing each one as Lizzie said "Arthur, you
fool, you fool," the tears running down her cheek as
Arthur's knobby knees wobbled in his referee's
shorts, and his black-striped filthy shirt wet from the rain
looked like a convict's. What did I know?
I thought it meant something. I thought
no one would ever be happy again. I thought
if I were Uncle Arthur I'd never again
come out from the dark basement where he raised canaries,
the cages wrapped in covers Aunt Lizzie sewed,
and where, once, when I was very small and because Uncle Arthur
loved me or loved his skill or both he slowly removed the cover
from a cage and a brilliant gold bird burst into song.

For Ganesha, Hindu God of Good Fortune
—and for Gerald Stern

In a week I'll be leaving
the only place I've ever been happy
living alone, I'll leave the red hills
of Birmingham and my monastic life where
I've written poems in silence and reread
Richard Farina and some other books
we used to live by, and every morning
washed the blue salt-glaze Japanese bowls
I've eaten my rice and grits from,
and I'll be leaving you, Ganesha, with your
broken tusk in your right hand and
the sweet rice cake (your favorite food)
in your left, as I drive due north
away from the Museum of Art, and
I'll think of you, god of wisdom
and good fortune, so much like my own
clumsy life and good luck lately.
The ancients report that you were
decapitated "in an unfortunate accident,"
that the gods gave you an elephant's head.
They said that you broke off your left tusk
to write the sacred books for the gods,
and you sit tonight in the dark Museum
with a self-satisfied grin, and the tusk
in your right hand and sweet rice cake
in your left, having done what you could
in improbable circumstances, as I sit
on my porch with a glass of Semillon and

a bowl of rice, watching the clouds
and the moon rising, and I will remember you
when I pray for the ones I love,
elephant face, grotesque and serene, and
when I leave here on the interstate
worrying my loose tooth, speeding away
from the barbecue at Dreamland,
and the blue tiled pools in the garden, and
the rough cabin where Ted sang Puccini to himself
because he was so happy cooking steaks while
I sat drinking wine on the deck, and away
from the carp pool in the Birmingham
Japanese garden where the fat man
with a camera asked me to photograph
himself and his friend—his charge—the kid
with palsy, whose head lolled from side to side
as they stood on the bridge and waved above the water,
while the carp, the koi, swam in schools around
around and around the little pond.

Oh Ganesha, I know happiness is fragile, I know
we disappear like the mallow flowers by the roadside
in spring, I know how clumsy we are,
but I'll think of you as I leave, driving home
as the insane Alabama drivers going 90
flip me a finger as they pass and
I'll flip one back because I'm glad
to have been in my silence, and now to leave it,
oh cripple and fool and holy one.

Alicia Suskin Ostriker

Alicia Suskind Ostriker's 13th poetry collection, *The Book of Seventy*, won the 2009 National Jewish Book Award for Poetry. Earlier collections have received awards from the Poetry Society of America, the San Francisco Poetry Center, the National Endowment for the Arts, and the Rockefeller Foundation, among others; she has twice been a finalist for a National Book Award. As a critic, Ostriker is the author of several books on poetry and on the Bible. She teaches in the Low-Residency MFA Poetry program of Drew University and lives with her husband in Princeton, N.J.

Stream-Entering

Though reluctant
when his mother insists
            on joining the sangha

the Buddha admits
women too are capable
            of stream-entering

Reading these words
it is not that suddenly
            I enter the stream

it is more that I become
aware of its coolness and of
            myself pleasantly wading

then the sea appears
heaving between continents
            grey, horizonless

death-cold currents
day and night, and I
            would be a drop

Sonnetina: The Storm

You know the way on a rainy night
when the noise wakes us we lie in bed
smiling at each other, the way

enjoyment spills through us
like after quiet satisfying sex, you know
how we stay awake listening to lashing rain

fierce wind, fierce wind and lightning crack
thunder tumbling and crumbling to nothing

so when you are gone and I am alone
if a storm keeps me awake
I pull sheet and blanket under my chin

like a child with a bedful of animals
a child with a secret that makes her laugh,
the secret of the storm.

The Blessing of the Old Woman, the Tulip, and the Dog

To be blessed
said the old woman
is to live and work
so hard
God's love
washes right through you
like milk through a cow

To be blessed
said the dark red tulip
is to knock their eyes out
with the slug of lust
implied by
your up-ended
skirt

To be blessed
said the dog
is to have a pinch
of God
inside you
and all the other dogs
can smell it

Gaia Regards Her Children

Ingratitude after all I have done for them ingratitude
is the term that springs to mind

yet I continue to generate
abundance which they continue to waste

they expect me to go on giving forever
they don't believe anything I say

with my wet green windy
hot mouth

Nancy Pagh

Nancy Pagh lives in Bellingham, Washington, and teaches at Western Washington University. She is the recipient of an Artist Trust Fellowship, and her work has appeared in numerous publications. *At Home Afloat*, her study of women's travel language at sea, was published in 2001; and her chapbook, *After*, in 2008. *No Sweeter Fat*, her first collection of poems, won the 2006 Autumn House Poetry Prize.

Blackberries

I would like to write you a poem about fat ladies
but you prefer to read of blackberries.

There are eight hundred sixty-four poems about blackberries
published in English; where is the harm
in another?

So let's say that the wildest fat ladies
grow on low runners that snake
unplanted along the driest hillsides
of coastal British Columbia.
The tight knot of their fruit
is smaller than all others, and shaped
like the bud of your own coldest nipple.

I heard a Sixteenth-Century Italian printer
despaired the destruction of cuttlefish
and began making his books with the juice
of fat ladies.

A transplanted Himalayan variety of fat lady
ripens in cow pastures late in the autumn.
It hangs in black clumps
among serrated yellow leaves, tasting
like barbed wire, hatred, and the mineral note
of self abnegation; your tongue thrills
to meet such darkness.

Royalty used to reserve the color of fat ladies
just for itself, but now
the CEOs all favor a striking red tie.
The American president follows suit.

Fat ladies travel many miles
in the gut of a bear
to colonize the bright waste of clearcuts.
I would like to read the diaries
kept on one of these passages.

Have you ever noticed that the biggest fat ladies
are just beyond your reach?

Fat ladies do not taste
like salmonberries. Salmonberries do not taste
of salmon. Fat ladies taste good
when you are standing near the Nooksack River
watching the salmon
or watching the places you wish there were salmon.

Fat ladies permanently stain everything
except your tongue.

An overripe fat lady drops in your palm
with the slightest touch.
If you try to blow off the roadside dust
you will break its tender skin
and miss the holy communion
of eating the roadside dust.

Oh that first day, that first day you notice
the fat ladies have withered and dried on their vines:
a regret more tart
than the small unripe segments
of the first fat lady
you ate that summer.

Again and again the fat ladies push
in to every unclaimed corner of the neighborhoods,
reminding the soft palates of children
there really are things in this world
so sweet and so free.

There are so many fat ladies; where is the harm
in sprinkling one with sugar
to watch the materialization
of Homer's wine-dark sea?

Ten Reasons Your Prayer Diet Won't Work

1.
Praying to god that you will be thin
instead of eating
only burns eleven calories
at average fervency.

2.
Jesus had large love handles.
I know in the pictures he is skinny
and White
with slightly Italian-esque features,
but he understood the value
of keeping on a few extra pounds
to tide him over in the desert.
If you are a child of god
this runs in your family.

3.
All food miracles create *more*:
more loaves, more fishes, more wine, more manna....
When you ask god to do something about fat
expect multiplication.

4.
The only time you used to talk to god
was giving thanks before high-caloric meals.
Your fat cells remember this
and begin to swell
even at the mention of his name.

5.
God has stock in Doritos.

6.
Eventually you will tell yourself
that god created you this way
and who are you to disagree?

7.
Contrary to popular belief,
eating is not a mortal sin *per se*
and god believes in free will.

8.
Bread and wine. Communion would suggest
god endorses the Mediterranean Diet
instead.

9.
Blasphemy, to waste German chocolate cake.

10.
God is characterized by excess;
your only proof that god exists
is that the natural world is more than it has to be.

Perhaps the closest you've come
to acting in her perfect image
was building your sacred hips.

Anchoring

With my hands touching you,
a memory of my father
crouched on the bow, on his toes,
the soles of his sneakers toward us—
lowering flat gray anchor and chain,
hand over hand, twenty feet of it,
then soft quiet rope.
He waves one hand to me, the eldest,
to say *put her in reverse.*
Chain draws out across the sea floor
as we drag for a catch.
He motions *stop*, cleats the line.
This subtle, elongated instant I wait for—
a rope drawn to its limit—
the perceptible springing back,
                              anchored.

Watching others anchor and fail: the charterers
who stand on the deck and throw their anchors,
a twirling mass of metal and chain.
The people with money, boat shoes,
black hats with gold braid,
drinking all day from nautical cups
with red and blue anchors.
My father sits, saying *Look at that would you
just look at that* and assures us all
judgment comes to those unfamiliar with "scope."
And that night, or another, it does—
an easterly wind at three a.m.
drags them off to hell.
Or at least, in the morning, they're gone.

That was long ago, only faintly connected
to your sand-brown body—

these patches of hair like coiled gold weeds,
ridges and rib bones are half-buried stone.
My hand travels slowly
charting useless planes,
a soft stretch of belly where nothing can catch.
The ledge of a forearm,
the hinge near your groin
are places to settle in for the night.

I hold you at arm's length a moment,
an elongated instant—
me drawn to my limit—
then perceptibly spring back,

                                    anchored.

I Believe I Could Kneel

I believe I could kneel
in so many quiet places
where the pale sponge of moss
would surely reach above
my hips as I sank down and down
as the deer must in their beds
kneeling once, then once again
to lower themselves front and back
before closing their glistening eyes.

I think I am the kind of person
down on one knee and shifting my weight
my whole life long
but capable of sinking far, and deep,
to the bottom of something
that might replace the religion I discarded
or make me really live in this body
or waste my life.

I would like to live my way into being
someone who stands back up
and runs toward that holy forest.

Gailmarie Pahmeier

Gailmarie Pahmeier, originally from rural Missouri, has been a Nevadan for 25 years. She currently teaches creative writing and contemporary literature at the University of Nevada where she has been honored with awards for her teaching. Among her poetry collections are *The House on Breakaheart Road* from University of Nevada Press, *West of Snowball, Arkansas,* and *Home* from Red Hen Press, and *Shake It and It Snows,* winner of the 2009 Coal Hill Chapbook Prize.

Homegrown Roses

Everyone has a story to tell
that's set inside a bar. I remember
the long year I loved a boy from school,
how every day at five o'clock we met
at George's Lounge, how we became familiar,
the aging lady bartender calling
out in her clear voice—*Miller, Miller Lite*—
before that big door eased shut behind us.
I also recall being conscious
of the clock, how in the world of the tavern
you are always alive in the future,
even if it's only ten or fifteen
minutes, long enough to know the baseball
game you're watching is behind you, that if
you hope hard enough your team can still score,
there's time and plenty of it. Imagine,
too, one chilled summer night when I was young
and fleeing my first divorce, found myself
at the End of the Trail in Dayton, Nevada.
I met a man who bought me drinks, who fed
the jukebox till I thought it would burst,
held me close enough to hear his heart.
I don't remember when we decided
to pretend—this is a bar story,
after all—but we told the other patrons,
four tired cowboys and a black-eyed woman,
that we'd just been married, this was our
honeymoon and we were happy.
One of the cowboys wandered outside,
broke a rose from a battered bush, placed it
in a beer bottle, a gift for the bride.
I still have it. And now every year or so,
when I return to my truck in the dark
after work, I find a single rose anchored

under the wiper. My friends think I should
be afraid of this, as if this flower
were a dead chicken or a stalker's signature.
But it's just a rose and all it means
is that I'm forever joined to a man
who'll never know my real name, a man
I couldn't possibly pick out in a crowd.
Now, your turn. Tell me one of your stories.

Hometown Girl at 30

Someone more romantic might say
it has to do with the rhythm of spoons,
the toy piano sound of silverware
tossed onto a table. Someone else might
say it has to do with the way I move
across the floor, my thick-hosed legs aching
to be quick. All I can say is I like

waiting tables where truckers gulp my strong
coffee, tell lies they hope will loosen
my grip, lure me into their cabs come dark.
Sometimes I'm sorely tempted, and I've gone
to a few who were young and good-looking
and on their way to somewhere I might get
a card from. I like the big button

I wear pinned to my chest—*Try Our Famous
Cherry Cheesecake*—I like the way I make
things shine (napkin dispensers, the easy
necks of catsup bottles, the long counter
I rest my body against). I like the noise
of Alvie in the kitchen singing
"Delta Dawn," the sweet smell of onions

Roberta chops for chili, I love knowing
I'm at home here, another small town girl
with big dreams. I love knowing that someday
I will walk out of here on the arm
of someone with promise, that everyone
will miss me, will say, *Whatever happened
to that local gal who told those stories?*

Home Maintenance

Sometimes my father's hand shakes, sends fat drops
of paint to splatter my patio.

He's fond of this work, and I like the way
this man feels in the sun, healthy and honest
and responsible. I work next to him
on the shorter ladder, my hair sticky
against my neck. He says, *This heat's a bitch.*
I say, *Wears my ass out.* I'd like more talk,
but it's too hot, too hot to wrap our mouths
around vowels, urge consonants into
the air. We'll finish my house by Saturday,
my father will go home, live through another
familiar summer in his own backyard.
We both know he'll never be back, that this
job is his last large gift, that he will tell
my mother about the heat, tell her
this paint will last seven years at most,
that he worries about who will help me
next time, who will work beside me in the sun,
who will love me in ways simple as sweat.

A Home Full of Color

> *"Y'all have no idea how much it costs to look this cheap."*
> —Dolly Parton

I, too, believe in makeup, believe in
the luxurious artifice of color
that couldn't possibly come from within.
I want my eyelashes as long as spiders' legs,
my cheeks the startled tones of too much—
sun, drink, fevered loving—and my mouth
a darker, more defined wound. I love

most the men who aren't afraid, who'll kiss
my red lips straight on, take the color
onto their own, leave it there until
some other woman touches a tissue
to her tongue, rubs out my being there.
It is, indeed, expensive to be cheap.

Think of Jezebel, alone at her dressing
table, her meticulously rendered
applications—hands, hair, face, feet. She knows
they are coming to kill her, that her blood
will bracelet the hooves of horses,
perhaps even imagines her hands and feet
gnawed from their limbs but still lovely,

lovingly tendered, an offering of sorts.
I've lived long enough to know what can happen
to a face, to the body earned and deserved.
Applying makeup is a way of saying,
here's who I am, enhanced and ready for
anything. Come on now, come on and kiss me.

Linda Pastan

Linda Pastan is the author of 13 volumes of poetry, most recently *Traveling Light* (W. W. Norton, 2011). Her awards include the Dylan Thomas Award, a Pushcart Prize, the Alice Fay di Castagnola Award from the Poetry Society of America, the Bess Hopkin Prize from *Poetry* magazine, the Maurice English Award, the Charity Randall Citation of the International Poetry Forum, and the 2003 Ruth Lilly Poetry Prize. Two of her collections of poems were finalists for the National Book Award and one for the *Los Angeles Times* Book Prize. She was on the staff of the Bread Loaf Writers' Conference for 20 years, and from 1991 to 1995 she was Poet Laureate of Maryland.

Rain

A rage of rain
on the tin roof
a hammering
as of a thousand
carpenters:
water spilling
from the cup
of the sky, baptizing
houses and trees:
bright sheets
of water
blowing about
in the wind
like translucent laundry.
The ground is losing
its firmness—
each step
a sinking in,
a pulling out.
I long
for the barreling
sound of water
to cease;
for umbrellas
to fold their merciful
wings; for the sun
to come back
and wring itself out,
so the world—

like some shaggy
drenched beast—
can shake itself
dry.

Ars Poetica

"Well, less is more, Lucrezia..." Robert Browning

I am working towards
the one line poem,

the shortest distance
between two points,

from past to future,
for instance,

from copper-colored autumn
to winter.

But one word
might be better,

for isn't a single bullet
to the head enough?

Or one shaft of sunlight
through the trees—

that celestial finger
pointing?

I'll remove the restless
back and forth of verbs,

the obfuscating
adjectives.

It's nouns that matter:
leaf; child; wave—

the single one that splinters
on the empty sand.

but maybe even one word
is too much,

maybe a silence
that is infinite

is what I'm after, a poem
that reverberates

on the virgin page
the moment

before language
is invented.

snow shower

come look
improbable
flakes

are falling
out of the
sky

the size
of flowers
without

their stems
magnolias
perhaps

the size of doilies
of porcelain
cups

they disappear
straight through
the earth

leaving only
a wintry scent
behind

Norah Pollard

Norah Pollard, the daughter of Seabiscuit's jockey, Red Pollard, has been a folk singer, waitress, nanny, teacher, solderer, print shop calligrapher, and sometime secretary. She has received the Academy of American Poets Prize and for several years edited *The Connecticut River Review*. She lives in Stratford, CT.

The Sum of a Man

In autumn,
facing the end of his life,
he moved in with me.
We piled his belongings—
his army-issue boots, knife magazines,
Steely Dan tapes, his grinder, drill press,
sanders, belts and hacksaws—
in a heap all over the living room floor.
For two weeks he walked around the mess.

One night he stood looking down at it all
and said: "The sum total of my existence."
Emptiness in his voice.

Soon after, as if the sum total
needed to be expanded, he began to place
things around in the closets and spaces I'd
cleared for him, and when he'd finished
setting up his workshop in the cellar, he said,
"I should make as many knives as I can,"
and he began to work.

The months plowed on through a cold winter.
In the evenings, we'd share supper, some tale
of family, some laughs, perhaps a walk in the snow.
Then he'd nip back down into the cellar's keep
To saw and grind and polish,
creating his beautiful knives
until he grew too weak to work.
But still he'd slip down to stand at his workbench
and touch his woods
and run his hand over his lathe.

One night he came up from the cellar
and stood in the kitchen's warmth
and, shifting his weight
from one foot to the other, said,
"I love my workshop."
Then he went up to bed.

He's gone now.
It's spring. It's been raining for weeks.
I go down to his shop and stand in the dust
of ground steel and shavings of wood.
I think on how he'd speak of his dying, so
easily, offhandedly, as if it were
a coming anniversary or
an appointment with the moon.
I touch his leather apron, folded for all time,
and his glasses set upon his work gloves.
I take up an unfinished knife and test its heft,
and feel as well the heft of my grief for
this man, this brother I loved,
the whole of him so much greater
than the sum of his existence.

Narragansett Dark

for my father

They led the horses away.
They tore down the fences.
The wrecking ball brought down
the grandstand, the clubhouse.
They plowed under the track kitchen,
the tack shop, the bettors' windows.
They burned the green barns.

When there was nothing of Narragansett
but a great empty space, the moon
glittered over it like a Vegas sign
and the wind blew dust across
900 acres to the Newport-Armistice roads.
The next day they paved.

Black asphalt covered the scent
of hay and the horse.
They built a drugstore,
a store for linoleum, and they
threw up subdivisions, aqua and mustard

and pink, whose mailboxes rusted
before they were sold.
Then they built a nursing home

where now the old jockey lay in a narrow bed.
He did not know where he was
so the irony was lost to him,
but he knew his wife would come
and wash him and light him a cigarette
and put the swatches of cotton
between his toes and pour him
a small cup of blackberry brandy.
Long nights alone, after the t.v. was
shut off and the brandy gone,
he'd listen for something.
All the long dark nights, listening.

One night a lean March wind
rattled the gate and his heart labored
in his breast and he rose up
for he heard what he heard—
their soft nickering and blowing, the thin
rustle of silks, the creak
of saddle and the tick
of hoof on stone.

And he left the bed and went out
to where they stood in the grasses.
He stood before them and
their breath fell on him like cloud
and he saw their great eyes pool the moon.
And the one waiting for him,
the one with an empty saddle,
was a bay.

He mounted up and they rode under the moon
and the wind flared the mane of his horse
and was hard and clean on his face.
The others galloped on either side, silently,
as if they were running on moss or flowers,
and he went with them where they took him
into the fields of night.

Kiss

I was the high schooler awkward and shy
coming from church
on an August morning

in the two-toned DeSoto with the
clank in the rear.
He was the gas pump boy
at the Texaco station who said
he needed to hear the clank
in action.

We are the kids who drive
the hot and dusty country roads
of Seekonk,
windows down, wind flicking
my hat's flocked veil, his arm
out the window holding up the roof.

Past corn stands, watermelon stands,
cows, crows, and barnsmell,
past miles of shade trees,
past old tin trailers rusting in the weeds,
to a small dirt clearing in the sun,
where rock ledge and pines surround us
like an amphitheater.
Here
he stops the car and turns
and, barely smiling,
takes off my little rosette hat
with the veil, my white crocheted gloves,
and lays them carefully on the dashboard.
I am not afraid.

His lips, burnt by the sun,
his hands, the nails oil-edged,
touch me everywhere.
The sun blazes. The yellow dress
with the Peter Pan collar falls away.
Wordlessly we cling and kiss,
sweat and touch. His body
smells of sweat and socks and gasoline.
Bits of tobacco from the cigarette
crushed in his shirt pocket
stick to my shoulders,
fleck my small bare breasts.

He shrugs from the shirt
with the Texaco star,
eels from his oily trousers.
His sweating body glistens
like a molted thing, and
there's a port wine stain

like a Maybelline kiss
high on his thigh near his cullions.

Bees. Sun.
The black and pungent pines.
Yellow haze burning off yellow fields.
When he covers me,
his love cry throws crows in the air.
I bloom in his arms like mimosa.

Dawn Potter

Dawn Potter is associate director of the Frost Place Conference on Poetry and Teaching, held each summer at Robert Frost's home in Franconia, New Hampshire. She is the author of two collections of poetry as well a memoir, *Tracing Paradise: Two Years in Harmony with John Milton*, which chronicles her strange project of copying out all of *Paradise Lost* word for word while living in the Maine woods. With her husband, photographer Thomas Birtwistle, she has lived in those woods for the better part of two decades now, raising boys and livestock, hauling firewood, and reading books.

Nostalgia

It was darker then, in the nights when the cars
came sliding around the traffic circle, when the headlights
speckled with rain traveled the bedroom walls
and vanished; when the typewriter, the squeaking chair,
the slow voice of the radio stirred the night air like a fan.
Of course, the ones we loved were beautiful—
slim, dark-haired, intent on their books.
The rain came swishing against the lamp-lit windows.
The cat purred in his chair. A clock sang,
and we lay nearly asleep, almost dreaming,
almost alone, nearly gone—the days fly so;
and the nights, like sleep, disappear without memory.

Why I Didn't Finish Reading David Copperfield

Bus three's eight-track tape player chunks into gear,
it's Frank Zappa again, crooning huskies and snow,
and down the back of my neck, a couple of bad boys

chant, "Mescaline, peyote, LSD." I've got this book
splayed on my lap, poor Mr. Peggotty, it's not like
I don't feel for him, I just can't keep my mind off

those bony elbows and white hands, those tender,
spotty faces. Glance up in study hall, sure enough,
beautiful bad boys are scrawling "Skynyrd"

all over the chalkboard, the teacher's slipped off
to the supply closet, everyone knows he's got
Mrs. Kay jammed up against a stack of manila paper,

but where is my true love? I worry all the time
I'll end up with nothing, even Barkis-is-willin' won't save me
a smile, I'll be stuck on the bus with Miss Murdstone,

driver shrieking she'll play "The Sound of Music" twice a day
for the rest of the year if those tramps in the back seat
don't keep their hands where she can see them.

I could lay my head on this vinyl seat and cry,
even Little Em'ly has more fun than I do, not one bad boy
in the whole world wants me, I'll never brush my clumsy

lips against his open mouth, taste his sweet smoky breath,
and every time I pick up this book, my mind starts wandering
in circles like an old dog that can't find a good spot to sleep,

you hear his nails clacking back and forth across the kitchen floor,
and it just makes me so sad, sitting here on the bus wishing
I was holding hands with a boy in a Kiss t-shirt, my own wild Steerforth.

I don't care if he dumps me after a week . . . I don't care.
All I want is to give him everything he asks for, I'd lay myself down
in the falling snow to feel the weight of his heart,

and Little Em'ly, if you really needed me, I swear I'd finish your story.
Maybe you've floated too long in the cold, or the wind's wrong,
but right now I have no idea what you're screaming about.

Eclogue

> Look, oxen now bring home their yoke-suspended ploughs,
> And the sun, going down, doubles growing shadows;
> But I burn in love's fire: can one set bounds to love?
> —Virgil

A marriage worth of minutes we've stood
side by side, staring into the hooded depths
of your 1984 Dodge Ram pickup truck,
watching the engine chitter and die
for no apparent reason. I feel a crazy,
ignorant joy: here we go again, sweetheart,
struggling in harness over yet another
crappy mystery. Do you? I can't say I'll ever
know one way or the other what your thoughts
will do, though twenty years ago I made you cry
when I dumped you for the jerk down the hall,
and I'll never get over it, the sight of you,
cool autocrat, in tears for a dumb girl
who happened to be me.

Now I'm the one who cries all the time,
you're the one not walking away from me
down the hall. Just the same, you imagine
walking away, I'm sure of it; maybe when you're
dragging another snow-sopped log to the chainsaw
pile, or we're curled in bed waiting for a barred owl
to stammer in the pines, the barn dog shouting back
like a madwoman. It's not that being here
is misery; it's more like marriage is too much
and not enough at the same time: the trees crowd us
like children, our bodies betray a fatal longing.
What's left for us, at forty, but dismay
till labor shakes us back into our yoke.
Work, work, that puritan duty—yet
how beautiful the set of your shoulders
when you heave a scrap of metal siding
into the trash heap. Our bodies linger
this side of lovely, like flowers under glass.
We drive ourselves to endure; on my knees
in the hay mow, stifled and panting,
I plant bale after bale in place: you toss,
you toss, I shove, I shove. We keep pace,
patient and wordless; the goats in their pen
blat irritably. In the yard our sons quarrel.
Mourning doves groan in the eaves.
Long hours ahead, till our job is done
and another begins.
Hunting scattered chickens in the bug-infested dew:
I watch you crouch along the scrubby poplar edge,
then circle back between the apple trees,
white hen skittering ahead, luminescent in the shabby
dark. Suddenly she drops her head and sits,
submissive as a girl. You've got her now; tuck up her feet
and carry her back home, then squat to mend the ragged fence.
A breath of sweat rises from your sunburnt neck,
salt and sweet. My love. Marry me, I say. You cast
an eye askance and shrug, I did. How odd it seems
that this is where we've landed: chasing chickens
through the woods at twilight, humid thunder rumpling
the summer sky, dishes washed, a slice of berry pie left
cooling on the counter. I've been saving it for you.

Liam Rector

Liam Rector was the founder and director of the graduate Writing Seminars at Bennington College. His books include three collections of poems: *American Prodigal, The Sorrow of Architecture* and *The Executive Director of the Fallen World.* He died in 2007.

In My Memory Eddie

Great-Uncle Eddie
Came to see us in the country.
Eddie looked exactly

Like Fred Astaire, floating
Fred Astaire (and Eddie
For some reason had on

A tuxedo, top hat, and spats).
I loved Eddie.
At eight I was already

Gone to the movies,
And Eddie looked exactly
Like a world just beyond,

Like a well-lit city just over
The hill. (I could not imagine
How Eddie came out of anything

Resembling our family.)
Eventually
Eddie hanged himself: just kicked out

The stool beneath him and, after
What I imagine was a brief struggle
On a lonely day for Eddie, Eddie

Was gone. And when I asked
My grandmother what would make Eddie
Do such a thing, she, in a moment

Of uncharacteristic candor,
Said Eddie simply could not stand
Getting older. I did not know it

At the time, but Eddie
Had already transported me
(Much as Astaire transported,

Much as startling art transports)
Towards the city, no matter
How much I loved the country.

(My grandmother said before I left
She could understand how I felt
About Eddie, and she apologized

For allowing me to so often sit up late with her
And experience
What she suddenly called

"Too many movies.")
And now that I live
In New York City,

Where nights
Of top hats, champagne,
And limousines actually are

Part of life, I, when really dressed,
Always raise a glass to Eddie.
I raise a glass to Eddie and to a time

When men believed so deeply
In style (or at least in
Their clothes) (or at least in the movies)

That when those men died (at least
When they chose to exercise
The option of ending themselves

By hanging)
They had the decency,
Before they kicked out their stools

(And I have documentation
To support this),
They had the damned decency

To make sure
They died with their hats on.
And these days I find

My greatest transport (outside
The movies, where I still live)
By remembering such days

As when Eddie
Came to visit us
In the country.

Alberto Ríos

Alberto Ríos, born in Nogales, AZ, is the author of eight books of poetry, three collections of short stories, and a memoir about growing up on the border called *Capirotada*. A National Book Award finalist and recipient of the Western Literature Association Distinguished Achievement Award, Ríos teaches at Arizona State University.

Refugio's Hair

In the old days of our family
My grandmother was a young woman
Whose hair was as long as the river.
She lived with her sisters on the ranch
La Calera— the Land of the Lime—
And her days were happy.

But her uncle Carlos lived there too,
Carlos whose soul had the edge of a knife.
One day, to teach her to ride a horse,
He made her climb on the fastest one,
Bare-back, and sit there
As he held its long face in his arms.

And then he did the unspeakable deed
For which he would always be remembered:
He called for the handsome baby Pirrín
And he placed the child in her arms.
With that picture of a Madonna on horseback
He slapped the shank of the horse's rear leg.

The horse did what a horse must,
Racing full toward the bright horizon.
But first he ran under the *álamo* trees
To rid his back of this unfair weight:
This woman full of tears
And this baby full of love.

When they reached the trees and went under,
Her hair, which had trailed her,
Equal in its magnificence to the tail of the horse,
That hair rose up and flew into the branches
As if it were a thousand arms,
All of them trying to save her.

The horse ran off and left her,
The baby still in her arms,
The two of them hanging from her hair.
The baby looked only at her
And did not cry, so steady was her cradle.
Her sisters came running to save them.

But the hair would not let go.
From its fear it held on and had to be cut,
All of it, from her head.
From that day on, my grandmother
Wore her hair short, like a scream,
But it was long like a river in her sleep.

In My Hurry

The curious lavender attentions to itself of the jacaranda
Stopped me, as through the leaves and small avenues

In late summer I made my way in love toward you.
The tree's flowering was an intimacy I had not earned,

A color of undergarment or something from the better
Pages in the book already underlined by classmates.

It was lavender or lilac, something from the hundred blues,
This color without rank and without help, standing there,

Giving me the gift over and again but high up, outside
My reach, which made my desire to touch it all the more.

The color and the tree, the moment and the lateness of season,
They joined in a gang of what I could see was a tangle of sinew,

So much muscle in search of the cover-skin of an arm,
The tree itself seeming all at once an arm unleashed,

Strength itself gone wild in its parts to the sky.
This was an arm that had stopped me—

How could I not have seen it? This tree was an arm
And more than arm, its muscle strung in everything

So that the tree—everything about it—the tree
Made itself of arm and leg, leg and neck, at angles,

At stops and starts and in bends, everything broken,
Everything but the lavender, which was flower,

So much lavender coming from what was left, what must be
A mouth, a thousand mouths, at once speaking

The lavender or the lilac, the blue, understood language.
These were match-tipped words asking the impossible of me,

Whatever I imagined the impossible to be: a bowl of cherries
In winter, or that I might come again by this place and stop.

Absent of reason, I could agree to anything addressing a tree.
The cherries were not much, I know, but what they meant,

Born of this exotic, all lavender and muscle, held me.
It was an equal and other necessity, calling to me in my hurry.

It was a tree in wild color calling to a tree in wild color,
And the lavender, I think you know what the lavender is.

The Gathering Evening

Shadows are the patient apprentices of everything.
They follow what might be followed,

Sit with what will not move.
They take notes all day long—

We don't pay attention, we don't see
The dark writing of the pencil, the black notebook.

Sometimes, if you are watching carefully,
A shadow will move. You will turn to see

What has made it move, but nothing.
The shadows transcribe all night.

Transcription is their sleep.
We mistake night as a setting of the sun:

Night is all of them comparing notes,
So many gathering that their crowd

Makes the darkness everything.
Patient, patient, quiet and still.

One day they will have learned it all.
One day they will step out, in front,

And we will follow them, be their shadows,
And work for our turn—

The centuries it takes
To learn what waiting has to teach.

Pattiann Rogers

Pattiann Rogers has published 13 books, most recently *Wayfare* (Penguin, 2008) and *Firekeeper, Revised and Expanded Edition*, (Milkweed, 2005). *The Grand Array*, her selected essays, was published in 2010 by Trinity University Press. Rogers is the recipient of two National Endowment for the Arts Grants, a Guggenheim Fellowship, and a Literary Award from the Lannan Foundation. She is the mother of two sons and has three grandsons. She lives with her husband, a retired geophysicist, in Colorado.

The Snow of Things

I don't know if Jesus ever walked
in snow, through a storm of snow
blowing icy pieces stinging against
his face, in his eyes, snow melting
and freezing again in his hair until
it hung in stiff cords on his shoulders,
against his forehead. I've never seen
him pictured that way.

I don't know if he ever witnessed snow,
Jesus, wrapped in robes that couldn't
keep out a winter wind of the mildest kind.
He would have had to swaddle his feet
in layers of cloth and around his sandals
to walk through the snow of a mountain
pass, using his staff along the narrows
of slippery rocky paths,

Once in a May storm, I saw a hummingbird
hovering momentarily outside the window,
caught in a late spring freeze and snow-filled
fog. He was tiny irridescent feathers of green
and rose. He was a flittering bead of living color
taking off against the grey monument of winter.

I wonder if people would have followed
Jesus, climbing a mountain through the snow,
gathering around him there to listen, the wind
screaming its own beatitudes, whipping up
sudden gusts and shifts of snow descending
again over them like night. Hooded,
crouched down close together and sleeted

with snow, they might have resembled
a flock of sheep huddled on the hillside.

Once I saw a work of art lying abandoned
in the hoarfrost and snow of a forest clearing,
Van Gogh's *Starry Night* lying frayed among
the stiff and rattling grasses, that deep swirling
blue sky of bursting suns and splitting stars slowly
being buried by pearl on icy pearl of drift.

He could have told them the parable
of the blindness of snow-filled fogs
and white-outs, or the parable of the linking
prisms and pattern of any single flake,
or the parable of the transfiguration
by snow of needles, thorns, and jagged
stones. The breath of his words might
have been seen as a holy ghost of warmth
in the paralysis of that killing cold.

I don't know if Jesus ever witnessed snow.
It may never have snowed in Galilee,
although it is written that he rose
to heaven in "raiments white as snow."

Co-evolution: Flowers, Tongues, Talents

1.

All those tongues lapping and sucking,
licking and probing, the flurry-hover
of feeding hermit hummingbirds
and clearwing moths, bee and butterfly
flutter on shaky petals, and the pinpricks
of bat claws, the shiver and rub of furry
heads and bodies pushing into the deepest
crevices for nectar, coming up dripping
sugar and powdered with pollen
for the next one—the lesser long-nosed bat
plunges with its bristly tongue, perfect
to sweep the sweetness of the saguaro
blossom, and the hawk moth's tongue
delves exactly to the far bottom end
of the comet orchid's narrow nectary,
and bumble bees with magic keys
are opening everywhere snapdragons
with magic locks.

2.

In those early days, when we came
upon flowers—dawning blues, golds
and violets, startling scarlets and pinks
growing in among the monotonous
greens—we were happy. Their perfume
rose spicy, sweet, nostalgic with sun-
and-moon fragrances. We fed,
though they were not food, left them
to bloom in our scratched-out plots.
Their seeds, mixed with the others,
we scattered and sowed.

And they thrived, all the while
cultivating the gentleness they required
in the bones of our hands, a finer
finesse in the discernment of our eyes,
urging our genes to a greater yearning
for beauty, an empathy with the vulnerable
in the muscle of our hearts.

3.

I would be a night pollinator,
my fur-covered wings of skin spread wide,
flying north from Mexico over the deserts
toward the mad musky fragrance
of the organ pipe cactus, melding
with its flowers swelling now
into their full budding.

I would be still, stationary, a blossom
of the lightest shade of lavender,
smooth as white in the night, scented,
sedate, rigorously accessible, undone
on the tip of the tallest stem.

In the Silence Following

After a freight train lumbers by,
hissing steam and grumbling curses,
metal screeching against metal, it passes
into the night (which is the empty
shadow of the earth), becoming soft
clinking spurs, a breathy whistle, low
bells clanking like tangled chains,
disappearing as if on lambskin wheels.

Something lingers then in the silence,
a reality I can't name. It remains as near
to a ghost as the thought of a ghost
can be, hovering like a dry leaf spirit
motionless in a hardwood forest absent
of wind, inexplicably heraldic. It is closest
to the cry of a word I should know
by never having heard it.

What hesitates in that silence possesses
the same shape as the moment coming
just after the lamp is extinquished
but before the patterned moonlight
on the rug and the window-squares
of moonlight on the wall opposite
become evident. That shift of light
and apprehension is a form I should know
by having so readily recognized it.

After the yelping dog is chastened
and a door slams shut on the winter evening
filled with snow and its illuminations,
someone standing outside in the silence
following might sense not an echo
or a reflection but the single defining
feature of that disappearance
permeating the frigid air.

When all the strings of the chord
are stilled and soundless, the hands
just beginning to lift from the keys,
when the last declaration of the last
crow swinging down into the broken
stalks of the corn field ceases, when
the river, roaring and bucking
and battering in its charge across
the land, calms its frothy madness
back to bed at last, then suspended
in the space of silence afterward
may be a promise, may be a ruse.

Kay Ryan

Kay Ryan became the U.S. Poet Laureate in 2008. Her most recent books are *The Best of It, New and Selected Poems* (2010), *The Niagara River* (2005), *Say Uncle* (2000), and *Elephant Rocks* (1996). Her awards include the 2004 Ruth Lilly Poetry Prize from The Poetry Foundation, a Guggenheim Fellowship, an Ingram Merrill Award, and a National Endowment for the Arts Fellowship. Ryan's work has been selected four times for *The Best American Poetry*. Her poems and essays have appeared in many journals and anthologies, have been used in the funny papers ("Boondocks"), and one was permanently installed at New York's Central Park Zoo. She lives in Marin County, California.

Blandeur

If it please God,
let less happen.
Even out Earth's
rondure, flatten
Eiger, blanden
the Grand Canyon.
Make valleys
slightly higher,
widen fissures
to arable land,
remand your
terrible glaciers
and silence
their calving,
halving or doubling
all geographical features
toward the mean.
Unlean against our hearts.
Withdraw your grandeur
from these parts.

The Fabric of Life

It is very stretchy.
We know that, even if
many details remain
sketchy. It is complexly
woven. That much too
has pretty well been
proven. We are loath

to continue our lessons,
which consist of slaps
as sharp and dispersed
as bee stings from
a smashed nest,
when any strand snaps—
hurts working far past
the locus of rupture,
attacking threads
far beyond anything
we would have said
connects.

The Best of It

However carved up
or pared down we get,
we keep on making
the best of it as though
it doesn't matter that
our acre's down to
a square foot. As
though our garden
could be one bean
and we'd rejoice if
it flourishes, as
though one bean
could nourish us.

Grazing Horses

Sometimes the
green pasture
of the mind
tilts abruptly.
The grazing horses
struggle crazily
for purchase
on the frictionless
nearly vertical
surface. Their
furniture-fine
legs buckle
on the incline,
unhorsed by slant
they weren't
designed to climb
and can't.

Sheryl St. Germain

Sheryl St. Germain is of Cajun and Creole descent. Her poetry books include *Going Home, The Mask of Medusa, Making Bread at Midnight, How Heavy the Breath of God, The Journals of Scheherazade,* and *Let It Be a Dark Roux.* She has published a book of translations of the Cajun poet Jean Arceneaux, *Je Suis Cadien,* and *Swamp Songs: The Making of an Unruly Woman,* essays about growing up in New Orleans. She directs the MFA Creative Writing Program at Chatham University in Pittsburgh.

Addiction

> *in memory of my brother,*
> *Jay St. Germain, 1958–1981*

The truth is I loved it,
the whole ritual of it,
the way he would fist up his arm, then
hold it out so trusting and bare,
the vein pushed up all blue and throbbing
and wanting to be pierced,
his opposite hand gripped tight as death
around the upper arm,

the way I would try to enter the vein,
almost parallel to the arm,
push lightly but firmly, not
too deep,
you don't want to go through
the vein, just in,
then pull back until you see
blood, then

hold the needle very still, slowly
shoot him with it.
Like that I would enter him,
slowly, slowly, very still,
don't move,
then he would let the fist out,
loosen his grip on the upper arm—

and oh, the movement of his lips
when he asked that I open my arms.
How careful,
how good he was, sliding
the needle silver and slender
so easily into me, as though
my skin and veins were made for it,
and when he had finished, pulled
it out, I would be coming
in my fingers, hands, my ear lobes
were coming, heart, thighs,
tongue, eyes and brain were coming,
thick and brilliant as the last thin match
against a homeless bitter cold.

I even loved the pin-sized bruises,
I would finger them alone in my room
like marks of passion;
by the time they turned yellow,
my dreams were full of needles.

We both took lovers who loved
this entering and being entered,
but when he brought over the
pale-faced girl so full of needle holes
he had to lay her on her back

like a corpse and stick the needle
over and over in her ankle veins
to find one that wasn't weary
of all that joy, I became sick
with it, but

you know, it still stalks my dreams,
and deaths make no difference:
there is only the body's huge wanting.

When I think of my brother
all spilled out on the floor
I say nothing to anyone.
I know what it's like to want joy
at any cost.

Sestina for the Beloved

I would wake at night to their breath,
the sound of them together, their want,
the smell of their thighs and bones,

even thousands of miles away I could feel him undress
her, could hear his voice speaking
her name. It is not my name, which is difficult.

What he had with the two of us was not difficult,
it was as easy as night's breath,
as easy as me not speaking,
not saying what it was I wanted
most, not saying I wanted to undress
only for one man, only for one to know the bones

of me, the bones of my mouth, the bones
of my feet, of my heart, even the difficult
bones of my eyes and sex, only one to undress
my voice, only one to sing my breath,
only one to know the forest of my want,
to know there is only one who is speaking

my name in dreams, speaking
my body as if even voice had bones.
What I want is uncompromising, what I want
is difficult,
is like wanting water to offer breath,
is like wanting fire to undress

itself, is about possession undressing
itself, is about what it means to be speaking
at all, is about belonging like breath
to the beloved, the one whose bones
are inside you like so many difficult
hearts, the only one you want to want

so much that all there is of living is that want.
I cannot tell you it will be easy to undress
your heart only for me, that I will not be difficult,
that some days and nights you may feel as if you are speaking
to no one, that some nights your bones
won't ache for the touch of another, the sweet breath

of the unknown, the undressed breath
of one less difficult, a bone-
want that I will recognize, whose ache I will honor and sweeten
          with my love, my many, many breaths.

Bread Pudding with Whiskey Sauce

French bread goes stale quickly,
like all intensely pleasurable things:
brothers die young and beautiful,
a mother's smile disappears
to sorrow, passion dies to sex,

but sorrow can be transformed
into bread pudding. Break
the bread into small bits
as if you were a priest,
and this the bread for communion.
The prayer you will say
has to do with remembering
what it was like to eat it
on the street in Paris, a baguette fresh
from the boulangerie, a good
loaf, how it made all the day's pain
worth it, the crust brown and hard,
but not too hard, the inside soft
and white and cool, you could squeeze
it like a sponge, oh holy sponge
of God! it speaks, it sings
in your mouth, it fills you for
little money—

Scald milk until you can smell it, and the smell
enters your body the way it did
when you were a baby and your mother
put a finger between your lips
and her nipple to break the suction,
and in your sleep you could smell
the milk, still warm on her nipple.

The milk must smell like that
before it is ready.

The bread goes into the scalded milk
which will enter it like one who
cannot be denied, will transform
the dry hard pieces into soft moist bits.
Add raisins and peach halves.
Beat eggs with sugar and cinnamon,
freshly grind allspice and nutmeg.
It will smell like Christmas,
it will smell like your mother's
happiness. Mix it all together,

bake. The house will fill
with goodness, with the smell
of grace.

Make a whiskey sauce with brandy,
sugar, eggs and milk. Eat the pudding
warm with the sauce poured
over it. The raisins will be swollen
and full of the milky, bready juice:
they will burst open in your mouth
when you bite. The bread will be
warm and fruity, sweet
and spiced as you wish you could
make your life, the peaches will be
a surprise when you bite into them,
and the brandy cream will warm
you like sun, like sheets,
like your father's breath,
your mother's perfume.

If you close your eyes
you may almost be able to remember
summer, a pool of cool water,
the voice of your dead brother,
a smile on your mother's face.

Ruth L. Schwartz

Ruth L. Schwartz is the author of five books, including *Edgewater*, a 2001 National Poetry Series selection, and *Dear Good Naked Morning*, which won the 2004 Autumn House Poetry Prize. The recipient of more than a dozen national awards, Schwartz teaches at Ashland University. She lives in Oakland, California, where she has a private practice in psychospiritual healing and leads Conscious Relationship workshops.

Come with Me

Come with me up to the rim of the city, the ridge of hill
which waits for us, forbidding, forgiving, implacable,
its naked bruises dry as stones in summer wet as soup of mud
in winter, forcing our feet up through rungs of bone,
sucking them down like a last proposal—saying
There is no other world
for us to love, only this one,
fantastic disaster—
where vultures stand beside the fallen
head of deer as at the head
of some great table, one by one waiting their turn
to sip the nectar of the eye.

The nectar of the I:

above the Eladio's Bail Bond billboard, its grinning
promises, its opened metal doors—*Lo Sacamos
Del Bote Hoy*. Above the city storefront churches, *Temple of Love*
boarded and sealed, *Temple of the Word*,
the cars hiked up on rusted wheels in shaggy driveways,
the slinking cats with oil-dragged tails, who cry and cry
for food, but run when we come near—

Where is my life?

Is it in Socios Garage, grimy, unheated, impatient as tires are
levered onto my car, or is it in the five-week-old pit bull
I hold while I wait, because it's there, because it shakes
with cold or fear, groans like a dying man until I wrap my scarf
around the tremble, and it rests? Is it in the dog outside, already

trained and chained, the years of meanness layered onto him, the heart
which doesn't speak, but snarls? Or in what hasn't happened yet?
And where does it go when I leave, the puppy whimpers back to its kicked
cardboard, when I drive away?

Come with me like the junkie pounding
on the window of the pickup,
If you love me, open the door.
If you love me, open the door.
If you ever loved me, open the goddamned door—

until I think she must be right, the door itself is damned.

Now she screams off down the street,
staggers, crumples to the curb.
The truck speeds through the light, swerves, backs up.

Sometimes that's all I want: to love you,
whoever you are.

Below us the ruthlessly quarried water,
two deer nosing their way to the far shore
to drink.

It's spring; even the dumpsters gleam.
A woman climbs inside and digs,
uncovering a whole Big Mac, still wrapped;
I watch her hand it to her man
the way a bride forks cake into the mouth
of her new husband, in the kind of light which lives
between two faces, and refuses nothing.

Sex

It's the church of pleasure and sorrow.
All its intricate windows have been smashed.
It holds the places where the stars
opened inside us, blood on shattered glass.
It holds the light between us,
brighter than anything—
except for the equal measure of darkness,
sealed inside our bodies,

which eclipses it.
O stubborn animal, celestial, transforming.
O spasm which loves nothing but itself,
aware of nothing but itself, grateful to nothing.
O firefly which asks, What do you most want?
as it sputters out.

Trees in Wind

How sure they are, the trees in wind,
gangly, manic, drugged, exuberant; rustling,
reckless, lost; wringing a thousand hands
over a thousand graves; placing long fingers
to long lips, saying Hush, all is not lost
that you think is lost; saying There are costs
you have not yet paid. They know more than you
want to know, you who want to know

everything. They know more than that and aim
to tell it all night long, in song you can't repeat
or translate; Don't forget, they say, and pray, equally
to the gods of wind and ground; chance and purpose;
air and failure; gods of all things fallen, their limbs
block the way, arrow toward the way.

Highway Five Love Poem

for Anna

This is a love poem for all the tomatoes
spread out in the fields along Highway Five,
their gleaming green and ruddy faces like a thousand
moons prostrate in praise of sun.
And for every curd of cloud,
clotted cream of cloud spooned briskly
by an unseen hand into the great blue bowl,
then out again, into a greedy mouth.
Cotton baled up beside the road,
altars to the patron saint of dryer lint.
Moist fudge of freshly-planted dirt.
Shaggy neglected savage grasses
bent into the wind's designs.
Sheep scattered over the landscape like fuzzy confetti,
or herded into stubbled funnels, moving like rough water
toward its secret source.
Egrets praying in the fields like
white-cloaked priests.
A dozen wise and ponderous cows
suddenly spurred to run, to gallop, even,
down a flank of hill.
Horses for sale, goats for sale, nopales for sale, orange groves for sale,
topless trailers carrying horses,
manes as loose and lovely as tomorrow in our mouths,
and now a giant pig, jostling majestic in the open
bed of a red pickup,

and now a fawn-colored coyote
framed between the startled fruit trees
who looks directly at me before loping back
into the world he owns.
Even the bits of trash are alive,
and chase each other in the wind, and show their underwear.
Even the sparrows hop like the spirit,
sustain themselves on invisible specks,
flutter and plummet, rise straight up like God.

Perseid

August meteor shower

While they're here I hold them
like my breath. They deepen the sky
like blood in my body, I'm glad to offer
my body like this—a small craft
over fields of water,
where light can fall, be lost, be caught,
be held.
I'm naked in my chair,
facing the window.
If I were outside I'd want to look up
and see someone naked in every window.
I think we need
the difficult river, we need the absence of tenderness
so love can come like shooting stars
if it comes.

Tim Seibles

Tim Seibles is the author of *Hammerlock, Body Moves*, and *Hurdy-Gurdy*. His newest collection of poems, *Buffalo Head Solos*, was published by the Cleveland State University Poetry Center in 2004. A former NEA fellow and winner of an Open Voice Award from the 63rd Street Y in New York City, he teaches courses for Old Dominion University's English Department and MFA in Writing Program.

Four Takes of a Similar Situation
or *The World Mus Be Retarded*

Fine as that Mexican mommy was?
Had me thinkin *jalapeño, hot tamale, arroz*
con pollo an' every other Spanish food
I ever heard about. Hell, I gotta
little bit of a accent just looking at'er, homebrew.
Yes, indeedy, sweetie, that girl's stuff
was **sho-nuff** meaty. Talkin 'bout
leave that girl alone—is ya crazy?
Even them gay cats be leanin when she bust in!
Had that cinnamon-colored skin
all squeezed into that tight yellow jump-suit
and that smooth-ass salsa-fied strut:
make a brotha wanna do them no-hand push-ups, yo—
make you wanna put ya shoes on backward
And run over yourself, make you
mus gotta getta new car, a new pair a'pants
or at leas' a new attitude.

Fine as that sista was?
Wit them tight-ass jeans ripped up jus right—
you know the kind: look like somebody
let Tony the Tiger customize them bad boys
till it was just a cryin shame
how them big choclit thighs come screamin
outta there. Shee-it! I was so bent over looking
I coulda tied my shoes wit my teeth—and
she saw that I was seein and she gave me one a'them
uh-huh, yeah looks, like she knew
that I **betta** know she got all the groceries

in one bag. Home-slice, if that honey
had got a holt'a me it'd been
Humpty-Dumpty all over again—
all the king's horses and all the king's men
woulda jus shook their heads and said, *Yeah, mothafucka,*
you shoulda **known** *you wasn't man enough.*

Fine as that lady was?
Big as China is, they couldn't fit
no more fine behind the Great Wall
than Ms. Asia had in her lef earlobe. I won't even
tell you about that thin little light-blue top
she was wearin—**no** bra   **no**where
no how, home-page!
Nipples hard as trigonometry too—
makin that serious jailbreak. Yo,
I gotta cramp in my gums jus from tonguin
the maybe's, baby! And we most certainly do **not**
wanna discuss that black satin sheet a'hair
she had sheenin till a brotha mus gotta
wear shades. And had the nerve to have them rich,
full-bodied Maxwell House lips—damn near
like a sista. Yeah, you can do the *The Monkey*
and the *Philly Dog* too, but you can't tell me
that that Chinese Chile wasn't sho-nuff bad.
Talkin' bout who I should and shouldn' be checkin out:
The whole world mus be retarded.

Fine as Ms. white girl was?
Fuck all y'all crazy mothafuckas!
I don know if she was prejudice or not,
but the honey had them big, strong-ass
white girl calves—and one a'them slit skirts
that talk to ya when she walk—
and backed it up witta little bit a'bootie:
I'm telling you dead-up, yo—I was ready
to forgive the sins of her fathers right then and **there**!
Had that kinda curly, halfway frizzy red-brown hair.
She coulda been Jewish, Scottish, Octoroon, Italian—
only her hairdresser knows, hometown, but
if the honey had said, *looka'here, mista,*
I think I wanna waltz—brotha, you betta know
I had my dancin shoes wit me.

The Caps On Backward

It was already late inside me.

City air. City light.
Houses in a row.

14-year-olds. Nine of us.
Boys.

Eight voices changed. Already rumbling
Under the governance of sperm.

But *his* voice, bright as a kitten's
tickled our ears like a piccolo.

So, we'd trill ours up—*What's wrong, man?*
Cat got your balls? Then watch him shrink
Like a dick in a cool shower.

Every day. Bit by bit. Smaller.

I think about it now—how bad he wanted to be
with us   how, alone with the radio

he must have worked his throat
to deepen the sound.

The blunt edge of boys   teething on each other.
The serrated edge of things in general.

Maybe he spilled grape soda on my white sneaks.
Can't remember.

But I knocked him down, gashed him with my fists.

It was summer. A schoolyard afternoon.
Older boys by the fountain.

Yeah, kick his pussy ass.

Nobody said it, but it was time.
We knew it   the way trees know shade
doesn't belong to them.

The low voices knew.
And the caps on backward.

It must go something like this:

First, one cell flares in the brain. Then
the two cells next to that. Then more and more.

Until something far off begins to flicker.
Manhood, the last fire lit before the blackening woods.

The weak one separated from the pack.

The painted bird. The bird, painted.

Latin

Words slip into a language the way
white-green vines slide between slats in a fence.

A couple opens the door to a restaurant,
sees the orange and black colors everywhere

and the waitress grins, "Yeah,
a little Halloween overkill, huh."

Overkill, a noun for all of us
fidgeting under the nuclear umbrella—

but for that instant, it just meant too many
paper skeletons, too many hobgobbled balloons.

———————

I know a woman who is tall with dark hair
who makes me think of honeysuckle

whenever she opens her legs. Not just the flower
but dew-soaked music itself   *honeysuckle*   like a flavor.

And I remember the first time years back
when LaTina told me what it was we had

between our eight-year-old front teeth
that April afternoon, our hands wet

with rain from the vines. "Honey sickle," she said,
while the white flower bloomed from the side of her mouth,

and I had a new sweetness on my tongue and a word
I'd never heard before. How was it decided in the beginning?

This word   for *this* particular thing,
a sound attached to a shape or a feeling forever.

————————

All summer long the cicadas don't know
what we call them.

They sneak from the ground every year after dark,
break out of their shells right into the language,

and it holds them like a net made of nothing
but the need to make strange things familiar.

All summer long they rattle trees like maracas
until they become part of our weather—

quiet in rain, crazy in hard sun,
so we say *those cicadas sure make enough noise, huh.*

And the noise of that sentence   heard ten-thousand times
becomes a name for *us* the cicadas keep trying to say.

————————

I think about dying sometimes,
not the sudden death in the movies—

the red hole in the shirt, the eyes
open like magazines left on a waiting room table—

not that, but withering slowly like a language,
barely holding on until everything

I ever did or said   is just gone, absorbed
into something I would never have imagined—

like Latin. Not lost completely, but moved away
from that bright, small place

between seeing   and naming,
between the slow roll of ocean

and the quick intake of air
that would fill the word *wave.*

Rebecca Seiferle

Rebecca Seiferle was awarded a Lannan Foundation Poetry Fellowship in 2004. She is the author of four poetry collections, most recently *Wild Tongue* (Copper Canyon, 2007), and two book-length translations: *The Black Heralds* (Copper Canyon, 2003) and *Trilce* (Sheep Meadow, 2002). Her collection, *Bitters* (Copper Canyon, 2001), won the Western States Book Award and a Pushcart Prize. Her poetry, translations, and essays have appeared in over 25 anthologies, including *Best American Poetry 2000*, and her poetry has been translated into several languages. The founding editor of *The Drunken Boat*, www.thedrunkenboat.com, she teaches at the Art Center Design College in Tucson, Arizona.

The Shearing

Each hour they grow fewer, the splayed
lipped, white drift of the apple blossoms
falling to wind, late frost, and 90 lumens
of the brilliance of paper falling, shredded
to the floor, even incised with the black burning
of someone else's sacred defoliation, love is not
transitory enough but snail-like shapes
self to shell, or hooks like scorpion tail
in crevice or niche, long past luck or life.
Who wants to love forever? Love should fall
like the apple blossoms, die at the kiss
of a bee, learn to perish, come to an end.

Bitter Herb

I had to lie down in the earth myself,
plowing the sand
with my belly, propelling myself
under the wire fence
that kept us apart. I'd stood there,
for a long time on the other side, just
clinging to a post, until the sheriff said
someone would have to cross over
and identify the body. Through
the gauntlet of the earth—the scrambling
weeds, the willows striking my shoulders
like whips—I crawled and bent
and shuffled until I was beside my brother—
his face as if someone had taken it apart
and put it back together in an awry

riddle of wood. Death was a riddle
to Gilgamesh when he went looking for a way
to bring his brother, Enkidu, back to life.
He was told to find *the plant*
of opening, a mysterious herb
that grew by the banks of a stagnant pond,
like this one, at the edge of a desert waste,
and was warned that it would prick his own hand
as he cut free its bitter root. On the way back
Gilgamesh stopped to rest and bathe;
as he drifted back into himself, full
of relief, reverie, and rescue,
a snake came out of the grasses
and swallowed the herb of eternal life.
But these waters, near where my brother lay,
were still and empty. The plant of opening,
rose-colored, ambrosial, did not shimmer
like a prism in the murky depths. My brother
had aimed at his own heart, not once,
but twice, firing down that pathway
of the soul. And the only sign
of a snake was his discarded skin.
When I said "Yes, that is
my brother, Clinton Seiferle,"
I heard the fingers of the dead snapping
around me. They would not let me touch him.
He was still evidence, the last witness
to the story they thought they would find
in the gleanings of his fingernails,
in his shirt as if shredded by a swarm of bees
from the powder burns, in the ground seething
with ants, the flies swarming and settling
upon him, his dead dog that lay at his feet.
He had come to the edge of that abyss
where fear came out of the water
and consumed whatever could have
brought him back. Three days later,
I'm the only one who comes back
to life, realizing that I'm still
wearing the same clothes, my jeans
prickly with nettles. As I slip out
of the black and stinging fabric, I find
the pockets are full of sand. How can
I give this earth to the waters? For touching
these fine grains, these sparkling abrasions,
it seems I touch all that remains
of the lost face of my brother.

Homophobia

I could say that discovering such ugliness
in a friend is like standing on my own porch,
barefooted, ready to jump into the sweet grass,
still soft with spring newness, and finding coiled—
its outline broken by fractals of sand—the blunt
venomous head of a prairie rattler,
lying in wait, striking out at whatever
comes within range of its desire or fear.
Throwing itself forward, the snake
would be as certain of its normality as my friend is,
coiled around the memory of the man who died,
rattling with indignation at the news
that he died of AIDS, and I, I could be the mouse,
frozen with timidity, having blundered
on an exceptionally beautiful morning
into this toxic stare, struck dead on the spot,
the hypodermic lullaby poisoning my conscience
as much as muscles of my throat and heart. But
the snake is beautiful, those diamonds etched
along its spine as newly green as the fragrant sage,
and the mouse, the mouse being swallowed
would become of use, its cells, mother
and father of new snakeskins, and I could turn
back, refrain from jumping off the step, and the snake
would slide into the grass, its body a long sigh
breathing itself away, leaving me to thank heaven
for such a glimpse, and such a narrow escape.
The snake would not, as my friend does,
keep flinging itself at a dead man, talking about
how repulsive it must have been, how shocking
to imagine the lovemaking of two people
of the same sex, though she keeps imagining
it again and again. As if she held her soul
in an artificial grip, forcing its jaws open
to the naked drip and chill—though a snake,
so pried upon a petri dish,
would be milked of all its poison.

Muse

In later years, my daughter said to me
that when she was little and before
sister and brother, growing up in that trailer
that bordered the desert, she thought there was someone

else who lived with us, and it was only later that she knew
there was no one else, just the poetry, that other child that I was always
	singing to,
nursing in my arms, chanting, as I passed back and forth between those
	rooms.

Faith Shearin

Faith Shearin's first book, *The Owl Question*, won the May Swenson Award and a second, *The Empty House*, was published by Word Press. She has received fellowships from the Fine Arts Work Center in Provincetown, the National Endowment for the Arts, and the Barbara Deming Memorial Fund. She has been a visiting writer at the Interlochen Arts Academy, Carver Center for the Arts and American University. Recent work appears in *Ploughshares* and *North American Review* and has been read aloud on Garrison Keillor's "Writer's Almanac." She lives with her husband and daughter in Kitty Hawk, North Carolina and Baltimore, Maryland.

Shopping

My husband and I stood together in the new mall
which was clean and white and full of possibility.
We were poor so we liked to walk through the stores
since this was like walking through our dreams.
In one we admired coffee makers, blue pottery
bowls, toaster ovens as big as televisions. In another,

we eased into a leather couch and imagined
cocktails in a room overlooking the sea. When we
sniffed scented candles we saw our future faces,
softly lit, over a dinner of pasta and wine. When
we touched thick bathrobes we saw midnight

swims and bathtubs so vast they might be
mistaken for lakes. My husband's glasses hurt
his face and his shoes were full of holes.
There was a space in our living room where
a couch should have been. We longed for

fancy shower curtains, flannel sheets,
shiny silverware, expensive winter coats.
Sometimes, at night, we sat up and made lists.
We pressed our heads together and wrote
our wants all over torn notebook pages.
Nearly everyone we loved was alive and we

were in love but we liked wanting. Nothing
was ever as nice when we brought it home.
The objects in stores looked best in stores.
The stores were possible futures and, young
and poor, we went shopping. It was nice
then: we didn't know we already had everything.

Retriever

My father, in middle age, falls in love with a dog.
He who kicked dogs in anger when I was a child,
who liked his comb always on the same shelf,
who drank martinis to make his mind quiet.

He who worked and worked—his shirts
wrapped in plastic, his heart ironed
like a collar. He who—like so many men—
loved his children but thought the money

he made for them was more important
than the rough tweed of his presence.
The love of my father's later years is
a Golden Retriever—more red

than yellow—a nervous dog who knows
his work clothes from his casual ones,
can read his creased face, who waits for
him at the front door—her paws crossed

like a child's arms. She doesn't berate him
for being late, doesn't need new shoes
or college. There is no pressure to raise her
right, which is why she chews the furniture,

pees on rugs, barks at strangers who
cross the lawn. She is his responsible soul
broken free. She is the children he couldn't
come home to made young again.

She is like my mother but never angry,
always devoted. He cooks for his dog—
my father who raised us in restaurants—
and takes her on business trips like

a wife. Sometimes, sitting beside her
in the hair-filled van he drives to make
her more comfortable, my father's dog
turns her head to one side as if

thinking and, in this pose, more than
one of us has mistaken her for a person.
We would be jealous if she didn't make
him so happy—he who never took

more than one trip on his expensive
sailboat, whose Mercedes was wrecked

by a valet. My mother saw him behind
the counter of a now-fallen fast food

restaurant when she was nineteen.
They kissed beside a river where fish
no longer swim. My father who was
always serious has fallen in love with

a dog. What can I do but be happy for him?

The Name of a Fish

If winter is a house then summer is a window
in the bedroom of that house. Sorrow is a river
behind the house and happiness is the name

of a fish who swims downstream. The unborn child
who plays in the fragrant garden is named Mavis:
her red hair is made of future and her sleek feet

are wet with dreams. The cat who naps
in the bedroom has his paws in the sun of summer
and his tail in the moonlight of change. You and I

spend years walking up and down the dusty stairs
of the house. Sometimes we stand in the bedroom
and the cat walks towards us like a message.

Sometimes we pick dandelions from the garden
and watch their white heads blow open
in our hands. We are learning to fish in the river

of sorrow; we are undressing for a swim.

Deborah Slicer

Deborah Slicer lives with her horses and cats near Missoula, Montana. Her poems have appeared in several magazines and have been featured on Garrison Keillor's radio program "The Writer's Almanac." *The White Calf Kicks* won the 2003 Autumn House Poetry Prize. She teaches philosophy at the University of Montana.

Mousey and Me

If you think like a Holstein
who's stood cramped in a grey stall

all six months of winter, waiting
for the first buttercups to push up snow in the pasture

like clabber rising through milk,
then you know the penalty

for swatting the bony man in thick glasses
with a piss-soaked tail

that stings like fire thrown in his face:
You get a beating with

whatever's handy—the bucket, a filthy rope,
his fists—on your rump

and maybe all over the head.
Sometimes, when the pain is unbearable

his brothers will have to stop him, throw him into a snowbank,
with his pride.

(Why do you do it, anyway?
                    Who knows...
He's such an easy target.)

When he leans his strawberry blonde head against you
as he's milking,

mumbling all his heartache
into your belly, usually

the extra weight there's all right.
But when it gets meaner,

when he threatens to move into Floweree and
get rid a all a ya !

then it's not so easy to stand there, take it, or
the strap.

His freckled hands are a fact of life,
and at least they're efficient. Now and then

there's sugar in those fists
that he makes you work a little for—

haul a wagon of muck from the barn
after he's grappled an hour just to teach you the harness,

maybe lower your head down
like you're grateful, demure,

act interested in the neighbor's prize bull, even though he's certifiably
stupid.

That man?
Mousey and me knew him about the same.

After Metaphysics, or When the Fly Leaves the Flybottle

Just when I'm ready to call in the day and put it to bed without supper
you send the mockingbird who plays with his musical zipper,
exposing the World's underlife.
You send perfume from the autumn olive
whose septillion flowering ears are full of bees
singing songs for the revolution.
Out back Jake's Creek is speaking in tongues—
Missed you-missed you-missed you.

You wear me down, obsessively
rubbing your hands along my better judgment,
kissing the upturned noses of all my higher principles, until
my clothes are big as a mast sail,
until my longing leavens one thousand wedding cakes,
my longing is an undertow, and all the tourist beaches are posted: Danger.

Come for me—I'll break off my arms and will them to a body
of water, hang my legs up in overalls at night

so they won't come after us, feed
English to the birds in sweet pats of butter.
Then our loving gets raucous—
white moths yapping their wings—you wag, you
    wag in the little fingerbowl of me.

Your verbstem assumes declensions of mythic proportions.
My vowel sounds open on the south-most *hallelujah* side of the mountain.
Then metaphysically speaking we've stopped speaking
metaphorically—Silence

nuanced as a landscape in snow.

December 10
    —B.

Last night a single goose flew over the house,
throwing her voice out ahead of herself:
a stone
skipping out across still water.

A joy ride.

Then she followed the beautiful sound
across a meadow of moonlight and snow,
a clean bowl
waiting to be filled with the most delicious thing.

Pastoral

Let the roadside go to chicory
and gall-
of-the-earth, and the hillside go
to clover
and everlasting
pea, and the road itself
to the barred belly of the blacksnake
and the tarot belly
of the tortoise,
while burdock and poke
choke the corn
out of the fields,
and morning glories run wild
over the immaculate gardens—
let thistle grow tall
and defiantly purple.
And let there be no noise,

just the pileated woodpecker
screeching
like a wild monkey,
heat,
and the wind stumbling through a long row of pines,
the unabashed turning
of leaves
asking
the wind's *blessings, blessings, blessings.*

Gerald Stern

Gerald Stern, born in Pittsburgh, Pennsylvania in 1925, is the author of 15 books of poetry including *This Time: New and Selected Poems*, which won the 1998 National Book Award and a book of personal essays titled *What I Can't Bear Losing*. He has won the Ruth Lilly Prize and the Wallace Stevens Award, and his *Early Collected: Poems from 1965–1992* was published by W. W. Norton in the spring of 2010.

Casals

You could either go back to the canary
or you could listen to Bach's unaccompanied Suites
for which, in both cases, you would have the same sofa,
and you will be provided with a zigzag quilt to sleep
under and a glass-top table and great fury,
for out of those three things music comes;
nor should you sleep if even the round muscles
below the neck fall loose from their stringy moorings
for you would miss a sob and you would miss
a melody á la red canary
and á la white as well and á la canary,
perched, as the cello was, on top of a wooden box
and a small musician perched on top of the cello
and every night a church full of wild canaries.

In Beauty Bright

In beauty-bright and such it was like Blake's
lily and though an angel he looked absurd
dragging a lily out of a beauty-bright store
wrapped in tissue with a petal drooping,
nor was it useless—you who know it know
how useful it is—and how he would be dead
in a minute if he were to lose it though
how do you lose a lily? *His* lily was white
and he had a foolish smile there holding it up like
a candelabrum in his right hand facing the
mirror in the hall nor had the endless
centuries started yet nor was there one thorn
between his small house and the beauty-bright store.

Died in the Mills

Then, fifty dollars for a Hungarian
say a black dress to go to the funeral
and shoes with soles for the three oldest, that leaves
a dollar fifty for the feast but I'd say
what a dollar was worth then you could have
a necktie if you wanted and paprikash
for twenty or thirty and strudel with apples and nuts
and violins—he favored the violin—
and it is not just poets that love meadows
and take their sneakers off and their socks to walk
on the warm rocks and dip their tender white feet
in the burning freezing water and then bend down
precariously to pick up a froglet and sight
the farthest lonely tree and note the wind
moving quickly through the grasses their last summer.

Norman Riding

All that morning he had a merciful attitude
and this is what made him remember the swamp maple
that blocked the sunlight from his kitchen window
though it was idiotic to remember a tree that
anyhow labored over its own death and hung on
like some mad ninety-five year old on pills;
and the crash itself was gracious for the tree
could still bend, and when it cracked a hundred
things went flying and he who rode it he went
flying too, with bladed saw, his two arms
either cheering or keeping the branches away
from his sawdust glasses, all of which enlightened
his whole yard and set his other trees free;
though how pathetic a giant is on the ground
covered with ants he hates and here and there
a squirrel or a bird ignoring him as it nibbled
and gobbled and drank and spit and chewed as if
they all were eating and drinking at a funeral,
only the corpse was lying dead in the dirt
with his skin peeling and his hair blowing and his mouth
opening on its hinges, the great creases
clarified by the sun, the song insane.

The Farewell

Who can account for my glove, God save him, give him
a prize, bring him a goat, where are the bats
to go with my balls and where are the gloves, the webbed

and oiled and pocketed, where are the mothers
who waited for us when we got off the street cars?
Where was the war? Why is there a basket of
softballs beside my wooden pig, and wasn't I
an expert at counting the troops on their side and ours?

What does it mean to march Diagonally
the way the Americans did in Barcelona
on their way to the harbor where every woman
came out to show her gratitude and every
balcony was full, and every street
was covered in flowers, and horses and trucks were smothered
since grief is shown that way and they may have sung
or they may have marched to the ships without a word
though mostly crazed and compromised for they were
communards of a sort among the ugly who
hated peasantries of any sort and
gave short shrift to grief, including the dead
softball team and the four broken gloveless fingers
among the stages of grief, even the songs
one of the stages since grief is a dead wolf
lying on its side and a bird eating
the black intestines—and the bird eaten—for they
have to die too, witness the smell in the woods,
witness the cat, witness Birdie her sticks up,
her eyes X's, witness the ghosts being lowered
seventy years later nor button nor regalia.

Virgil Suarez

Virgil Suarez is working on a new collection of poems entitled *Indigo* about the 90-mile trek Elian Gonzalez and his mother undertook to the United States. His most recent collection of poems is *90 Miles: New and Selected* published by the University of Pittsburgh Press. When he is not writing, he is out riding his motorcycle up and down Florida's blue highways. He lives in Key Biscayne and watches out for hurricanes and balseros.

A History of Rain

There's something mind-numbing about waking
    up to rain on a Monday afternoon. Its drip-drip
sounds filtering in through the windows.

I remember those days in Cuba when up early
    for school, I knew that the rain would not
make it any easier on me. I waited for my parents

to take me to school, already dreading the hour.
    Gang boys' harassment enough, and now rain.
I hated the rain's mocking fall, its sounds,

Its own slickness on the streets, light blurring
    on the windshields of cars. I've always thought
of blue dying, a terrible melancholia gripping

the spirit. I remember my hatred of wet. Frogs
    in Havana ready to croak from some dark V
of a plantain frond. The unexpected, a skidding

of tires through our soggy lives.
    I hear it now, beyond my study, its beckoning—
Its power over me more than what I can say here.

Death breathes in the sound of rain. You hear it too?

La sangre llama

A flash-flicker of light on the back of a leaf,
when one carp gobbles up air on a pond's surface,
bubbles pop, small ripples form, in my hands

the hardness of pebbles, a rock in the chest
when bad news comes from the sick island,
la isla, the only one I know about, care about,
a lover's map of nostalgia, how penumbra
and solitude whip themselves into a coil
of longing for what can never be, must not
be remembered, how the child walks back
each day, from school, from church, a song
of the lost on his lips—what lasts here?
                         Bliss
of *exilio*, a man who can never find his way
back. The sight of water makes him dizzy,
his eyes blink out the images of a life lived
between splendor and shadow, between anger
and the cut of a serrated knife, *la sangre amarga*
on the horizon.
                  When he dreams at night,
he visualizes all those who've followed him here,
through the darkness, through so much water,
to arrive in this shelter where one sigh crumbles
this temple to remembrance he's built blow
by blow, memory by memory, inextinguishable
fire, hot embers from which he rises, burns anew.

After Lorca's "The Ballad of the Sleepwalker"

In this liquid world of the tropics, seen by your own
      eyes, verdigris is precisely the color. Where water
ebbs and flows over river rock, worn smooth, flushed

      with a patina of lichen, mossy tufts kissed in cracks.
The palm trees are regal in their new dress of fronds.
      Okay, *verde* like its coconuts. A snapping turtle

suns on a half submerged log, its head an arrow, still
      under its heavy, duckweed-veiled carapace. Who
would mistake it for a rock? This panorama's radiance

      is what must have driven the crew in Columbus' ships
to dive in and swim ashore. The history of their journey
      drowning in their mouths. Call it Green Surrender.

At midday, white light blanches the sand, the water,
      turning everything gauze. This silken filter.
Heaven's color. True color exalted in the eyes of God.

Jaibas

The Cubans on Key Biscayne
know them as *jaibas*, these bluish

crabs that appear en masse
on the steamy roads, between

the medians, under the beige
tendril-like roots of the mighty

banyans, by the coconuts palms—
they invade the key on a mating,

eating spree once a year—such
urgency in the scuttling ways—

squashed by the cars, they stink
up the place. One day here,

gone the next. Beachcombers
fill buckets with them, take

them home to boil, eat—
the crabs simply want to cross

from one end of the shore
to the other, find a mate.

How can the Cubans
not be jealous? Unlike these crabs,

their own water crossings
have never been this easy

or portentous.

Julie Suk

Julie Suk's books include *Heartwood, Medicine Woman, The Angel of Obsession,* and *The Dark Takes Aim* (Autumn House Press, 2003). She lives in Charlotte, North Carolina.

Where We Are

Three a.m., the house a foreign country I wake in,
same language but a different inflection,
a creak on the stair a harbinger,
this jolt into insomnia an alert.

In an etching by Goya, demons perch on a bedpost
and clamor for the sleeper's heart.

Long ago we knelt for prayers
but those children have slept for years,
dreams merging, child into beast.
                    Somewhere
a truck explodes and bodies bloom
with the fleshy extravagance of peonies—
                    forgive me,
not petals but a scream settling on entrails,
bone, meat, our betrayals piling in gutters.

It should be obvious where the fault lies,
yet we continue to build there, the structure
collapsing into itself, the century in ruins.
                    Somewhere
a trail remains, linking our inlands,
the path to summers in the mountains
where a halo of hummingbirds
crowns the feeder,
rock hectored by a snow-fed river,
mist from the falls beading our hair.

Moving as we do from the body
and its parochial demands to lessons of love,

you might say we succeed as often as not,
on call even as we sleep.
                              Even as we sleep,
the cry of a puma cracks the night.

Rounds

When I held my first son,
how perfect he seemed.
Driving home late,
we would sing rounds
O how lovely is the evening
his head nodding to my lap.

Blessings on that third
of our lives spent in sleep,
the plots of the day
left dangling.

Once I drove by a woman
clinging to a viaduct's ledge,
police, priest, and the curious
crowded below, the road
curving past into a benign
vista of cows and trees.

Blessings on those moments of reprieve
grabbed before dropping into nightmare.

How could my son fracture,
unaware of the split?
Ominous, the day I waited
on his porch, cake in hand
as if food could assuage
a mind reeling off.

Get out! Get out! The door slammed.
What I dread is a stand-off,
barricades, guns, police
with no choice but to shoot.

Blessings on the daughter
who ripens with a life
that turns us around again,
this time, we hope,
the helix of notes
descending in tune.

For a while we let pass
what Aeschylus said,
how at night
the pain that can't forget
falls drop by drop
upon the heart.

The moon floats off,
the dog whimpers under the steps.
How lovely the evening
with a child on my lap,
a circle of us singing
heedless of the dark taking aim.

Divorce

A tornado rips
the skin off a town.

In the aftermath
silence.

Someone facing you
wants to speak but can't quite
articulate the bad news.

A roof set down miles away.
A tattered sleeve flapping
from a stripped branch.

Everything gone
gone the woman sobs
plucking at this this
and this remnant.

Stalking

I could barely see,
but shot at what moved,
followed blood on the leaves
to the place the buck fell,
the body still warm,
eyes not yet glazed.

Kneeling down
I slit the throat
and pushed away
in case he kicked—

the way the dying do,
protesting to the last
regardless of pain.

Baby, my father used to say,
squeeze the trigger gentle-like.

Blood on the kitchen floor,
the smell of neat's-foot oil,
a clean stock.

I relish the flesh
of roasted venison,
its pungent taste
bursting on the tongue.

There isn't a bone
I wouldn't gnaw
to marrow, and suck.

Hungry, hungry—
remember that when I ease
up to you.

Geode

Admit it, we're drawn to the mysterious
like this geode opened after long darkness.

A rim of agate around amethyst—
clutch of daggers, flashy lights.

What a surprise to find
the basic compounds long-solidified.

Desire, envy, spite—aren't we all here?

Geodes smoldering in a river bank.
The most coveted disclosure—

a crevice opening on murderous thoughts
vitrified, the knife stilled before the plunge,
the bomb imploding into smoky quartz.

Soil and sand are fraught with minute crystals.

Forgetful of who we are,
we walk over ourselves every day.

Mary Szybist

Mary Szybist grew up in Williamsport, Pennsylvania. Her first collection of poems, *Granted*, was published in 2003 by Alice James Books, and was a finalist for the National Book Critics Circle Award. She is the recipient of a Witter Bynner Award from the Library of Congress and a fellowship from the National Endowment for the Arts. Her poems have appeared in *Virginia Quarterly Review, Poetry, The Kenyon Review*, and other journals. She is a graduate of the University of Virginia and the Iowa Writers' Workshop, and she lives in Portland, Oregon where she teaches at Lewis & Clark College.

The Troubadours etc.

Just for this evening, let's not mock them.
Not their curtsies or cross-garters
Or ever recurring pepper trees in their gardens
Promising, promising.

At least they had ideas about love.

All day we've driven past cornfields, past cows poking their heads
Through metal contraptions to eat.
We've followed West 84, and what else?
Irrigation sprinklers fly past us, huge wooden spools in the fields,
Lounging sheep, telephone wires,
Yellowing flowering shrubs.

Before us, above us, the clouds swell, layers of them,
The violet underneath of clouds.
Every idea I have is nostalgia. Look up:
There is the sky that passenger pigeons darkened and filled up—
Darkened for days, eclipsing sun, eclipsing all other sound with the
    thunder of their wings.
After a while, it must have seemed that they followed
Not instinct or pattern but only
One another.

When they stopped, Audubon observed,
They broke the limbs of stout trees by the sheer weight of their numbers.

And when we stop we'll follow—what?
Our *hearts*?

The Puritans thought that we are granted the ability to love
Only through miracle,
But the troubadours knew how to burn themselves through,
How to make themselves shrines to their own longing.
The spectacular was never behind them.

Think of days of those scarlet-breasted, blue-winged birds above you.
Think of me in the garden, humming
Quietly to myself in my blue dress,
A blue darker than the sky above us, a blue dark enough for storms,
Though cloudless.

At what point is something gone completely?
The last of the sunlight is disappearing
Even as it swells and waves.

Just for this evening, won't you put me before you
Until I'm far enough away you can
Believe in me?

Then try, try to come closer—
My wonderful and less than.

Annunciation as Fender's Blue Butterfly with Kincaid's Lupine

> *"Fender's blue butterflies may soon be extinct. . . .*
> *. . . Kincaid's lupine, a threatened plant species in the*
> *Pacific Northwest, is the only available host plant. . ."*
> —CNN

But if I were this thing,
my mind a thousand times smaller than my wings,

if my fluorescent blue flutter
finally stumbled

into the soft
aqua throats of the blossoms,

if I lost my hunger
for anything else—

I'd do the same. I'd fasten myself
to the touch of the flower.

So what if the milky rims of my wings
no longer stupefied

the sky? If I could
bind myself to this moment, to the slow

snare of its scent,
what would it matter if I became

just the flutter of page
in a text someone turns

to examine me
in the wrong color?

The Lushness of It

It's not that the octopus wouldn't love you—
not that it wouldn't reach for you
with each of its tapering arms:

you'd be as good as anyone, I think,
to an octopus. But the creatures of the sea,
like the sea, don't think

about themselves, or you. Keep on floating there,
cradled, unable to burn. Abandon
yourself to the sway, the ruffled eddies, abandon

your heavy legs to the floating meadows
        of seaweed and feel
                the bloom of phytoplankton, spindrift, sea-
        spray, barnacles. In the dark benthic realm, the slippery neckton
    glide over
the abyssal plains and as you float you can feel
                that upwelling of cold, deep water touch
        the skin stretched over
                your spine. You can feel
fished for and slapped. No, it's not that the octopus
                wouldn't love you. If it touched,

if it tasted you, each of its three
hearts would turn red.

Will theologians of any confession refute me?
Not the bluecap salmon. Not its dotted head.

Philip Terman

Philip Terman is the author of *The House of Sages, Book of the Unbroken Days*, and *Rabbis of the Air*. A professor of English at Clarion University, he lives with his wife and two children outside Grove City, Pennsylvania.

As My Child Climbs the Apple Tree, I Think of the Ancient Sephardic Poet Jehudah Halevi

And the child climbs the apple tree, limb
by hesitant limb, my hands cupping the air
just beneath her torso. Already a tooth
is on the loose, her tongue working it back
and forth, her fingers prodding, anticipating
its absence. She branches up and crouches
in her nest of limbs, an exotic bird, surveys
the yard from her new advantage: a fawn
slowly crossing the road, delicate steps
naïve to our enormous machinery. Confused
season—bees sizzling in their coupled bodies,
the wind tearing at the willow, robins returned
and disoriented, my daughter's restlessness,
and my own—settle down. Enough
of this unpredictability. Kill us, or change us
forever. But the swallows roosting under our roof,
swooping in and out, their nests small apartments
tucked inside our openings, our rooms filled with
their sexual song. We live in a complicated
harmony, like those male and female orioles
pecking their hours at the image of their tree
in our living room window instead of weaving
hay into a crown, readying eggs for their legacies.
I watch and record spring's convocation until
hunger stirs my loved ones, their blood spinning
their bodies into this waking world. Now
my wife's hoe *clicks-clicks-clicks* not unlike
the *tap-tapping* of the woodpecker in the upper
echelons. And the ancient poet said: *Remember
the days of longing.* This spring, I think, is preamble:

I have sought thy nearness, the poet claimed,
that name whose dwelling is infinite space, like
that field where the fawn thinks she's alone.
She doesn't hear us noticing her privacy, now
staring into the rustlings, now lifting her nose
into the almost-rain. And the poet concludes:
Seek the too-wonderful, the deeply-hid. And
my daughter, still perched in her apple tree,
observes bits of a robin's cracked eggshell
scattered in the shadows beneath her. She wants
to try to fit the pieces together and return it
to its nest. She squiqqles down, reaches two arms
toward me—an embrace, a hoisting up and
a twirling behind my back, the gradual easing
of her hips onto my shoulders, her hands patting
my head in the thrill of her ascendancy, this
small body I balance, this little life I lift aloft.

Mrs. Titus

Open wide!,
she'd plead, not like a dentist:
Sing!

So we croaked and crooned
our thin suburban scratches
that disappeared

into her celestial reach,
such a pure soprano
she muted our mumbles

and even the bad boys
considered castration.
Operatic portly, but in our elementary

school fashion we said *fat*
and nicknamed her *tit-us*
because hers were two pillows,

small hills protruding
out of her always-blue dress.
Curly hair, thick glasses,

round balloon face.
Once a week, a break
from penmanship, spelling bees,

recitation of dates,
show and tell,
our attention was hers.

To hold all that voice
her body needed such heft,
a sphere of sound

held and measured,
stilling the classroom noise,
holding our tongues dumb.

Heads tilted slightly, one ear cocked.

Reach down! Deeper!
From the diaphragm!
The blood! The soul!

If one of us was so soft
as to be almost silent
she would slide over,

grasp one ear and wiggle,
press her lips deep
into the crevice like a kiss

and bellow as if across
a canyon: *I can't heeeeeear you!*
In spite of ourselves

she roused us—and still,
when my words don't carry,
I feel the grip and clench

of familiar stubby fingers
and the sonorous
urgings of a sweet mouth.

Hasidim in New Square, New York, Hear Carp Speaking Hebrew

Latest miracle, back of a local fish market:
A carp opened its mouth and declared:
I am the soul of a dead childless Hasid!
I was sent to do good deeds on earth!

It spoke first to its executioner, Luis
Nivelo, one of the non-believers, just

as it was about to be gutted: *The fish
is talking!* Nivelo screamed. Zalmen

Rosen, his boss, rushed into the room
and the fish, in the ancient tongue, confirmed—
*Yes! I'm the soul of a departed Jew,
come back to relieve your burdens,*

*to heal your sick of heart, to give strength
to the weary*—then slid into the fish pile.
Attempts to recover it were fruitless,
one carp looking so much like another,

the way they can slip and slide until lost
among the school. When the workers called,
in their ache to re-affirm, why didn't it respond?
Why didn't it raise its voice out of the heap

of its inarticulate brethren and distinguish itself
again? So it was sold with the rest.
Some believe it was as the parting of the Red Sea,
as the giving of the commandments.

Reports spread: a carp spoke God's word.
The Messiah is coming, such was the rumor.
The local rabbi decreed: to honor this wonder
everyone should eat carp for a week.

The Stocking Bank

My father would sock his money away
in fat bundles shoved tightly inside the toes
of his size fourteen black stockings—I'd
sneak into the top drawer and examine
each rolled-up pair until I discovered
the one with bills bulging, then slowly unfold
the frayed nylon, thinned from wear,
still smelling of sweat, smooth my small
hand along the inside and gingerly loosen
out the wad until it was a pulsing animal
in my palm—hundreds and fifties and
twenties and tens and ones, carefully arranged,
facing the same direction, this stockpiled
treasure of a son of a Depression wage
laborer, securing his earnings in small fists,
what his waking hours amounted to.
I'd count them slowly in astonishment.

Sue Ellen Thompson

Sue Ellen Thompson is the author of *This Body of Silk*, *The Wedding Boat*, *The Leaving*, and *The Golden Hour*. She has been a Robert Frost Fellow at the Bread Loaf Writers' Conference, Visiting Writer at Binghamton University, and resident poet at The Frost Place in Franconia, New Hampshire. She lives in Oxford, Maryland, and teaches at The Writer's Center in Bethesda.

The Visit

I gave her some change, everything
I could dredge from the bottom of my purse,
to buy a cold drink at the college snack bar
the day of the open house for prospective
students. She took the coins without
touching my palm and disappeared
down the long corridor, her loose pants
scooping the dust from the floor,
her sneakers scuffed almost bald
of their suede, and I thought *This is how
she will leave me a year from now—*
my money loose in her fist, my breasts
on her father's body, my tears locked
in her father's eyes. When she returned,
she slammed the money down on the table
before me and said, *What the hell can I get
for sixty-five cents?*

　　　　　　She walked off
in the direction of the car, turning
her baseball cap backwards, the way
she did as a child bent over a coloring book,
not wanting so much as a shadow to fall
between her and her intent. I should have done
what my mother did, I should have rubbed soap
into the carpet of her tongue, but I didn't.
In silence I drove her all the way down
the New York Thruway, the Mass Pike,

91 South—her head flung back
on its hinges, her mouth ajar, sleeping
the way an infant sleeps when the evening's
last feeding is over—so furious
and blessed was I to have her in my sight.

In the Apartments of the Divorced Men

The apartments of the divorced men are small,
you can stand in the doorway
and see their whole lives as through a convex lens,

the way a fish sees all the ocean. Or
they are large, one room opening into another
until it seems the whole white winter sky

has settled on the walls. The apartments
are not what you'd expect, they are neat
as pins, and to enter them

is to endure that brief, accidental pain.
They are proud of everything, the divorced men,
proud of the clean white microwave,

the CD player with its growing audience of disks,
the futon that bears the furrow of their sleep
upon its back. They will show you

photographs of their children when they were young,
stepping from the doors of miniature cars,
pajama bottoms on backwards, or give you

a full tour of the kitchen cabinets, each of which holds
an item or two of use. And when it is time
for you to leave, they will follow you

to the top of the stairs, the door,
and stand there while you drive away,
their faces behind the wood, the glass—

looking like the faces that you've seen
in all the papers: the proud, pained soldiers torn
from their homes and sent out into the world
for a reason you must read on and on to understand.

Dr. Colin Simms

We were living in England, where for fourteen
weeks I didn't know I was pregnant. Then
I rolled over in bed one morning
and felt a fist beneath me. My boyfriend

was in the upstairs bathroom, taking a shower.
An American acquaintance persuaded her doctor to meet
with us the next day. We took the Underground,
thrilled and silenced by the possibility.

There was an open fire at one end of the room,
a Persian rug and, behind his desk, a bay
window overlooking Harley Street. Afternoon
tea was served, and he called us by my maiden name.

Slipping behind a lacquered screen, I undressed.
Then he examined me: *Oh my yes.*

In Praise of Cancer

For giving her those first six weeks
of summer, doing crosswords on the porch
in a kimono worn so thin the morning light

and birdsong could move through it. For drowsy
afternoons in chemo, reading magazines,
and for the nurses who could slip a needle

underneath the paper of her skin as easily
as a lover's name into a conversation.
For allowing us to see her as a girl again,

a stringbean, then a downy-headed infant,
curling in upon herself for sleep, and finally
as something luminous, desiring. For sending us

the unseasonable snow that dawdled
in the autumn foliage the day we drove
through the White Mountains past

Robert Frost's house, pausing long enough
for her to say, *And that has made all
the difference.* For the afternoon I brought her

home, exhausted, from the hospital and laid
her down to nap on that same porch—
the screens dissolving now in late

October's radiance—and for the sleep
she sank into so gratefully a smile
shone like water on her thin, dry lips.

For taking what it had to take so casually
at first—an appetite for olives, windfall
hair. For being quick and greedy at the end.

The Blue Blanket

Toward the end, my father argued
with my mother over everything: He wanted
her to eat again. He wanted her to take

her medicine. He wanted her
to live. He argued with her in their bed
at naptime. He was cold, he said,

tugging at the blanket tangled
in my mother's wasted limbs. From the hall
outside their room I listened

as love, caught and fettered, howled
at its captors, gnawing at its own flesh
in its frenzy to escape. Then I entered

without knocking, freed the blanket
trapped between my mother's knees and shook
it out once, high above

their bodies' cursive. It floated
for a moment, blue as the Italian sky
into which my father flew his bombs

in 1943, blue as the hat I'd bought her
for the winter she would never live
to see. My father's agitation eased,

my mother smiled up at me, her face
lucent with gratitude, as the blanket
sifted down on them like earth.

John Samuel Tieman

Born in St. Louis, John Samuel Tieman has lived in Mexico and the West Indies and served in the U.S. Army in Vietnam. A certified teacher since 1975 with a Ph.D. from St. Louis University, he teaches in the St. Louis Public Schools. His collections of poetry include *Morning Prayers* and *A Concise Biography of Original Sin*.

Clean

Today 1/11/96 sober six years and
I say morning prayers without speaking
I make the coffee while my wife rises
I listen without weeping at a sad ballad

The sound of the snow on the roof is
important, important as fresh bread
or the neighbor warming her car
important as a plan or an empty chair

That's why this morning six years
later to the day I hear the slight
chimes of the Angelus bells hear
the ash settle in my fireplace

hear the beauty of my wife's sigh
as she sits cross-legged on the edge
of the bed and asks half-aware
why I'm alive at this hour

Editing

> —*for Denis Lane*

This other Nam vet comes to see me and wants me to see
his manuscript. He brings this nosh, some bagels, so I say
OK, let's see it—Yea, OK, I'll read it. So we got some time till later so we swap
some Nam stories. He says
    This is what's pitiful, man. I'm visitin' Jim Mills,
this fuck-up all wounded you see. It's this hospital, Nha Trang. From a distance
it's all this commotion. But so what? It's Nam. I got directions to Jim Mills and
I got to pass this commotion. I start up some stairs, begin to look a little into this

second floor when halfway up the flight I see nuthin' but runnin' feet and screams.
Just runnin' feet, some bunches of blood pools and some screams. I got to turn
before I see completely in and there's the nurse all white right there
at the door. I got to ask Hey What The Hell Lady? but she's just sittin', just
sittin' at this desk. Imagine report
writin' at the door of the screams. So I look.
The screams are a dozen guys—I can't tell black from whose white and they're all
runnin' and bangin' walls and leavin' whole body—I mean the full body on the wall
blood stains and they're naked 'cause all the napalm left was
no skin. Nuthin'. Not even no boots.
So I beg the nurse
Do Somethin'! But she says Any More Morphine And They'll Die! Finally I see
she's just as freaked and fakin' calm and nobody knows what to do so I go off on
her when one guy runs up at my face and he's just goin' Mama Mama Mama
Mama Mama Mama Mama Mama Mama Mama Mama Mama Mama and like that.
(I always feel bad for that nurse 'cause she's maybe 23 and in charge of a
platoon of the dead or what's left.) So I walk off, find some quiet and just stuff
my mouth with my fatigue shirt and scream till I can't stop. And when Jim Mills
later asks What's that back there man? I say, you know how we said, Don't mean
nuthin', man. It just don't mean nuthin'.

Prodigal

When I think of myself at 10 or 15, I think of Our Lady
Of Perpetual Help, Her promises of mercy which made me
believe my faith would stop
my father from drinking, my mother from screaming. So I'd light
one more candle, say one more rosary, bargain
one more deal with Jesus, promise, like my mother promised
my dad, You give me peace or I'll give you hell. Between 16
and 40, I lit no more candles, prayed no novenas, kept no promises
except one: to be that angry bastard who abandons God.
Hear me now God. It took me decades to regain my faith, sanity,
sobriety. Now my father's dead, my mother 88, and again
for them I pray, except this time I make no promises.

Basho in St. Louis

awake all night long
I listen to autumn wind
howling down the hill
and past the cathedral bell
it sways gently for a dirge

•

when you stepped out
of the shower this morning
I kissed you long
enough for you to leave
wet impressions on my shirt

•

a spider gets caught
in the washing machine tub
I think of freeing it
but can't avoid its sting
thus does life yield to my Tide

•

students are somber
a long rain washes the streets
there is little wind
outside there is soft thunder
inside the sound of pencils

•

this morning I found
a Mass card for an old friend
dead now 14 years
I don't know where the time went
sitting here all afternoon

•

rereading your note
I'm still confused by all
the words we didn't say
I take a bite of my lunch
the silence of sour and salt

•

found poem / standardized test

22. Whose turn is it now?

        a Turn left there.
        b They both turned.
        c It's my turn.
        d The wrong way.

•

we undress for love
and for ten seconds the dusk
makes us young again

Jim Tolan

Jim Tolan is the author of the chapbook *Fresh Fruit and Gravity* (Far Gone Books). His poems have appeared in a wide range of publications, including *American Literary Review, Atlanta Review, Bellevue Literary Review, Indiana Review, MARGIE,* and Poets.org. Originally from Chicago, he received his PhD in creative writing from the University of Louisiana-Lafayette and is currently an Assistant Professor at the City University of New York. He lives in Cobble Hill, Brooklyn.

Blood Sport

1
When I was a boy, my father would tighten
his stomach and invite me to punch him
as hard as I could. Pounding away,
I'd give him my best shot,
again and again. It was useless.
He was invincible, and I was very small.
2
When I turned seven, I asked my father
if I could marry Mom when I was older.
He was never home. Why should he care?
He only laughed.
3
Still a boy, I raced into the bathroom
while my father was shaving and belted him
right in the gut. He grunted, doubled over,
and I ran like hell to my mom
only to have her demand that I apologize.
4
Back in the bathroom, I told him I was sorry.
He turned to me, blood trailing down his throat.
I was a man and would marry as I pleased.

Giggles before the Void

I could take her ass
and put it in a box by the window

and every morning I'd open the box
and tickle her ass with a goose feather

and giggle

but sooner or later she'd want it back
and I'd be stuck with an empty box

and a bald goose

and every morning after that I'd have to get up
and feed that goose

and look for something to put in the empty box.

Evening Trees

My grandfather was a storyteller who died
when I was young. He would take me
for walks among the evening trees and know
they were alive, pulsing with the life
that was his story. I run my hands
against the rough bark of an aged oak,
railroad spikes marking its trunk, and feel
my grandfather, his stories of lost children
stolen in the woods, when no one was there
but the wind and a thousand blinking eyes.

The Purple Crayon

I find a jumbo Crayola in the new used couch today, purple,
like in *Harold and the Purple Crayon*, the children's book
I once believed was named after my dad,

                              and I am sixteen
again, driving him home one more last time from the bar
at Ted's Log Cabin, where he's been since lunch, closing in again
on the indoor martini record, double digits no big thing,

when, stopped at the corner of Lewis and Grand, he flings
open his door and lets loose all over the road. No usual
drunken puking, this one's laced with lots of bloody
coagulum, olives, bifocals, and false teeth.

                              I throw
the two-tone Dodge into park, fish his specs and teeth
out of the mess, and drive him to St. Therese and two weeks
in detox before the next new lifetime of *Hi, I'm Hal T and I'm. . .*

My dad's story and a crayon, a lie I've been telling for almost
twenty years. My mother was driving. It was one of the few times
she wouldn't go get him by herself.

                                    She is the one who dipped
into what his body emptied to rescue the only help he had ever
admitted to needing, she who drove him to the hospital,
who stayed with him despite all those drunken years,
who loved him more than I have ever known how to love.

I'm thirty-two and still want to be the hero, want to be the one
reaching into the retch, the one making the necessary gesture,
not the pimpled boy in the back seat, his mouth open,
unable or unprepared to act, Hamlet still considering the ghost.

I loved my father and did nothing, sat there, hating myself
for loving this chance to see what he'd been hiding and holding
inside all those years, what he'd been watering and drowning in turn.

Natasha Trethewey

Natasha Trethewey is author of *Beyond Katrina: A Meditation on the Mississippi Gulf Coast*, and three collections of poetry, *Domestic Work, Bellocq's Ophelia*, and *Native Guard*—for which she was awarded the Pulitzer Prize. She is the recipient of NEA, Guggenheim, Bunting, and Rockefeller fellowships. At Emory University she is Professor of English and holds the Phillis Wheatley Distinguished Chair in Poetry.

Photograph of a Bawd Drinking Raleigh Rye
—E.J. Bellocq, circa 1912

The glass in her hand is the only thing moving—
too fast for the camera—caught in the blur of motion.

She raises it toasting, perhaps, the viewer you become
taking her in—your eyes starting low, at her feet,

and following those striped stockings like roads,
traveling the length of her calves and thighs. Up then,

to the fringed scarf draping her breasts, the heart
locket, her bare shoulder and the patch of dark hair

beneath her arm, the round innocence of her cheeks
and Gibson-girl hair. Then over to the trinkets on the table

beside her: a clock; tiny feather-backed rocking chairs
poised to move with the slightest wind or breath;

the ebony statuette of a woman, her arms stretched above
her head. Even the bottle of rye is a woman's slender torso

and round hips. On the wall behind her, the image again—
women in paintings, in photographs, and carved in relief

on an oval plane. And there, on the surface of it all, a thumb-
print—perhaps yours? It's easy to see this is all about desire,

how it recurs—each time you look, it's the same moment,
the hands of the clock still locked at high noon.

Incident

We tell the story every year—
how we peered from the windows, shades drawn—
though nothing really happened,
the charred grass now green again.

We peered from the windows, shades drawn,
at the cross trussed like a Christmas tree,
the charred grass still green. Then
we darkened our rooms, lit the hurricane lamps.

At the cross trussed like a Christmas tree,
a few men gathered, white as angels in their gowns.
We darkened our rooms and lit hurricane lamps,
the wicks trembling in their fonts of oil.

It seemed the angels had gathered, white men in their gowns.
When they were done, they left quietly. No one came.
The wicks trembled all night in their fonts of oil;
by morning the flames had all dimmed.

When they were done, the men left quietly. No one came.
Nothing really happened.
By morning all the flames had dimmed.
We tell the story every year.

Miscegenation

In 1965 my parents broke two laws of Mississippi;
they went to Ohio to marry, returned to Mississippi.

They crossed the river into Cincinnati, a city whose name
begins with a sound like *sin*, the sound of wrong—*mis* in Mississippi.

A year later they moved to Canada, followed a route the same
as slaves, the train slicing the white glaze of winter, leaving Mississippi.

Faulkner's Joe Christmas was born in winter, like Jesus, given his name
for the day he was left at the orphanage, his race unknown in Mississippi.

My father was reading *War and Peace* when he gave me my name.
I was born near Easter, 1966, in Mississippi.

When I turned 33 my father said, *It's your Jesus year—you're the same age he was when he died.* It was spring, the hills green in Mississippi.

I know more than Joe Christmas did. Natasha is a Russian name— though I'm not; it means *Christmas child*, even in Mississippi.

James Tyner

James Tyner received his MFA in Creative Writing from Fresno State in 2009, and considers himself new to poetry. Tyner has won the Andres Montoya Scholarship, the Larry Levis Prize, the Ernesto Trejo Poetry Prize, was a finalist for the Ruth Lilly Fellowship and the 2008 Winning Writers War Poetry contest, and won the 2008 *Coal Hill Review* Chapbook contest with his book *The Ghetto Exorcist*. A struggling pacifist, he writes about the violent gang world he came from, his multicultural background in Los Angeles and the California Central Valley, and the effects of violence on his world.

After Jumping Some Kids and Taking Their Money, 1988

We buy Cheetos and Fanta
with the money we stole.
Took it as they cried,
pried it loose with kicks to stomach
and stomps to the face.
Fingers grow orange
from the powder of our breakfast
and stomachs pop out
between ribs and belt buckles
as the soda slides down.
And Whooser laughs,
cheese staining his teeth,
his breath coming heavy
through busted lips.
I laugh also, lips stinging
from salt, from blood,
from smiles as we eat.
This is what we are given,
the children of the ghetto,
this is what we inherit,
a breakfast of chips,
skin pocked with dirt and scabs,
backs resting loosely
against graffitied alleys
as we laugh at fights,
at money stolen,
at the blood that drips loosely
down my left arm
and puddles.

Hollywood Trash

We pull monsters from the trash.
Claws, teeth, the rubber foam
of alien heads and demon bodies
lying still among empty wrappers
and rotten food. Everything
just waiting to be found.
I am ten here, and my father
jabs a mop handle into the pile,
searching for glass and the looseness
of garbage, so we don't slip or fall
too deep into it. We collect monsters,
throw them into black sacks slung
over our shoulders. From beyond
the trash, a door slams, and someone
shouts, "Fucking Mexicans, get out
of the trash." And I am happy.
Rotten milk pools around my left
foot, and I forget about this werewolf
as it drops from my hands,
these hands that are white,
not like my mother's, not like
my stepfather's, as he lifts me up,
and we run to the car,
pieces of Hollywood
over our shoulders.

Bones in the Grapevines

We pulled it from the earth, soil
dripping from it, coloring
more gray than white. Long,
crusted, tips broken off so we
could see the gray honeycombs
of marrow inside. "Dog?"
My cousin, Juan, shook his head,
and stories we grew up on,
things we heard, came back.
Family said that white guy,
the one who owned these fields
before us, the one with the belt,
the buckle with diamonds and bullhorns,
would beat the field workers for being
too slow, not filling boxes quickly
enough, sometimes even to death.
Our parents would scare us,
make us clean rooms or go to bed
with visions of belt buckles glinting,

leaves slowly picked from thin branches,
till they became a switch, to peel
skin, peel back to blood and bone.
There are workers in the field now,
and we can hear a song coming
from them, mixed motor of the tractor,
black heads bobbing above green lines
of the fields. Juan, colors of his Raiders
jersey soaking up so much sun the heat
pours from him, his skin so brown,
almost black now from too much summer,
takes the bone, throwing it at the workers.
"Fucking wetbacks!!" The bone falls
somewhere in vines and dirt, lost.
Juan's Raiders hat has fallen off,
and his hair glistens from Vaseline
used to keep his curls straight,
plastered to his skin, his skull.

At a Barbecue for R.C. One Week after He Is Out of Iraq

He laughs and tosses back
another shot of whiskey.
There are questions about cousins,
how is Lisa doing, she still drinking,
did Eddy finally marry that big
bitch, heard Monica is in L.A. now.
I fill him in, crack open another beer
chaser, and tell what stories I can.
I am light here, keeping things brief,
smiling, avoiding the heat from his skin,
the pocks and purple circles
that tighten his face, mar it.
A curl of scarred flesh lifts up
from the collar of his shirt,
hanging like a question
I can't ask. And suddenly the food
is done, barbeque finished,
mom calls out to get the kids
ready to eat, and his face fills
with an emptiness, jaw loosens
and he is muttering now, about kids,
something about so many goddamn
kids. He asks me if I know what
the color of brains really is,
and I answer that the ribs
are getting cold.

Jean Valentine

Jean Valentine is the author of ten books of poetry, most recently *Break the Glass* (Copper Canyon, 2010). She lives and works in New York City.

High School Boyfriend

You were willing to like me, and I did something,
and blew it,
and your liking me would have saved me,
and my liking you would have saved you,

that was the circle I was walking around,
pushing a bar that moved a wheel
down in the dark, holding my breath,
naked in a long hard army coat of you,
hating my feet, hating my path…

Today my tongue is a fish's tongue,
kissing my friend's light breastbone, his chestnut down;
full of tears, full of light, half both,
nowhere near my old home: no one anywhere
is so wrong.

Barrie's Dream, the Wild Geese

"I dreamed about Elizabeth Bishop
and Robert Lowell—an old Penguin book
of Bishop's poetry—a thick china cup
and a thick china sugar bowl, square,
cream-colored, school stuff.
                    And Lowell was there,
he was talking and talking to us,
he was saying, 'She is the best—'

Then the geese flew over,
and he stopped talking. Everyone stopped talking,
because of the geese."
                    The sound of their wings!
Oars rowing, laborious, wood against wood: it was
a continuing thought, no, it was a labor,
how to accept your lover's love. Who could do it alone?
Under our radiant sleep they were bearing us all night long.

Snow Landscape, in a Glass Globe

in memory of Elizabeth Bishop

A thumb's-length landscape: Snow, on a hill
in China. I turn the glass ball over in my hand,
and watch the snow
blow around the Chinese woman,
calm at her work,
carrying her heavy yoke
uphill, towards the distant house.
Looking out through the thick glass ball
she would see the lines of my hand,
unearthly winter trees, unmoving, behind the snow...

No more elders.
The Boston snow grays and softens
the streets where you were...
Trees older than you, alive.

The snow is over and the sky is light.
Pale, pale blue distance...
Is there an east? A west? A river?
There, can we live right?

I look back in through the glass. You,
in China, I can talk to you.
The snow has settled; but it's cold
there, where you are.

What are you carrying?
For the sake of what? through such hard wind
and light.
            —And you look out to me,
and you say, "Only the same as everyone; your breath,
your words, move with mine,
under and over this glass; we who were born
and lived on the living earth."

Judith Vollmer

Judith Vollmer is the author of three full-length collections of poetry—*Reactor* and *Level Green* (University of Wisconsin Press), and *The Door Open to the Fire* (Cleveland State University Press)—and the limited edition collection *Black Butterfly*, awarded the Center for Book Arts Prize. She is the recipient of grants from the National Endowment for the Arts and the Pennsylvania Council on the Arts, and residency fellowships from Yaddo and the American Academy in Rome. Vollmer co-edits the poetry journal *5 AM*.

Early Snow

It was coming down hard so the teacher motioned the flute
then the piano quiet and the children sang

a cappella, teacher's voice was gone, they screaked and worked
their lungs & shoulders like gulls, they swooped and cranked

it up, it was wonderful being all alone,
they could hear pauses, one by two by one, then she

ran to the edge of the world, opened it and thrust the dark
sleeve of her dress out & down into the whirlpools

and when a flake landed crisp & complete on the black
wool she ran to every desk then back for more until

she showed every voice a new jewel, an alien, autotelic
shape. What would you like to be, or who, or would you

go with the wind sweeping the parking lot & small bank of trees.

Spill

Before, I spoke of clear things,
shadows on white tile, men in paper suits
mopping the radiated water with Kotex pads
trucked in through the security dock, 1960. Now
I see blurry grasses swaying in dusk, the starless

sky & vaporous shapes of a Pennsylvania
town behind wire fences, there in the misty
place beyond the woods. I hear a truck
sputtering with cheap gas, & boot soles
slapping cement. *Is that my Uncle Ray*
running toward the truck, away? No, he's inside
with his men cleaning the burning place
protecting the core. Dawn is a swollen eye
they work toward. Those must be cattails
waving over the marshland, those must be geese
making that slapping leather sound of flight.

She Kept Me

wrapped & close & fragrant
in her incense of strange lemon soap.
She carried me down, all the way down
into her solitude, lace & bones was all
she was under the t-shirt
faded to watered black silk, thin
as her night veils, dreams

of wet earth, spring, Amsterdam
where she hung with the houseboat boys,
loading bricks of blond hash safely on;
she nursed their sore throats with concentrations
of aspirin & oranges. Spent her money on
artcards & books with blue wrappers.
Whores in windows moved
their lips like bright candies
and petals drifted down

onto my dark woven shoulders
& the three weeks we had,
hotels, of course, also her parents'
canalside perch where I held her
while she read her Stendhal, her Colette,
the stitches of my devotion
weight she counted on
for *quiet, let's find the exact point of focus, now that's desire,
isn't it?* O it is sex, mother
of all creative energies, books, & companion views.

I liked her
in the cool air of her balcony nights.
I was left on a train and once in a musty café.
I was handed down, yes, but never
taken up so fondly.

Thom Ward

Thom Ward's poetry collections include *Small Boat With Oars of Different Size, Tumblekid, Various Orbits, Fog in a Suitcase, The Matter of the Casket,* and *Etcetera's Mistresses.* His vices include golf, martinis, chicken wings, and reading.

Logos

He had once heard from someone somewhere that the root of the word metaphor is *to carry beyond.* If that was so, all he knew or thought he knew was much like fog in a suitcase. No, it wasn't like fog in a suitcase, it was fog in a suitcase. And how it got there was still a mystery or so he fooled himself into believing. And what it might accomplish and what it could not remained unfathomable. Furthermore, that word—unfathomable—remained outside the suitcase. He was quite sure he didn't know its root, had never approached its etymology, nor who might come by to pick it up and carry it off. The word, that is. Though just as easily the suitcase, the suitcase with its fog, the past, present and future swirling about, this way and that. Much like how a poem races around and around trying to catch something like its silhouette, how it tries to catch the silhouette itself. Now that was something he could understand, or, at least, fool himself into believing. But it didn't do much to make sense of the suitcase or the fog. No, he would have to leave that to somebody else. Surely it wouldn't be long before someone would come by to pick it up and carry it off, this suitcase with its fog, black handle and small black wheels. Thus, freeing him, at least for now, of those things full of metaphor and those things unfathomable. Leaving him here, where he'd always wanted to be, where what he thought he knew was nothing of what he understood—a wooden table, a wooden chair, sliced toast and a chunk of butter, the spoon he swirled about, this way and that, inside a white teacup.

Road Test, Defiance, Ohio

Even the rearview mirror is nervous, she thinks, and the tires will leap from the curb when this boy grips the wheel, pulls out. Quarter-to-three with all its clouds. So much to process, like the time she overheard a man say to his peers, Yep, that tree may be distinctive, but it couldn't handle a lynching. Turn right by the oak, she tells the boy. How many of these assessments had she presided over? Isn't happiness the really bad stuff that might have happened, but didn't? Stop here and begin your K-turn, she says, thinking how in October the maples will pucker up again, how objects in the mirror are more dangerous than they appear. Turn left, turn right. Sitting in the Plymouth years ago, the dark garage, her brother trying to locate the keyhole and her mother suddenly blurting out, I bet you could find it if it had hair around it. Sharp work with that K-turn, she says, You know what's next. There's a name each gust of wind is known by before it yanks its first leaf from the branch. Only the roots know this name, she was sure of that, watching him hit the blinker, check his blind spot, methodically negotiate the crucial parallel park. You're doing fine, she says, remembering the time her father kicked his briefcase down the stairs while her mother kept on drying the dishes, looking out the window at the ironwood. Turn right, turn left. Each grain of sand in the hourglass must be terrified of heights, she thinks. What's the chance a few of them might fall so far they'll scuff like her mother's heels on the kitchen floor. Pull over by the chestnut, she tells him, this boy with his scrawny whiskers and zits. That was better than before, that was good.

Anticipation

Nothing was coming down the road. Still, he went out in the middle of the night to meet it. Slippers he had remembered but not his glasses. Wind from the south and the sky exhausted with blotches, the silhouettes of houses almost confused with the suggestions of trees. At least the air was tepid, stripped of the aroma of local road kill. What a strange word, aroma, as if scent or fragrance weren't enough. He thought of socks forced into mandatory pairings, how one might take up a T-shirt and suffocate the other, like Cain, then escape through the dryer's aluminum shaft and adopt a life of nefarious behavior. The Greek verb *muo*, he recalled, to shut the eyes completely, the root for the noun mysticism. If he had a Labrador and a loaded rifle, he'd look more distinguished, almost aristocratic, standing in scarlet pajamas near the broken yellow line. The commotion of crickets in the pasture to the east. An occasional porch light and the familiar telephone poles, kings who cannot wander, extending their arms to the dark. Right about now, he thought, a flank steak would be sufficient, seared over the grill, medium rare. It was simple to retrace his steps, walk across the lawn toward a door he had left open, that part of his brain reminding him how glasses make for a certain blindness and truth is all about context, how nothing was coming down the road tonight or tomorrow or any night after, and that it was going to be quite difficult to get back to sleep with so much nothingness, so assuredly, on its way.

Charles Harper Webb

Charles Harper Webb's most recent collection is *Shadow Ball: New and Selected Poems*, published by University of Pittsburgh. Recipient of grants from the Whiting and Guggenheim foundations, he teaches at California State University, Long Beach.

Cocksucker

I thought it was a myth, tied with *motherfucker*
for the World's Most Disgusting Thing.
Just because some poor kid couldn't throw a ball,
or run, or talk without a lisp, didn't make him
a fairy, fruitcake, queen, queer, pansy, homo,
flaming fag—didn't mean he would do *that*.

My opinion made some say I must be one, and let me
practice the right cross-left hook Dad taught me.
When Sammy Blevins, Taft High's choir teacher,
got the spirit and proclaimed he'd been "an evil
Sodomite till saved by Jesus' love" (Jesus Gonzales,
jokers sneered)—I admitted *cocksuckers* were real.

Still, I had doubts until Del Delancey hired me
to play guitar for the Delmations, and we caught rainbow
trout and wrote neo-doowop and roomed together
on the road, and I had girls stay over, but he never did,
and when the band broke up, he said, "I love you, Chuck,"
and cried, certain I'd hate him. "It's hell," he said—

the hot iron boiling in his gut, the dark well
where, like that unkillable giant in Grimm's Tales, he hid
his heart. Remembering times I'd called some slow
driver or loudmouth drunk a cocksucker, I said,
"It's no big deal, Del." But I edged away.
"They do it up the Hershey Highway like I like it,"

he wrote from Mexico—to punish me?—and he was gone,
folded and packed into the chest where I keep painful things

safe, out of sight. But then today I heard a joke
about a cork soaker, a Coke stocker, and a sock cutter.
When I told my wife, she said, "A good cocksucker's
what I pray to be."

                    Please, God, take care of Del.
Lead him safely through the long valley of AIDS.
Give him health, a hacienda, and a man
who worships him and does everything he likes.
Tell him for me—dream, telepathy, vision, it's up to You—
Del, my friend, you cocksucker, I loved you too.

Tenderness in Men

It's like plum custard at the heart of a steel girder,
cool malted milk in a hot bowling ball.

It's glimpsed sometimes when a man pats a puppy.
If his wife moves softly, it may flutter like a hermit thrush

into the bedroom, and pipe its pure, warbling tune.
Comment, though and it's a moray jerking back into its cave.

Dad taught me to hide tenderness like my "tallywhacker"—
not to want or accept it from other men. All I can do

for a friend in agony is turn my eyes and, pretending
to clap him on the back, brace up his carapace with mine.

So, when you lean across the table and extend your hand,
your brown eyes wanting only good for me, it's no wonder

my own eyes glow and swell too big for their sockets
as, in my brain, dry gulleys start to flow.

Vikings

Overran my boyhood dreams—fierce
Blond beards, slab-chests,
Biceps gripped by bronze bands,
Dragon ships which terrorized my ancestors,
Weak Britons who whined to Christ:

No match for Odin, and the hard hammer
Of Thor. While other kids clutched
Toy guns and grenades, I swung

My plastic war ax: immune to bullets,
Refusing to die. While they dreamed

Of rocketing through sunny skies,
I dreamed of fjords, their crags and storms
Matching my dark moods, my doubts
Of God, my rages and my ecstasies.
I snuck in twice to see *The Norseman,*

Wincing but bearing it as the Saxon king
Chopped off Prince Gunnar's right
Hand. I gloried in the sulking gods
And ravens and great trees, roots
Reaching underground to realms

Of dwarfs and trolls. I gloried in the runes
On shields, the long oar strokes
That sliced through ocean cold as steel.
I gloried in the Valkyries, bearing slain
Heroes to the mead halls of Valhalla

To feast and fight and fondle blonde
Beauties forever, while we sad
Methodists plucked harps and fluttered:
Sissies mommy had to dress
For Sunday school. The day before

Christmas vacation, when Danny Flynn
Called me "a fish-lipped fool,"
I grabbed a trashcan lid and slammed
It like a war shield in his face,
Then leapt over his blood and bawling

And—while teachers shrilled their whistles,
And Mr. Bean, the porky principal,
Scurried for his ax—thrust my sword-
Hand in my shirt and stalked out
Into the cruel winter of third grade.

Patricia Jabbeh Wesley

Patricia Jabbeh Wesley is a survivor of the Liberian civil war of 1989–2003. Her books of poetry are *Becoming Ebony, Before the Palm Could Bloom: Poems of Africa, The River Is Rising* and *Where the Road Turns.* Her work has appeared in numerous American and international publications. She teaches English, Creative Writing, and African Literature at Penn State University, Altoona, Pennsylvania, where she lives with her family.

To Set Everything Right

Legend keeps the story of the Grebo women
who were going to wash all that salt out of the Atlantic.
Villagers from all over Grebo country spent years
boiling buckets of salt water away—
All that arrogance coming from women,
women, who were just women—
Women, wanting to set the ocean
right once and for all?

They decided to end all that flapping and foaming,
the way a man foams when a woman
stands her ground. Women came down
from Yederobo, Gbanmakeh, Tugbakeh, Manolu,
Gedetaabo, Gbanelu, Taakeh, Galloway…
women, their lappas flying in the salty breeze,
down the Cape in Gbanelu.
And when the men saw all this fussing,
they laughed, and thought of ways to put
all that feminism to rest.

If they came down from all these towns,
what then would they do with their husbands?
What would they put in their husbands'
bowls for feed? Fix them to drink?
To wash with?—Women, like ants,
washing away buckets and pails of salt

day after day, month after month,
forgetting to birth babies all those years,
just washing out the salty ocean,
but it was no use—oh how the washing

of the Atlantic kept their babies from
growing up, kept their husbands from farming,
from eating, from laughing,
kept their sons from coming out to be men...
—Just one woman dashed her pail away
and picked up her baby, and every woman followed...
to feed the men, to cook that spicy
palm butter that can put a man to sleep,
to smoke tabadu tender and smelly,
so the bone cracks under a man's teeth,
without cracking a tooth...

The Morning After: An Elegy

My husband and I gather our remaining lives
the morning after. I snatch away memories
of childhood, adolescence, college, where my life

was a bittersweet of books, boys, my father's
discipline, politics, and the whole world spread
out, awaiting me. This morning's bombing

is again rocking our lives and our home. A single
suitcase will have to bear all this pain.
It is August 1, 1990, right after a number no

one could count were massacred in deep sleep;
today, taken before today. They lay all over
St. Peter's Lutheran, in the aisles, on the solid

wood pulpit, twisted, in classrooms on top of one
another, a child here, a mother there, a father here,
a baby there, a heap here, a few there, our tattered

history. Where was God at two o'clock in the morning?
How did those soldiers push aside church doors,
reason, God? And is there anyone who can tell

my wide-eyed children how a single order could
put hundreds to death? To explain how hundreds
of troops could empty hundreds of bullets while

the world sits by? So we pack boxes of books, pots,
suitcases of clothes, stereos; we fold mattresses
and chairs, shutting blinds, windows, turning

off waterless taps so if water ever returns while
we're gone, this home will not become a river.
These new circumstances of our lives now gather

mucus in my throat. All this time, our three starving
dogs are watching; no barking, no jumping, are they
also wondering if someone will explain where

we're going? One last wave for my watchdogs before
refugee camps, starvation, then flight for America.
But everyone couldn't come to America, you see.

When My Daughter Tells Me She Has a Boyfriend

When my daughter tells me she has a boyfriend now,
at college, where we send our children so they can
grow up some more, I ask her, "Is he black...or...
white...?" There is just silence, no phone clicking,
no whisper. No pauses are allowed between a mother
and her daughter who has gone to college
to find herself among many lost people.

"What sort of question is that?" she sighs.
The phone has learned how to talk back
in many ways. "Is he tall or short? Are his eyes
large and round and brown like the walnut
just before it becomes meal? Are they green-green
or are they blue, pale, after the color of sky
just before gray settles in upon them in September?"
"Mom..." my daughter is weeping now.
My daughter has learned to weep at last
about the things that really matter.

"Are you racist?" My daughter cries into the phone.
Only a phone knows how to ask such questions.
It is only a far-away phone, a far-away daughter

taking liberty with phones, asking
a perfect mother if she is racist.

"Racism is something that happens to me," I say.
Doesn't a mother have the right to know,
to know it all, to have it all plain and simple on the table,
all the things one needs to know?
Whether my daughter is bringing home a tall
black boy, so dark, his skin sparkles,
a boy with hair he spends many nights
grooming so it loses all its nappy?

But my daughter tells me she's going home
with her boyfriend—home to his mother,
another woman, a white woman who will
stand at her doorstep hugging
my first girl-child, the daughter of a bull,
Jabbeh *Cho, Koo-oo-koo-oo*, an off-shoot
of Nganlun, where the spring water bubbles
at noonday in March. My daughter from
Seo Paton, the woman from Wah, losing her way
in a land where we are all trying to find ourselves.

My daughter, the women from Seo are hot like pepper.
They do not run off to meet their boyfriend's mother
just like that, girl. But in America,
a girl can hop on a car or plane, on a truck, or whatever
to meet her boyfriend's family at eighteen,
before her mother has looked the boy over,

before the elders sit in upon the whole idea
of a boyfriend, to see if it's taboo to marry a boy
from another clan. "What are his people like?
Who is his father? Does his father come from
a great people, a great clan?" I wanted to ask.

In America, a child at eighteen can drive a car,
run over a deer at two o'clock in the morning,
gather their belongings at noon, and move
out, at sixteen. I have heard it all.

My girl child whose beauty shines like the moon,
over the hilltops, over the forest when
the sun comes out in December, in Tugbakeh.
Nyeneplu, the beautiful, my daughter

running off to meet the other woman,
my daughter who reminds me of Neferteri
on her throne. My daughter, a woman like myself.
When I see that boy, I will cook him spicy pepper soup
so he knows how the dodo cries at night
just before the hawk has time to flee.

The Women in My Family

The women in my family were supposed
to be men. Heavy body men, brawny
arms and legs, thick muscular chests and the heart,

smaller than a speck of dirt.
They come ready with muscle arms and legs,
big feet, big hands, big bones,

a temper that's hot enough to start World War Three.
We pride our tiny strings of beards
under left chins as if we had anything

to do with creating ourselves.
The women outnumber the men
in the Jabbeh family, leaving our fathers roaming

wild nights in search of baby-spitting concubines
to save the family name.
It is an abomination when there are no boy children.

At the birth of each one of us girls, a father lay prostrate
on the earth, in sackcloth and ash, wailing.

It is an abomination when there are no men
in the family, when mothers can't
bring forth boy children in my clan.

Poem Written from a Single Snapshot

On the beach in Monrovia,
my children and I are building sandcastles.
You can see the Atlantic's waves in the distance,
fighting for a place to roll their way onto shore.
Waves are flapping in the wind

as the tide rises up and down.
Before we know it, we are in the middle of water.
Besie is two years old. MT, who is only
six months, clings a short arm around my knee.
He's staring at Besie and the sandcastle
she's erecting with her right foot.
This is how my mother taught me
to build a sand castle.
You put your foot down
and build mounds around it until
the castle becomes stable.
This is how we search for home.
You put your foot down in a place long enough
that new place becomes home.

Broken World

To every winning team, many more will lose—
Many defenders, goalies, linebackers, dribblers, attackers,

ball catchers, and now one lone, winning cup from which
no one will ever drink. To every war, there are no winners.

To every living, many more dead will go unmarked.
So many lives lined up for death; so much of what took

forever to build, goes up in some cloud. So many buried
alive or executed—a stray bullet, accidentally passing.

So many players who never knew the name of the game
they played, yet they played, without even knowing they

were playing until someone found them dead by the road-
side. Today, here are St. Louis Rams, walking away from

the Super Bowl, carrying the Super Trophy. Tennessee
watches with a tearful eye. But below the deep Atlantic

in Abidjan, a plane has just gone down. One hundred
and sixty-nine, gone down, and all this time, I was here

watching what Americans call *Super Bowl*. I do not know
the game; it is not even my game to lose or win, but my

heart pounds hard for the game. Sometimes, I can feel
my skin slowly becoming American. Is life a game you can

win or lose? Will winning warlords ever know the extent
to which they have lost their war? How can anyone count

those who have won and those who have lost our war?
How can anyone travel from town to town, from country

to country, from refugee camp to refugee camp, counting
our living? How could we dig up each shallow mass grave

for all the tens of thousands who were never counted?
Why should anyone want to count at all? Show me the trophies

of our war, so I will take you to a field, where all
the massacred still gather at night to bind open, bullet

wounds even though they are already dead. When warriors
come home from war, carrying on their hands trophies

of booty, all the bullets from their weapons, gone, do
we ask them to show us their scars? The after-war Dorklor,

with all its drumming and dancing, was never meant
to be merry—not even in their jubilation at victory.

You have only to watch the dancing warriors' feet to know.

Lori Wilson

Lori Wilson is the author of *House Where a Woman* (Autumn House Press, 2009). Her poems have appeared in various literary publications, including the *Poetry Daily* website, *Southern Poetry Review, Georgetown Review, Kestrel, Cerise* and *5 AM.* She works as a computer systems analyst in Morgantown, West Virginia, and is a student in the MFA Program in Poetry and Poetry in Translation at Drew University.

My Mother Likes to Tell

how when I was ten
she sent me to fetch a sweater
from the top right drawer of her dresser,
how when I came back I said,
the drawer was stuck
but I looked in the other eight drawers.

She thinks this is funny.
I think it's the distance
between a world where anything
not in its place simply *isn't*
and mine, where things are always
showing up where they don't belong,

the way yesterday in the check-out line
I saw the white hem of the clerk's undershirt
hanging untucked and wrinkled,
and you were suddenly there
at the edge of the bed,
shoulders hunched forward,

long arms reaching back
to peel the shirt over your head.

Green Glass Bird

From a box marked *Lillian's Desk*
I lift the green glass bird
I bought when I was seven,
the Christmas I was old enough
to buy her present myself
with two dollars my father
pressed into my hand.

I hold it up to the basement bulb,
remember how she kept it
on the coffee table all those years,
glass-to-glass, remember her hands
cradling its weight, remember
the bristle of rug on my arms,
my cheek, as I watched her wait
for late-afternoon sun to ignite
the green heart of that bird.

North Carolina, West Virginia,
Michigan—green glass bird
in and out of packing boxes,
onto the sill, the curio shelf, at last
her desk the winter and spring
of oxygen tanks and feeding tubes,
where it caught the inadequate light
until there were no more breaths.

In the basement with boxes
I rock on my heels,
cold bird cuddled to my neck
like a frightened cat. And I stroke it,
murmur *Stupid bird, poor fat green bird,*
a careless move could crack you
on this painted concrete floor.
Did you think it was you that she loved?
Poor bird, it was me.
It was me.

Slap

She was seven, she wouldn't
stop whining. I said *be quiet*
and she cried *but Mommy.*
Please be quiet.
But Mommy.
Enough.
Her lank yellow hair,
her damp face, she was seven.
It wasn't / I shouldn't have / I'll never (I never
did it again). No comfort
to say I was young, I was learning—
no one told me
that some days I'd want to upend the table,
hurl dishes, crawl under the couch.
Should I have walked out the door
down Darnell Hollow to 857
kept walking north if that's what it took?
I didn't. My hand (my own hand)—
her intake of breath
still wakes me some nights.

Michael Wurster

Michael Wurster was born in Moline, Illinois and currently resides in Pittsburgh with his two Siamese cats. He is a founding member of Pittsburgh Poetry Exchange and teaches at Pittsburgh Center for the Arts. His poetry collections are *The Cruelty of the Desert, The Snake Charmer's Daughter,* and *The British Detective.*

Newsboy

Newsboy
in his fifties
with wild hair
and gray clothing

shivering on the corner
of Fifth and Wood,
hands in pockets,
whistling

"Saint Louis Blues"
out of tune.

Inheritance

Who devises these seasons of knowing?
Roosevelt sat heads up, cigarette holder
clamped tightly between his teeth.
Young Kennedy ran into a tree.

Dreamt an argument with my daughter
in a maze of corridors leading
to a small space. Chaos on the stair,
memories of wet paint in the Old Soldiers' Home.

Pound in St. Elizabeth's. My father
in St. Elizabeth's. Olson enjoying
a country inn in Oxford, Maryland,
where I stayed several times years later,

the green lawn went right down to the water
of the bay. I feel a last child,
the one the sickle moon will cleanse.

Poem about America

In Clinton, Iowa
on the Mississsippi

there's a small ballpark,
Riverfront Park.

The team is called the Pilots.

The home run balls
go into the water
and down to New Orleans.

Those Missing Towers

Sartre said it's easy to
describe a presence, but hard
to define an absence.

On September 12, 2001,
New York City defines an absence
as a hole in the heart,

those missing towers in the skyline.

Dean Young

Dean Young's most recent book of poetry is *Fall Higher* (Copper Canyon, 2011). He is currently the William Kivingston Chair of Poetry at the University of Texas in Austin.

I See a Lily on Thy Brow

It is 1816 and you gash your hand unloading
a crate of geese, but if you keep working
you'll be able to buy a bucket of beer
with your potatoes. You're probably 14 although

no one knows for sure and the whore you sometimes
sleep with could be your younger sister
and when your hand throbs to twice its size
turning the fingernails green, she knots

a poultice of mustard and turkey grease
but the next morning, you wake to a yellow
world and stumble through the London streets
until your head implodes like a suffocated

fire stuffing your nose with rancid smoke.
Somehow you're removed to Guy's Infirmary.
It's Tuesday. The surgeon will demonstrate
on Wednesday and you're the demonstration.

Five guzzles of brandy then they hoist you
into the theater, into the trapped drone
and humid scuffle, the throng of students
a single body staked with a thousand peering

bulbs and the doctor begins to saw. Of course
you'll die in a week, suppurating on a camphor-
soaked sheet but now you scream and scream,
plash in a red river, in sulfuric steam

but above you, the assistant holding you down,
trying to fix you with sad, electric eyes
is John Keats.

Cotton in a Pill Bottle

I love the fog. It's not one hundred degrees.
It's not Mary sobbing on the phone or powder-
white mildew killing the rose. My father
lost inside it keeps pretending he's dead
just so he can get a little peace.
It's not made of fire or afraid of fire
like me, it has nothing to do with smoke.
There's never any ash, anything to sift through.
You just put your hand on the yellow rail
and the steps seem to move themselves.
It doesn't have a job to do.
It's morning all afternoon.
It loves the music but would be
just as happy listening to the game.
Still, I don't know what frightens me.
It doesn't blame anyone.
You'll never see tears on its cheeks.
It'll never put up a fight.
I love how the fog lies down in the air,
how it can get only so far from the sea.

How I Get My Ideas

Sometimes you just have to wait
15 seconds then beat the prevailing nuance
from the air. If that doesn't work,
try to remember how many times
you've wakened in the body of an animal,
two arms, two legs, willowy antennae.
Try thinking what it would be like
to never see your dearest again.
Stroke her gloves, sniff his overcoat.

If that's a no-go, call Joe
who's never home but keeps changing
the melody of his message.
Cactus at night emits its own light,
the river flows under the sea.
Dear face I always recognize but never
know, everything has a purpose
from which it must be freed,
maybe with crowbars, maybe the gentlest breeze.
Always turn in the direction of the skid.
If it's raining, use the rain
to lash the windowpanes or,
in a calmer mode, deepen the new greens
nearly to a violet. I can't live
without violet although it's red
I most often resort to.
Sometimes people become angelic when they cry,
sometimes only ravaged.
Technically, Mary still owes me a letter,
her last was just porcupine quills and tears,
tears that left a whitish residue
on black construction paper.
Sometimes I look at used art books at Moe's
just to see women without their clothes.
How can someone so rich,
who can have fish whenever he wants,
go to baseball games,
still feel such desperation?
I'm afraid I must insist
on desperation. By the fourth week
the embryo has nearly turned itself
inside out. If that doesn't help,
you'll just have to wait which
may involve sleeping which may involve
dreaming and sometimes dreaming works.
Father why have you returned,
dirt on your morning vest?
You cannot control your laughter.
You cannot control your love.
You know not to hit the brakes on ice
but do anyway. You bend the nail
but keep hammering because
hammering makes the world.

Acknowledgments

Addonizio, Kim: "Collapsing Poem," "Onset," and "The Moment" from *Tell Me* copyright 2000 published by BOA Editions, Ltd. Copyright © 2000 and used with permission of the publisher.

Anderson, Maggie: "And Then I Arrived at the Powerful Green Hill," "How the Brain Works," "Try," and "Beautiful War" copyright 2011 by Maggie Anderson. Reprinted by permission of the author.

Baca, Jimmy Santiago: "Tire Shop" from *Healing Earthquakes*, copyright 2001 by Jimmy Santiago Baca. Used by permission of Grove/Atlantic, Inc.

Beatty, Jan: "My Father Teaches Me Desire," "My Father Teaches Me Longing," "My Father Teaches Me Light," and "Modern Love" from *Boneshaker*, by Jan Beatty, copyright 2002. Reprinted by permission of the University of Pittsburgh Press and the author.

Berger, Jacqueline: "At the Holiday Crafts Fair," "The Magic Show," and "Celebrity Cooking," from *The Gift that Arrives Broken* copyright 2010. Reprinted by permission of the author and Autumn House Press.

Blair, Peter : "Discussing the Dream of Culture with Professor Kwaam," "November Full Moon," "The Day after the Coup," "Planting Rice with Nipun, Ubol Province" from *Farang* copyright 2010. Reprinted by permission of the author and Autumn House Press.

Bloch, Chana: "The New World," "Reprieve," "Sometimes I Want to Sink into Your Body," "Brothers," "The Messiah of Harvard Square," from *Blood Honey* copyright 2010 by Chana Bloch, reprinted by permission of the author and Autumn House Press.

Bosselaar, Laure-Anne: "After a Noisy Night" and "Plastic Beatitude" by Laure-Anne Bosselaar, from *The Hour Between Dog and Wolf*. © BOA Editions, Ltd., 1997. Reprinted with permission of BOA Editions. "The Pleasures of Hating" from *Small Gods of Grief*. © BOA Editions, Ltd., 2001. Reprinted with permission of BOA Editions.

Budy, Andrea Hollander: "In the Garden," "Ex," "Nineteen Thirty Eight," "Graveyard Shift," from *Woman in the Painting* copyright 2006 reprinted by permission of the author and Autumn House Press.

Campbell, Rick: "Fair Warning," "Road House," "Poetry Makes Nothing Happen," from *Dixmont* copyright 2008 by Rick Campbell, reprinted by permission of the author and Autumn House Press. "Heart of Dependent Arising" copyright 2010 by Rick Campbell, reprinted by permission of the author.

Clifton, Lucille: "the times," "moonchild," "what I think when I ride the train," "august," "study the masters," "to my last period," and "my dream about being white" from *Blessing the Boats, New and Selected Poems, 1988-2000* copyright 2000 by Lucille Clifton, published by BOA Editions and used by permission of the publisher.

Collins, Billy: "Consolation" and "Workshop" from *The Art of Drowning* by Billy Colliins copyright 1995. Reprinted by permission of the University of Pittsburgh Press. "Taking Off Emily Dickinson's Clothes" from *Picnic, Lightning* by Billy Collins copyright 1998. Reprinted by permission of the University of Pittsburgh Press.

Cramer, Steven: "The Benevolence of the Butcher" first appeared in *Memorious #9*, copyright 2010 by Steven Cramer, reprinted by permission of the author. "On Hold" first appeared in *Harvard Review* (Spring/Summer 2009), copyright 2009 by Steven Cramer, reprinted by permission of the author. "Sketches at the Hayden Rec Center" first appeared in *Ploughshares* (Winter 2006-2007), copyright 2006 by Steven Cramer, reprinted by permission of the author.

Daniels, Jim: "Short-order Cook" from *Show and Tell: New and Selected Poems* copyright 2003 by the Board of Regents of the University of Wisconsin System. Reprinted courtesy of the University of Wisconsin Press and the author. "Where Else Can You Go" from *Blessing the House*. © University of Pittsburgh Press, copyright 1997. Reprinted by permission of the University of Pittsburgh Press and the author.

Davis, Todd: "Craving," "Accident," "Puberty," "Theodicy" from *The Least of These*, Michigan State University Press, copyright 2010. Reprinted by permission of Michigan State University Press and the author.

Derricotte, Toi: "Boy at the Paterson Falls" from *Captivity*, by Toi Derricotte, copyright 1989. Reprinted by permission of the University of Pittsburgh Press. "Bird" from the poem sequence entitled "Two poems," "After a Reading at a Black College," "Not Forgotten," and "Shoe Repair Business" from *Tender*, by Toi Derricotte, copyright 1997. Reprinted by permission of the University of Pittsburgh Press.

Dickman, Matthew: "Some Days" from *All-American Poem*. Copyright © 2008 by Matthew Dickman. Reprinted with the permission of the *American Poetry Review*.

Dickman, Michael: "Scary Parents" from *The End of the West* copyright 2009 by Michael Dickman. Reprinted by permission of Copper Canyon Press.

Dobler, Patricia: "An Afterlife," "Field Trip to the Mill," "Your Language is Lost at Sea," "Uncle Rudy Explains the Events of 1955," "On Murray Avenue," from *Collected Poems* copyright 2005, reprinted by permission of the estate of the author and Autumn House Press.

Dobyns, Stephen: "Stars," "Wisdom," and "Leaf Blowers" copyright 2010 by Stephen Dobyns, reprinted by permission of the author.

Dove, Rita: "Hattie McDaniel Arrives at the Coconut Grove" from *American Smooth*, W. W. Norton & Company, New York, NY. © 2004 by Rita Dove. Reprinted by permission of the author. "Daystar," "Aircraft," "Straw Hat," and "Roast Possum" from *Thomas and Beulah*, Carnegie-Mellon University Press, Pittsburgh, PA. © 1986 by Rita Dove. Reprinted by permission of the author.

Duhamel, Denise: "How It Will End" copyright 2010, reprinted by permission of the author. "Oriental Barbie" from *Queen for a Day: Selected and New Poems*, by Denise Duhamel, copyright 2001, reprinted by permission of the University of Pittsburgh Press and the author. "Blue Beard's One-Hundredth Wife" from *How the Sky Fell* published by Pearl Editions, copyright 1996, reprinted by permission of the publisher and the author.

Dunn, Stephen: "Don't Do That" copyright 2010 by Stephen Dunn, reprinted by permission of the author. "The Sacred" from *Between Angels* by Stephen Dunn. Copyright 1989 by Stephen Dunn. Used by permission of W.W. Norton & Company, Inc. "Empathy" from *Different Hours* by Stephen Dunn. Copyright 2000 by Stephen Dunn. Used by permission of W.W. Norton & Company, Inc.

Eady, Cornelius: "Dance at the Amherst County Public Library" and "Almost Grown" from *Hardheaded Weather: New and Selected Poems* (New York: G.P. Putnam's Sons, 2008). Reprinted by permission of the author.

Emanuel, Lynn: "Dear Final Journey," "The Revolution," "The Murder Writer," "Ellipses," and "The Occupation" from *Noose and Hook*, by Lynn Emanuel, copyright 2010. Reprinted by permission of the University of Pittsburgh Press.

Emerson, Claudia: "Animal Funerals, 1964" appeared in *Tar River Poetry*. "Cold Room" appeared in *Poetry East*. "Secure the Shadow" appeared in *Blackbird*. All poems copyright 2010 by Claudia Emerson. Reprinted by permission of the author.

Fairchild, B.H.: "Rave On," "A Photograph of the Titanic," from *Early Occult Memory Systems of the Lower Midwest: Poems by B.H. Fairchild.* Copyright 2003 by B.H. Fairchild. Used by permission of W.W. Norton & Company, Inc.

Gaspar, Frank X.: "One Thousand Blossoms," "Hurricane Douglas, Hurricane Elida," "Bodhidharma Preaches the Wake-up Sermon" from *Night of a Thousand Blossoms.* Copyright 2004 by Frank X. Gaspar. Reprinted by permission of Alice James Books, www.alicejamesbooks.org.

Gay, Ross: "Summer," "Alzheimer's," "The Truth," and "Pulled over in Short Hills, NJ, 8:00 AM" from *Against Which* copyright 2006 reprinted by permission of CavanKerry Press.

Gibb, Robert: "The Writing Class," "For the Poets in the Prisons of America," "What the Heart can Bear," from *What the Heart Can Bear* copyright 2009 reprinted by permission of the author and Autumn House Press.

Goldberg, Beckian Fritz: "Wren," "Lie Awake Lake," "Fourth Month" from *Lie Awake Lake* copyright 2005, reprinted by premission of Oberlin College Press. "Story Problem" copyright 2011, reprinted by permission of the author.

Gontarek, Leonard: "Study/White," "Study/Trees," "Study/Crow" from *Déjà vu Diner* copyright 2006 reprinted by permission of the author and Autumn House Press.

Gridley, Sarah: "Posthumous" and "Summer Reading" were first published in *Slope.* "Work" and "Against the Throne and Monarchy of God" were first published in *NEO.* "Medieval Physics" was first published in *Kenyon Review Online.* Poems copyright 2010 by Sarah Gridley and reprinted by permission of the author.

Hales, Corrinne Clegg: "The Rich," "To Make It Right," "Forgiven," "'Young Nubian Woman'" from *To Make it Right* by Corrine Clegg Hales, copyright 2011. Reprinted by permission of Autumn House Press and the author.

Hamby, Barbara: "Ode to My 1977 Toyota" from *Babel*, by Barbara Hamby, copyright 2004. Reprinted by permission of the University of Pittsburgh Press. "I Beseech Thee, O Yellow Pages" from the poem cycle entitled "9 Sonnets from the Psalms" from *All-Night Lingo Tango*, by Barbara Hamby, copyright 2009. Reprinted by permission of the University of Pittsburgh Press. "Betrothal in B Minor" and "The Language of Bees" from *Delirium*, University of North Texas Press, copyright 1995 by Barbara Hamby, reprinted by permission of the author.

Harvey, Matthea: "The Golden Age of Figureheads," "If Scissors Aren't the Answer, What's a Doll to Do?," and "Inside the Good Idea" from *Modern Life: Poems* (St. Paul, Minn.: Graywolf Press, 2007). Reprinted by permission of the publisher.

Harvey, Yona: "To Describe my Body Walking," "Blessing Blue Crabs," "Discovering Girdles" copyright 2011 by Yona Harvey, reprinted by permission of the author.

Hasan, Raza Ali: From *67 Mogul Miniatures*, "#1," "#11," "#28," "#38," "#60," from *67 Mogul Miniatures* copyright 2008 reprinted by permission of the author and Autumn House Press.

Hass, Robert: "A Story About the Body," "The Apple Trees at Olema," "Misery and Splendor" from *Human Wishes* by Robert Hass. Copyright 1989 by Robert Hass. Reprinted by permission of HarperCollins Publishers.

Hayes, Terrance: "The Same City" from *Hip Logic* by Terrance Hayes, edited by Cornelius Eady, copyright 2002 by Terrance Hayes, reprinted by permission of the author and the Penguin Group (USA) Inc.

"Snow for Wallace Stevens," "All the Way Live," and "A Plate of Bones" from *Lighthead* by Terrance Hayes, copyright 2010 by Terrance Hayes, reprinted by permission of the author and the Penguin Group (USA) Inc.

Hazo, Samuel: "God and Man," "My Roosevelt Coupe'," "Toasts for the Lost Lieutenants," "Ballad of a Returnee," from *The Song of the Horse, Selected Poems, 1958-2008* copyright 2008, reprinted by permission of the author and Autumn House Press.

Hicok, Bob: "Bars poetica," "1935," and "Cutting edge" from *Insomnia Diary* by Bob Hicok, copyright 2004. Reprinted by permission of the University of Pittsburgh Press. "Solstice: Voyeur" from *This Clumsy Living*, by Bob Hicok, copyright 2007. Reprinted by permission of the University of Pittsburgh Press.

Hill, Mary Crockett: "A Theory of Everything," "All About It," "Pantoum for Attachment," "Young People Today," from *A Theory of Everything* copyright 2009 reprinted by permission of the author and Autumn House Press.

Hirshfield, Jane: "First Light Edging Cirrus" first appeared in *The Harvard Review*. "The Supple Deer" first appeared in *Orion*. "Narrowness" first appeared in *Times Literary Supplement* (UK). "A Hand is Shaped for What It Holds or Makes" first appeared in *The Georgia Review*. "Perishable, It Said" first appeared in *Poetry*. All poems copyright 2011 by Jane Hirshfield and reprinted with her permission.

Hoagland, Tony: "The News," "Suicide Song," "Phone Call," and "Two Trains" from *What Narcissism Means to Me* (St. Paul, Minn.: Graywolf Press, 2003). Reprinted by permission of the publisher.

Howe, Marie: "The Copper Beech," "Practicing," "What the Living Do," from *What the Living Do* by Marie Howe. Copyright 1997 by Marie Howe. Used by permission W.W. Norton & Company, Inc.

Jacobik, Gray: "The 750 Hands" and "The Tapeworm" from *Brave Disguises*, by Gray Jacobik, copyright 2002, reprinted by permission of the University of Pittsburgh Press. "Skirts" from *The Double Task* published by the University of Massachusetts Press, copyright 1998, reprinted by permission of the author.

Jarman, Mark: "Butterflies Under Persimmon," "In the Tube," "The Wind," and "Astragaloi" from *To the Green Man: Poems* (Louisville, Kentucky: Sarabande Books, 2004). Reprinted by permission of the publisher.

Jeffers, Honorée Fanonne: "Hagar to Sarai," "Confederate Pride Day at Bama (Tuscaloosa, 1994)," and "Don't Know What Love Is" from *Outlandish Blues* copyright 2003 by Honorée Fanonne Jeffers. Reprinted by permission of Wesleyan University Press.

Kaminsky, Ilya: "In Praise of Laughter," "Aunt Rose," and "My Mother's Tango" from *Dancing in Odessa*, published by Tupelo Press, copyright 2004 by Ilya Kaminsky, reprinted by permission of Tupelo Press.

Kelly, Brigit Pegeen: " Black Swan," "The Dragon," "Elegy" from *The Orchard* copyright 2004 published by BOA Editions, Ltd. Copyright © 2000 and used with permission of the publisher.

Kelly-DeWitt, Susan: "Egrets at Bolinas Lagoon," "Pomegranates," "Crossing the Mojave at Night" from *The Fortunate Islands* copyright 2007 by Susan Kelly-DeWitt, reprinted by permission of the author and Marick Press. "Apple Blossoms" from *To a Small Moth* published by Poet's Corner Press copyright 2002 by Susan Kelly-DeWitt, reprinted by permission of the author.

Kenyon, Jane: "Happiness," "Eating the Cookies," "Prognosis," and "Pharaoh" from *Otherwise: New and Selected Poems* (St. Paul, Minn.: Graywolf Press, 1996). Reprinted by permission of the publisher.

Kilwein Guevara, Maurice: "Doña Josefina Counsels Doña Concepción before Entering Sears" from *Poems of the River Spirit*, by Maurice Kilwein Guevara, copyright 1996. Reprinted by permission of the University of Pittsburgh Press. "Fast Forward" from *Autobiography of So-and-So: Poems in Prose*, copyright 2001 by Maurice Kilwein Guevara, reprinted by permission of New Issues Poetry & Prose and the author.

Kirschner, Elizabeth: "Why do I love the winter garden so?," "Once Mother came," "While boys milked my breasts," "In the psych ward," "While my words," from *My Life as a Doll* copyright 2008 reprinted by permission of the author and Autumn House Press.

Kitchens, Romella: "The Reflected Face of the Sea" and "Florida" copyright 2011 by Romella Kitchens, published by permission of the author.

Kooser, Ted: "Geronimo's Mirror" and "Laundry" from *One World at a Time*, by Ted Kooser, copyright 1985. Reprinted by permission of the University of Pittsburgh Press. "Selecting a Reader" and "Old Soldier's Home" from *Sure Signs: New and Selected Poems*, by Ted Kooser, copyright 1980. Reprinted by permission of the University of Pittsburgh Press.

Kumin, Maxine: "On Being Asked to Write a Poem in Memory of Anne Sexton," from *Selected Poems 1960-1990* by Maxine Kumin. Copyright 1996 by Maxine Kumin. Used by permission of W.W. Norton & Company, Inc. "Jack," from *Jack and Other New Poems* by Maxine Kumin. Copyright 2005 by Maxine Kumin. Used by permission of W. W. Norton & Company, Inc.

Krygowski, Nancy: "The Bus Comes, the Girl Gets On" and "Heaven, As We Know It" from *Velocity*, by Nancy Krygowski, copyright 2007. Reprinted by permission of the author and the University of Pittsburgh Press.

Laux, Dorianne: "Pearl," "Family Stories," and "Twilight" from *Smoke* copyright 2000 published by BOA Editions, Ltd. Copyright 2000 and used with permission of the publisher. "Dust" from *What We Carry* copyright 1994 published by BOA Editions, Ltd. Copyright 2000 and used with permission of the publisher.

Lea, Sydney: "The Vanishing," "Ars Vitae," and "Fathomless" copyright 2010 by Sydney Lea. "Ars Vitae" was first published in *Margie*. "Fathomless" was first published in *Pleiades*. Poems reprinted by permission of the author.

Lee, Li-Young: "The Hammock," "Words for Worry," "Praise Them" from *Book of My Nights* copyright 2001 published by BOA Editions, Ltd. Copyright © 2000 and used with permission of the publisher.

Levine, Julia B.: "Vigil" from *Ditch-Tender* copyright 2007 reprinted by permission of University of Tampa Press and the author. "Fontanelle," "Nights on Lake Michigan," and "My Gemini" from *Practicing for Heaven* copyright 1999 reprinted by permission of Anhingha Press and the author.

Levine, Miriam: "Candlewood," "Staying In," "Surfer at Wellfleet," "Aaron's Retreat," from *The Dark Opens* copyright 2008 reprinted by permission of the author and Autumn House Press.

Levine, Philip: "The Wandering Poets" first appeared in *Dossier*; "The Gatekeeper's Children" first appeared in *Poetry*; "Words on the Wind" first appeared in *The Georgia Review*; and "1934" first appeared in *The New Yorker*. All poems copyright 2009 by Philip Levine and reprinted by permission of the author.

Levis, Larry: "The Poet at Seventeen" and "My Story in a Late Style of Fire" from *The Selected Levis*, by Larry Levis, selected by David St. John, copyright 2000. Reprinted by permission of the University of Pittsburgh Press.

Limón, Ada: "Selecting Things for Vagueness," "Centerfold," "The Lost Glove," "The Firemen Are Dancing," from *lucky wreck* copyright 2006 reprinted by permission of the author and Autumn House Press.

Macari, Anne Marie: "Earth Elegy," "Praying Mantis," "Stellar's Sea Cow," "Sunbathing," from *She Heads into the Wilderness* copyright 2008 reprinted by permission of the author and Autumn House Press.

Margolis, Gary: "The Burning Bush of Basketball," "Lincoln on the Battlefield of Antietam, October 3, 1862," "On the Way to the Sitter's," "Self-Portrait in the Garden," from *Fire in the Orchard* copyright 2002 reprinted by permission of the author and Autumn House Press.

Matthews, William: "Housecooling," "The Cloister," "Mingus at The Showplace" and "A Night at the Opera" from *Search Party: Collected Poems of William Matthews*. Copyright 2004 by Sebastian Matthews and Stanley Plumly. Reprinted by permission of Houghton Mifflin Harcourt Publishing Company. All rights reserved. "Landscape with Onlooker" from *Time & Money: New Poems* by William Matthews. Copyright 1995 by William Matthews. Reprinted by permission of Houghton Mifflin Harcourt Publishing Company. All rights reserved.

McDougall , Jo: "Time Telling," "Dirt," "Why I Get Up Each Day," "Summer," "The Good Hand," "Waiting Room," "Cancer," "Tempting the Muse," "Luck," "What We Need," from *Dirt* copyright 2001 reprinted by permission of the author and Autumn House Press.

Merwin, W.S.: "Blueberries after Dark," "The Song of the Trolleys," "The Pinnacle," "No," "Little Soul," "Recognitions," "The Odds," and "To Paula in Late Spring" from *The Show of Sirius* copyright 2008 by W.S. Merwin. Reprinted by permission of Copper Canyon Press.

Mitcham, Judson: "Surrender," "The Multitude," "History of Rain," and "Writing" are reprinted from *This April Day* copyright 2003 with permission from Anhinga Press.

Nelson, Marilyn: "Egyptian Blue," "Bedside Reading," "Cafeteria Food" from *Carver: A Life in Poems* by Marilyn Nelson, copyright 2001. Published by Front Street Books, an imprint of Boyds Mills Press. Reprinted by permission of the publisher.

Newman, Dave: "The God in Walt Whitman," "9/11," "Bo Diddley" were published in *5am*. Poems copyright 2011 by Dave Newman. Reprinted by permission of the author.

Nye, Naomi Shihab: "Sure," "Lunch in Nablus City Park," and "Famous" were published in *Words Under the Words,* copyright 2005 by Naomi Shihab Nye. "Dusk" and "Swerve," copyright 2011 by Naomi Shihab Nye, were first published in *The Langdon Review*. All poems reprinted by permission of the author.

Ochester, Ed: "Changing the Name to Ochester," "Fred Astaire," "Monroeville, PA," "Retired Miners," "The Canaries in Uncle Arthur's Basement," "For Ganesha, Hindu God of Good Fortune," from *Unreconstructed, Poems Selected and New* copyright 2008. Reprinted by permission of the author and Autumn House Press.

Ostriker, Alicia Suskin: "Stream-Entering," "Sonnetina: The Storm," "The Blessing of the Old Woman, the Tulip, and the Dog," and "Gaia Regards Her Children" from *The Book of Seventy*, by Alicia Suskin Ostriker, copyright 2009. Reprinted by permission of the University of Pittsburgh Press.

Pagh, Nancy: "Blackberries," "Ten Reasons Your Prayer Diet Won't Work," "Anchoring," "I Believe I Could Kneel," from *No Sweeter Fat* copyright 2007 reprinted by permission of the author and Autumn House Press.

Pahmeier, Gailmarie: "Homegrown Roses," "Hometown Girl at 30," "Home Maintenance," "A Home Full of Color," from *Shake It and It Snows* published by Coal Hill Review, an imprint of Autumn House Press, copyright 2010 reprinted by permission of the author and Autumn House Press.

Pastan, Linda: "Rain" was published in *Valley Voices*. "Ars Poetica" was published in *Provincetown Arts*. "Snow Storm" was published in *Great River*. All poems copyright 2009 by Linda Pastan and reprinted by permission of the author.

Pollard, Norah: `"Narragansett Dark" and "Kiss" are from *Leaning In*, copyright 2003 by Norah Pollard, reprinted by permission of Antrim House and the author. "The Sum of a Man" is from *Death and Rapture in the Animal Kingdom* copyright 2009, reprinted by permission of Antrim House and the author.

Potter, Dawn: "Why I Didn't Finish Reading *David Copperfield*" and "Eclogue 2" from *How the Crimes Happened* copyright 2010. Reprinted by permission of CavanKerry Press and the author.

Rector, Liam: "In My Memory Eddie" from *The Executive Director of the Fallen World* copyright 2006. Reprinted by permission of University of Chicago Press.

Ríos, Alberto: "Refugio's hair," "In My Hurry," and "The Gathering Evening" from *The Smallest Muscle in the Human Body* (Port Townsend, Wash.: Copper Canyon Press, 2002). Reprinted by permission of the publisher.

Rogers, Pattiann: "The Snow of Things," "Co-evolution: Flowers, Tongues, and Talents," "In the Silence Following" copyright 2010 by Pattiann Rogers. Reprinted by permission of the author.

Ryan, Kay: "The Best of It" from *The Niagara River*, copyright 2005 by Kay Ryan. Used by permission of Grove/Atlantic, Inc. "Blandeur," "The Fabric of Life," "Grazing Horses" from *Say Uncle*, copyright 1991 by Kay Ryan. Used by permission of Grove/Atlantic, Inc.

St. Germain, Sheryl: "Addiction," "Sestina for the Beloved," "Bread Pudding with Whiskey Sauce" from *Let It be a Dark Roux, New and Selected Poems* copyright 2007 by Sheryl St. Germain, reprinted by permission of the author and Autumn House Press.

Schwartz ,Ruth L.: "Come with Me," "Sex," "Trees in Wind," "Highway Five Love Poem," "Perseid" from *Dear Good Naked Morning* copyright 2005 by Ruth L. Schwartz, reprinted by permission of the author and Autumn House Press.

Seibles, Tim: "Four Takes of a Similar Situation or The World Mus Be Retarded," "The Caps On Backward," "Latin" from *Hammerlock*. Copyright 1999 by Tim Seibles. Reprinted with permission of the Cleveland State University Poetry Center: www.csuohio.edu/poetrycenter/.

Seiferle, Rebecca: "The Shearing" from *Wild Tongue* (Port Townsend, Wash.: Copper Canyon Press, 2007). Reprinted by permission of the publisher. "Bitter Herb," "Homophobia," and "Muse" from *Bitters* (Port Townsend, Wash.: Copper Canyon Press, 2001). Reprinted by permission of the publisher.

Shearin, Faith: "Shopping," "Retriever," and "The Name of a Fish" by Faith Shearin, from *The Owl Question*. © Utah State University Press, 2002, reprinted by permission of Utah State University Press and the author.

Slicer, Deborah: "Mousey and Me," "December 10," "After Metaphysics, or When the Fly Leaves the Flybottle," "Pastoral" from *The White Calf Kicks* copyright 2003, reprinted by permission of the author and Autumn House Press.

Stern, Gerald: "Casals" first appeared in *Five Points*. "In Beauty Bright" first appeared in *Poetry*. "Casals," "In Beauty Bright," "Died in the Mills," "Norman Riding," and "Farewell" copyright 2010 by Gerald Stern and reprinted by permission of the author.

Suk, Julie: "Rounds," "Where We Are," "Divorce," "Stalking," "Geode," from *The Dark Takes Aim* copyright 2003 reprinted by permission of the author and Autumn House Press.

Szybist, Mary: "The Troubadours etc." first published in *Meridian*, "Annunciation as Fender's Blue Butterfly with Kincaid's Lupine" first published in *Cincinnati Review*, "The Lushness of It" first published in *Electronic Poetry Review*. All poems copyright 2010 reprinted by permission of the author.

Terman, Philip: "As My Child Climbs the Apple Tree, I Think of the Ancient Sephardic Poet Jehudah Halevi," "Mrs. Titus," "Hasidim in New Square, New York Hear Carp Speaking in Hebrew," "The Stocking Bank," reprinted from *Rabbis of the Air* copyright 2007 by permission of the author and Autumn House Press.

Thompson, Sue Ellen: "The Visit," "In the Apartments of the Divorced Men" reprinted from *The Leaving, New and Selected Poems* copyright 2001, reprinted by permission of the author and Autumn House Press. "Dr. Colin Simms," "The Blue Blanket," "In Praise of Cancer," reprinted from *The Golden Hour* copyright 2006 by permission of the author and Autumn House Press.

Tieman, John Samuel: "Clean," "Editing" from *A Concise Biography of Original Sin* published by BkMk Press, copyright 2009 by John Samuel Tieman; reprinted by permission of the author. "Prodigal" from *Morning Prayers* published by *The Pittsburgh Quarterly*, copyright 1998 by John Samuel Tieman; reprinted by permission of the author. "Basho in St. Louis" copyright 2011 by John Samuel Tieman; reprinted by permission of the author.

Tolan, James: "Blood Sport," "Giggles Before the Void," "Evening Trees," "The Purple Crayon" copyright 2010 by James Tolan, reprinted by permission of the author.

Trethewey, Natasha: "Incident" and "Miscegenation" from *Native Guard: Poems* by Natasha Trethewey. Copyright 2006 by Natasha Trethewey. Reprinted by permission of Houghton Mifflin Harcourt Publishing Company. All rights reserved. "Photograph of a Bawd Drinking Raleigh's Rye" from *Bellocq's Ophelia: Poems* (St. Paul, Minn.: Graywolf, 2002). Reprinted by permission of the publisher.

Tyner, James Paul: "After Jumping Some Kids and Taking Their Money, 1988," "Hollywood Trash," "Bones in the Grapevines," "At a Barbecue for R.C. One Week After He Is Out of Iraq" reprinted from *The Ghetto Exorcist* published by Coal Hill Review, an imprint of Autumn House Press, copyright 2009 by permission of the author and Autumn House Press.

Valentine, Jean: "Barrie's Dream, The Wild Geese," "High School Boyfriend," and "Snow Landscape, In a Glass Globe" from *Door in the Mountain: New & Collected Poems 1965-2003*, copyright 2004 by Jean Valentine. Reprinted by permission of Wesleyan University Press.

Vollmer, Judith: "Spill," "Early Snow," and "She Kept Me" from *Reactor* copyright 2004 by the Board of Regents of the University of Wisconsin System. Reprinted courtesy of The University of Wisconsin Press.

Ward, Thom: "Logos" was first published in *Denver Quarterly*, "Road Test, Defiance, Ohio" in TheBlueMoon.com and "Anticipation" in *Connecticut Review*. All three poems were included in *Fog in a Suitcase*, a leatherette chapbook published by Picadilly Press, copyright 2004 by Thom Ward and reprinted with his permission.

Webb, Charles Harper: "Cocksucker" and "Vikings" from *Shadow Ball: New and Selected Poems*, by Charles Harper Webb, copyright 2009. Reprinted by permission of the University of Pittsburgh Press. "Tenderness in Men" from *Liver* copyright 1999 by the Board of Regents of the University of Wisconsin System. Reprinted courtesy of The University of Wisconsin Press.

Wesley, Patricia Jabbeh: "To Set Everything Right," "The Morning After: An Elegy," "When My Daughter Tells Me She Has a Boyfriend," "The Women in My Family," "Poem Written from a Single Snapshot," "Broken World" reprinted from *The River Is Rising* copyright 2007 by permission of the author and Autumn House Press.

Wilson, Lori: "My Mother Likes to Tell," "Green Glass Bird," "Slap" reprinted from *House Where a Woman* copyright 2009 by permission of the author and Autumn House Press.

Wurster, Michael: "Newsboy," "Inheritance," "Poem about America," "Those Missing Towers" from *The British Detective*, published by Main Street Rag, copyright 2009, reprinted by permission of the author.

Young, Dean: "I See a Lily on Thy Brow," "Cotton in a Pill Bottle," and "How I Get My Ideas" from *Skid*, copyright 2002. Reprinted by permission of the University of Pittsburgh Press.

The Autumn House Poetry Series

Michael Simms, General Editor

One on One	Jack Myers
Snow White Horses	Ed Ochester
The Leaving	Sue Ellen Thompson
Dirt	Jo McDougall
Just Once: New and Previous Poems	Samuel Hazo ▲
Fire in the Orchard	Gary Margolis
The White Calf Kicks	Deborah Slicer • 2003
The Divine Salt	Peter Blair
The Dark Takes Aim	Julie Suk ▲
Satisfied with Havoc	Jo McDougall
Half Lives	Richard Jackson
Not God After All	Gerald Stern ▲ (with drawings by Sheba Sharrow)
Dear Good Naked Morning	Ruth L. Schwartz • 2004
Collected Poems	Patricia Dobler
A Flight to Elsewhere	Samuel Hazo ▲
Déjà Vu Diner	Leonard Gontarek
lucky wreck	Ada Limón • 2005
The Golden Hour	Sue Ellen Thompson
Woman in the Painting	Andrea Hollander Budy
Joyful Noise: An Anthology of American Spiritual Poetry	Robert Strong, ed.
No Sweeter Fat	Nancy Pagh • 2006
Unreconstructed: Poems Selected and New	Ed Ochester
Rabbis of the Air	Philip Terman
The River Is Rising	Patricia Jabbeh Wesley
Dixmont	Rick Campbell

The Autumn House Anthology of Contemporary American Poetry	Sue Ellen Thompson, ed.
Let It Be a Dark Roux	Sheryl St. Germain
The Dark Opens	Miriam Levine • 2007
The Song of the Horse	Samuel Hazo ▲
My Life as a Doll	Elizabeth Kirschner
She Heads into the Wilderness	Anne Marie Macari
House Where a Woman	Lori Wilson
When She Named Fire: An Anthology of Contemporary Poetry by American Women	Andrea Hollander Budy, ed.
The Working Poet: 75 Writing Exercises and a Poetry Anthology	Scott Minar, ed.
67 Mogul Miniatures	Raza Ali Hasan
A Theory of Everything	Mary Crockett Hill • 2008
Blood Honey	Chana Bloch
The Gift That Arrives Broken	Jacqueline Berger • 2009
The White Museum	George Bilgere
What the Heart Can Bear	Robert Gibb
Farang	Peter Blair
To Make It Right	Corrinne Clegg Hales • 2010
Where the Road Turns	Patricia Jabbeh Wesley
Coda	Marilyn Donnelly
The Autumn House Anthology of Contemporary American Poetry 2nd edition	Michael Simms, ed.

• Winner of the annual Autumn House Poetry Prize
▲ Hardcover

Design and Production

Cover and text design by
Kathy Boykowycz

Text set in Stone Serif fonts, designed
in 1987 by Sumner Stone

Printed by McNaughton & Gunn on
Nature's Book, a 30% recycled paper